You Can Garden Anywhere

1,317 Quick & Easy
Gardening Tips the Experts
Don't Want You to Know

Publisher's Note

The editors of FC&A have taken careful measures to ensure the accuracy and usefulness of the information in this book. While every attempt has been made to assure accuracy, errors may occur. We advise readers to carefully review and understand the ideas and tips presented and to seek the advice of a qualified professional before attempting to use them. The publisher and editors disclaim all liability (including any injuries, damages, or losses) resulting from the use of the information in this book.

The health information in this book is for information only and is not intended to be a medical guide for self-treatment. It does not constitute medical advice and should not be construed as such or used in place of your doctor's medical advice.

> "Let us consider how to stimulate one another to love and good deeds, not forsaking our own assembling together, as is the habit of some, but encouraging one another; and all the more as you see the day drawing near."
>
> Hebrews 10:24, 25

FC&A Publishing®
103 Clover Green
Peachtree City, GA 30269

Produced by the staff of FC&A

ISBN 978-1-935574-17-0

TABLE OF CONTENTS

Garden planning: simple steps to a dazzling design

Lessons in low-maintenance landscapes 2

Zone defense: make climate & conditions
    work for you 13

Timing tips for a gorgeous garden 20

Trouble-free borders & beds 25

Earthy matters: making the most of your soil

Secrets to building better soil 34

Composting: a pick-me-up for your plot 44

Fertilizer: quick & easy plant food fixes..................54

Mulch magic: the multi-purpose cover-up................61

Sharpen your gardening skills

Horticultural habits that save time & money 70

Techniques to keep tip-top tools 73

Super-simple seed starters 83

Plant expertise: buy for less, select the best 94

Propagation: free plants for life..100

Prune & groom: tough love for better plants 105

Tap into wise watering tips 113

The flower garden: best bets for bountiful blooms

Amazing annuals 122

Beautiful bulbs 132

Perfect perennials 142

The kitchen garden: excellent edibles for less

Fabulous fruits 154

Volumes of veggies..167

Superb herbs...199

Container plants: versatile home & garden accents

Potting like a pro...210

Goof-proof houseplants 223

Hale & hearty plant picks for outdoor living.................238

Windowsill wonders anyone can grow...........................246

Trees, shrubs & ground covers: pretty problem solvers

Sure-fire success strategies for shrubs...........................250

Tried-and-true tree tactics...............................258

Groundcovers: care-free yard solution 267

Vigorous vines & climbers for quick cover.......................269

Quick tips for luscious lawns

Lawn CPR: simple fixes to revive & restore 274

Seeding: the first step to a beautiful lawn.........................282

Watering dews and don'ts...............................287

Mowing mastery: keeping it groomed & growing.............291

Battle plan to wipe out garden foes

Win the war on weeds 296

Save your plants from pesky pests 305

Creative critter control 317

Add pizzazz with special garden features

Fun attractions: birds, butterflies & more 330

Make a splash with wonderful water 338

Fences, trellises & arbors: pretty & practical
    add-ons 346

Ins & outs of garden paths..355

Appendix: Plant Hardiness Zone Map

Appendix: Plant Hardiness Zone Map 362

Index

Index..365

GARDEN PLANNING

SIMPLE STEPS TO A DAZZLING DESIGN

Lessons in Low-Maintenance Landscapes

Top 5 tricks for a low-maintenance landscape. Trim the time you spend on yard work, and get back to enjoying your garden.

- Fill beds and borders with perennials and shrubs instead of annuals.

- Avoid fast-growing plants. They need pruning more often.

- Focus on native plants. They can better withstand local weather and pests, and generally need less care.

- Opt for hardscaping like gravel or a creeping ground cover instead of grass.

- Build landscape elements like retaining walls out of stone or brick instead of wood timbers. Choose man-made materials for decks and fences over wood.

Smart planning cuts watering woes. Make watering easy on yourself. Forget about hauling the hose to the farthest reaches of the yard. Plan your plantings so the thirstiest plants are closest to the house — and the water spigot. Or put them at the bottom of a slope, where they will benefit from rain runoff. Put drought-tolerant plants in beds farthest from the house or at the top of a slope.

The easiest plants you'll ever own

Want plants that grow better and need less maintenance? Go native. Native plants are tough but beautiful. They have survived your climate for hundreds, even thousands, of years without being babied. Put them in your landscape, and they'll do the same. Once established, they will rarely need watering or fertilizing. Plus, they're naturally resistant to local pests. You'll have a beautiful garden and spend less in the long run.

Crank up your curb appeal. Boost the market value of your home with these simple curb-appeal secrets.

- Choose only a few attention-grabbing plants for the front yard. Too many will leave it looking chaotic and confused.

- Pick plants for the front that have at least two seasons of interest, such as spring flowers, colorful fall foliage, or an interesting winter outline.

- Use evergreens sparingly. Their foliage adds winter interest, but too many can make the yard look dark and gloomy.

- Plant a tree of roughly the same size on each side of the house for symmetry. Or aim for asymmetry with a tree on one side and group of shrubs on the other.

- Frame the front door naturally. Place the biggest plants at each end of the house, then get progressively smaller as you landscape toward the entrance.

Limit materials for unified look. Don't use more than three different materials in your landscape. Smashing together too many types of stone, brick, tile, wood, or pavers can create visual chaos. Pick two or three and stick with them. The unified look will tie the garden together better.

Opt for odd numbers

Always group plants in odd numbers, not even. Odd numbers naturally look like a group to the human eye, whereas even numbers look separate and awkward. The exception — if you are planting a large, even amount of plants. If the group is big enough, your eyes won't be able to tell if you're seeing an even or odd number.

Best way to plan your landscape. Let tracing paper save you hours of time and years of headaches.

- Take photographs of the parts of your yard you want to landscape.

- Lay tracing paper over each photo.

- Sketch your designs on the tracing paper before you begin digging up the yard.

Create a separate drawing of what the garden will look like in five or 10 years, once the plants have matured. Research your plant choices, and find out how big you can expect them to get. Then draw them in accordingly. You can see at a glance if you've placed plants too close together or put too-tall specimens up against the house.

Free designs help shape your landscape. Beautify your yard with a quality plan for little or no cost.

- Snag free landscape designs from the Arbor Day Foundation at *www.arborday.org/trees/landscapedesign*. Plans range from a traditional knot garden to a flowering woods edge.

- Call the colleges and universities near you, and ask if they have a landscape design or horticulture program. You may be able to hire a student designer at a reduced cost.

- Sketch out your own ideas. Hire a landscape designer to look over them and make suggestions or corrections. You'll spend a fraction of the cost of having a whole plan drawn from scratch.

Put in plants you can eat while admiring. Work attractive edibles into your landscape. Plant an apple or pear tree as an ornamental in the front yard. Substitute blueberry bushes for boxwoods in beds and borders. Sow colorful varieties of herbs, like the purple "Red Rubin" basil, in a bed with other annuals. Not only can you graze while weeding and mowing — you'll also get plants that do double duty, pro viding both food and beauty.

Get the 'OK' to avoid delays

Failing to plan is planning to fail, especially if you don't plan for permits. A code enforcement officer can bring your landscape project to a screaming halt. Get approval before you start to guard against delays. Call your local zoning board or city council. Describe the work you want to do, and ask if you need any permits. Get a seal of approval from your neighborhood association while you're at it.

Patience pays off in new home. Give yourself one year to live in a new home before you begin redoing the landscape. Plants and twigs that look dead now may surprise you in spring with beautiful blooms. Bulbs may emerge in unexpected places, and perennial climbers could creep back to life.

- Take note of what plants sprout where around your yard and how they look in each season. Then you can better decide what to keep, what to move, and what to give away.

- Watch sunlight, too. Keep track of where it shines the most and least, and at what times of day, so you can select the right plants for those areas.

- Look for patches of poor drainage, pitiful views, and other pitfalls, and plan accordingly.

Help home shine with perfect-sized plantings. Don't hide your
home behind oversized trees and shrubs. Pick plants that are the perfect size for framing it, or prune the ones you have down to size. Measure the distance from the ground to the eaves. Doorway plants should be no taller than one-third of this height. Foundation plants at the corners should be no taller than two-thirds.

Insiders' secrets to nabbing free stuff. Gardening shouldn't cost a fortune, and if you have access to a computer, it won't. Little-known websites like the ones below are packed with advice on getting free plants, mulch, pots, tools, and more.

- For tips on snagging free plants, mulch, and pots, head to *www.frugalgardening.com*.

- Find a tool lending library near you at *en.wikipedia.org/wiki/ List_of_tool-lending_libraries*.

- No nearby tool libraries? Two more websites, *www.borrow tools.com* and *www.neighborgoods.net*, help people who live near each other connect to share tools as well.

Slow runoff down a slope. Turn troublesome terrain into a gardening opportunity. A series of terraces across a slope will slow the rush of water downhill and prevent erosion. Too much trouble to build? Simply put in plants that thrive under the special conditions a slope creates.

- For the top and incline, select perennials and shrubs with deep, dense root systems — think daylilies, California fuchsia, or any clump-forming, ornamental grass. Select varieties that enjoy dry soil.

- For the bottom, pick plants that don't mind occasional sogginess, since water tends to pool here.

Lighten up shady spots. You don't have to cut down all your trees to let in more light. Boost what nature already offers. Where the shade is cast by a building or fence, try the old-fashioned trick of whitewashing. The color white reflects light. Painting a wall white bounces light from the sun back into the garden, giving sun-hungry plants more of what they crave.

Hardy plant choices for hard-to-grow areas. You can find plants that grow in any sort of garden — whether shady, salty, or dry. Don't give up hope of having the garden of your dreams. Look for plants that thrive in these tough environments.

Land is	Try growing		
	flowers	shrubs	trees
dry	lavender artemisia coneflower	juniper Japanese barberry	eucalyptus Eastern red cedar
shady	geraniums impatiens columbine	hydrangea barberry mountain laurel	flowering dogwoods Western red cedar many types of maple
salty	dianthus iris, salvia, sedum	rosa rugosa bayberry, sumac	Southern red cedar white oak

Call your local extension office and ask them to recommend more plants. They'll know what grows best in your area.

Fix flaws in your yard with raised beds. Overcome almost any problem by growing plants in these easy-to-assemble structures.

- Build beds in low-lying, flood-prone spots to give flowers a fighting chance. Raised beds drain faster than the ground around them, which helps prevent water-logged roots.

- Liven up flat, boring pieces of land by adding height and texture.

- Garden even in salty or hardpan soil by installing raised beds and filling them with good dirt.

Learn how to build different types of raised beds in the *Trouble-free borders & beds* and *Volumes of veggies* chapters.

Keep invasives under control. It's tempting to stick an invasive plant in the yard. They grow fast and need little care. That's also what makes them invasive. Experts warn against letting these loners into your landscape. But if you must, take steps to keep them contained.

- Slide a large kitchen knife into the soil every few weeks and cut around the plants. This severs the spreading roots and tendrils, so they don't sprout elsewhere.

- Cut the bottom out of a plastic planter and sink it, or a wide piece of pipe, into the ground at least 10 inches down. Then plant inside the walls.

Play in the dirt to improve your memory

Working with plants can help keep you sharp into old age. Studies show that gardening has healing powers for people with Alzheimer's, improving their sleep, agitation, and cognition. It may also slow the loss of short-term memory in people starting to struggle with memory problems.

The key to guarding your memory — getting active enough in your garden for it to count as "moderate exercise." That means doing things that raise your heart rate and breathing. Do that for 30 minutes a day, five days a week to help keep your brain and body sharp.

Turn stone eyesores into alpine paradise. Make the most unsightly rock piles and crumbling stone walls a centerpiece of the landscape with alpine plants. Crevices between rocks and cracks in walls are perfect places for alpines. They grow best in thin soil with good drainage and plenty of sunlight. Stuff these nooks and crannies with a little dirt, and you're ready to grow. For planting ideas, see tips in the chapters *Superb herbs* and *Fun attractions: birds, butterflies & more.*

Well-placed trees trim heating and cooling. Shade trees can cut your summer cooling costs up to 30 percent and your winter heating bill up to 50 percent.

- Plant at least three large, deciduous trees on the south and west sides of your home to block the heat and keep it cooler in summer.

- Let these same trees warm your house in winter. They lose their leaves, letting in the strong sunlight from the south and west.

- Avoid planting evergreens on the south or west side, though. They will block the sun's light — and warmth — in winter, since they don't drop their leaves.

Natural windbreak warms home in winter. Slash your winter heating bill by planting a windbreak on the north side of your house. Evergreen trees and shrubs work best, since they keep their leaves and needles through the coldest months. A sturdy evergreen windbreak can slow wind from 35 miles per hour (mph) to about 10 mph by the time it reaches your home.

- Choose trees with low-growing branches and dense foliage to block the most wind.

- Place them close together.

- Find out how tall they will be at maturity, and plant no farther than twice that distance from the house.

Lower the heat all over the landscape. Cool down the entire landscape by planting shade trees near the driveway and patio so concrete, asphalt, and other hardscapes radiate less heat to the rest of the yard.

Situate trees to sidestep storm damage. Planting trees can be a tricky business in parts of the country prone to serious storms. Put them where they won't damage your home should they fall or lose a limb. First, find out how wide the tree's canopy typically grows. Divide that in half, then multiply by 1.5. The number you get is how far you should plant it from the house. For example, the plant tag on a white oak tree tells you the oak's typical spread is 50 feet. Take half of that — 25 feet — and multiply by 1.5. The resulting 37.5 feet is how far you should place the sapling from your house.

Tricks to make a garden look longer. Give your shallow garden more depth with a few visual tricks.

- Create beds that are wider at the front and narrow as they move away from where you like to sit.

- Fill those beds with large-leaved plants close to the sitting area. Use progressively smaller plants with smaller leaves farther down the bed.

- Do the same with paths. Make them wider at their start, and gradually narrow them as they move away.

- Plant a taller shrub or tree at the front of the garden and shorter ones at the back.

- Trim a long hedge so it's taller at the front and gets shorter as it stretches away.

- Opt for a smaller, or at least shorter, focal object at the end of the garden than a large one. The smaller one will seem more distant.

Beware beds near black walnut trees. Don't make the mistake of situating a bed or vegetable garden near a black walnut tree. The roots and leaves release a chemical, juglone, that prevents other plants from growing, so it doesn't have to compete for water and nutrients. Even raised beds can't solve this problem. Your best bet — let the tree be, and put your plants elsewhere.

Use forest to enlarge your yard. Blend the woods behind your home into the rest of your garden to make it look larger. Plant shrubs and small trees along the wood's edge. Place taller plants in the back, closest to the forest, and transition to the shorter ones in front.

Make more space with an optical illusion. Put your painting talent to work, and make good use of a walled-in garden. On one wall, paint a mural of an archway, open gate, or some other opening with a sweeping vista behind it. The illusion will lead the eye beyond the wall and make a tiny plot instantly feel more open and airy.

Add charm by framing free views

Don't have a wall to paint a mural? Frame views of the land beyond your own small plot — nearby woods, a far-off mountain, or even your neighbor's nicely landscaped backyard. Find something that captures your eye. Plant or prune trees to naturally frame that view, or put up an arbor to do the same. You'll get the benefit of a great view without the sweat or cost of maintaining it.

Create depth with color. Ask any expert, and they'll tell you cool colors seem to recede and warm colors seem to advance. The same goes for dark (receding) and light (advancing) foliage. Work these effects to your advantage.

- Fill a small garden with cool-colored flowers and foliage, like blues, greens, and violets, to create a sense of space. Use warm colors, like red, yellow, and orange, sparingly.

- Plant cool-colored flowers at the end of a short yard to give it more depth.

- Put warm colors, like red, yellow, and orange, at the end of a long, narrow garden to make it feel shorter.

- Plant white flowers against a backdrop of dark foliage to create the illusion of greater depth.

ZONE DEFENSE

MAKE CLIMATE &
CONDITIONS WORK FOR YOU

Special map for trees and perennials. The Arbor Day Foundation produces its own hardiness zone map for trees and perennials, based on an area's lowest average temperature. Look up your Arbor Day Hardiness zone by typing in your zip code at the website *www.arborday.org/treeinfo/zonelookup*.

Pick plants that beat your summer heat. Hardiness Zone Maps tell you which plants will survive your winters — but not your summers. For this, turn to the American Horticultural Society's (AHS) Heat Zone map. Heat Zones range from 1 to 12, based on how many days a year the temperature exceeds 86 degrees.

- Zone 1 averages less than one 86-degree day a year.

- Zone 12, on the other hand, tops 86 degrees at least 210 days a year.

Some nursery plants now include Heat Zone codes along-side Hardiness Zone codes. Find out which Heat Zone you live in, then pick plants that will thrive there. See the box *Point and click for instant zone info* to access the AHS Heat Zone website, or order a copy of the map for $9.95 by calling the AHS at 800-777-7931, ext. 119. You can download a free copy to your computer at *www.ahs.org/pdfs/05_heat_map.pdf*.

Get a better guide for gardening out west. The USDA Hardiness Zone Map is fairly accurate for the Eastern United States, but gardeners out West say it often falls short. It's based on lowest average temperatures, but many other factors affect plant survival — including elevation and rainfall. Tall mountain ranges in the West cause big swings in both. Many gardeners in these areas have come to rely on a different guide, the Climate Zone Map by Sunset magazine. Developed specifically for Western states, it may do a better job of helping you choose plants for your yard. Look up your climate zone for free online at *www.sunset.com/garden/climate-zones*.

Point and click for instant zone info

Climates change, and so do zone maps. You can see the latest versions without waiting for paper copies to come out. Jump on a computer and travel to these websites. Then type in your zip code or click on the picture of the map for a close-up look at your zone.

- United States National Arboretum, for the government's official Plant Hardiness Zone Map, at *www.usna.usda.gov/Hardzone/ushzmap.html*
- Plantmaps.com for an interactive USDA Plant Hardiness Zone Map and other plant, tree, and gardening maps and data at *www.plantmaps.com/usda_hardiness_zone_map.php*
- American Horticultural Society's Heat Zone Map at *www.ahs.org/publications/heat_zone_finder.htm*

Take zone maps with grain of salt. Zone maps are meant as guidelines, not gardening law. Microclimates in your yard may favor plants that normally wouldn't survive in your area. If Zone 7 plants have been thriving in your Zone 6 yard for years, don't pull them up. Relax and enjoy the envy of your neighbors.

4 factors that throw off zone guidelines. Wind, elevation, buildings, and exposure can raise or lower certain garden spots by a whole zone. If a plant that's supposed to thrive in your area seems to be struggling, see if these factors could be to blame.

- Wind-blown areas dry out plants fast, making them less tolerant of cold.

- Dips in the landscape trap cold air. Houses sitting at the bottom of a hill can be 20 degrees, or an entire zone, colder than homes at the top.

- Shady areas may be an entire zone colder in winter than nearby sunny spots.

- Cities tend to be 5 to 10 degrees warmer than the countryside, bumping you up into the next Hardiness Zone. Don't choose flowering plants that are borderline for your zone. A late frost can cost you a year's worth of blooms.

Smart shopping strategy guards against winter. Look for long-lived plants like trees, shrubs, and perennials whose labels say they can survive in the next-coldest zone from yours. The next time your area gets hit with an unusually chilly winter, you'll be glad you did.

Best ways to garden during drought. A water shortage can doom plants, but not if you follow these guidelines for survival.

- Water whole areas, not single plants. The dry soil near a plant will suck moisture away from its roots.

- Add another 2 inches of mulch around plants to help conserve water.

- Don't bother watering the worst-off plants. They may tug at your heart strings, but they will never fully recover. Save water for plants with the best shot at survival.

- Put off fertilizing. Added nutrients spur growth, which makes plants even thirstier.

- Cut back flowering annuals. They may rebloom if the rains return.

- Make perennials, trees, and shrubs a priority over short-lived annuals or vegetables. Their loss would leave a bigger hole in your landscape — and your wallet.

Salvage plants post-flood. Drenching rains and overflowing rivers needn't mean barren landscapes. True, you may lose this year's annuals and vegetables. But other plants can survive and thrive again.

- Prop up perennials, and they may regrow snapped stems next year.

- Stake trees and shrubs until they recover their strength.

- Wipe or hose the mud off plant leaves so sunlight can reach them and spur photosynthesis.

Keep plants warm with plastic jugs. Give delicate plants a fighting chance during cold snaps.

- Fill clear milk jugs with water, and set them on the north side of small, tender plants. This protects them from frost without covering them up.

- Paint the outside of detergent bottles or other containers with flat, black paint. Then fill with water and set inside cold frames or cloches. The black paint helps the water absorb more heat, keeping plants warmer at night.

- Fill clear soda bottles or milk jugs with dark liquid like stale coffee or flat soda and lay them on their sides between plants. The dark liquid will hold more heat from the sun.

Skip the blanket in garden bed

Fluffy blankets may conjure up thoughts of warmth, but they don't work on plants the way they do on people. Wrapping your favorite azalea in a heavy quilt won't save it from frost damage. A blanket will help, however, if you combine it with plastic. The next time you drape plastic sheets over plants, cover the plastic with a warm blanket to trap more heat.

Black plastic beats clear for winter warmth. Clear plastic blocks the wind just as well, but it can make plants too warm on cold, sunny days. The false warmth tricks the plant into sending sap into its buds. When the temperature drops again at night, the delicate buds can suffer more damage. Since black plastic reflects sunlight, it doesn't heat the plant as much. Instead, it traps heat from the soil and keeps it close to the trunk and limbs. That makes it a better bet for keeping plants warm during cold spells. Don't let the plastic rest on the plant itself. It can actually freeze the plant where it touches. Drape it over stakes, instead. Be sure to anchor the edges with hefty rocks, dirt, or tree limbs to stop wind from sneaking underneath.

Turn rusty hangers into homemade cloche. Make your own cloche — for free. Take several old wire hangers and straighten the hooks. Pull the hangers open so they form more of a diamond shape, rather than a triangle. Jab each straightened hook into the ground beside a plant. Next, drape plastic sheeting over the row of hangers. Bury the edges or weigh them down with rocks so the wind doesn't blow it off the wire frame.

Drive away the cold with old tire. Protect fledgling plants from wind and frost with an old tire. Lay it on the ground with the plant in the center. Punch holes in the bottom-side of the tire so water doesn't get trapped inside and begin breeding mosquitoes. The black rubber will heat up during the day, warming the plant into the night. On super-cold nights, stretch a plastic sheet over the tire's top to trap more heat.

Old umbrella provides perfect frost cover. Put broken umbrellas to good use in your garden. Open one and stick the handle in the dirt beside small plants to guard against frost. For bigger, bushier beauties, drape plastic over the umbrella and tuck in around the base of the plant.

Skip sprinklers during hard freeze

You've seen images of citrus growers running sprinklers to protect their fruit during a hard freeze. Should you do the same? Experts warn against it. Those growers use sprinklers specially designed for freeze protection. Regular sprinklers — like the ones for watering your lawn — spray too much water to guard against frost. You'd also have to run them constantly, until temperatures warmed enough to melt nearly all the ice off plants. By then, you'd be left with a soggy, swampy yard.

Plant-safe ways to de-ice paths. The salt and chemicals in de-icers can do a number on landscape plants. Even "kinder" chemicals like calcium nitrate or high-nitrogen fertilizer can burn plant roots and kill friendly soil organisms. Create naturally non-slip surfaces by:

- spreading course sand or clay cat litter over areas where you often walk. If you choose cat litter, get the basic kind, not super absorbent.

- laying leftover sheets of asphalt shingles on paths. Sprinkle some sand underneath the shingles to keep them from sliding.

Free insulation protects potted plants. Leftover Bubble Wrap can save your potted plants in winter. Simply line the inside of your greenhouse with it. Bubbled packaging material adds a layer of warmth to even the most humble greenhouse. Staple it to the inside of the windows, leaving about an inch of air space between the bubble sheet and the glass wall. Attach inexpensive furring strips to the window frames, if necessary, to give you the inch of separation.

Create quick and easy cold frames. Make cold frames right in garden beds, where the plants already grow. No need to build special, permanent structures. Line crop rows, beds, or borders with hay or straw bales laid end-to-end so they form a rectangle around a row of plants. Lay old windows flat on top of the bales for an instant cold frame. When the weather warms enough to take it down, you can use the bales for mulch.

Frame plants with extra insulation. Cold frames aren't foolproof against frigid temperatures. They may need a little extra help keeping plants safe on super-cold nights. Try adding another layer of insulation over the cold frame. Styrofoam sheets, old carpet, or thick layers of straw can all help.

TIMING TIPS FOR A GORGEOUS GARDEN

Pick the perfect time to plant vegetables. Some gardening rules sound more like folklore. "Plant corn when oak leaves are the size of a squirrel's ear," for instance. But there's a reason for those sayings — they're often true. Phenology, the science of studying when plants do things like bloom or leaf out, has a long track record of success. Watch for these cues in your own garden.

Plant this	When
peas	forsythia blooms
peas, lettuce, spinach, carrots, beets, other cool-weather crops	lilac leaves are the size of a mouse's ear
spinach, beets, carrots	dandelions bloom
bean, cucumber, squash seeds	lilacs enter full bloom
potatoes	first dandelion blooms or shadbush blooms
corn	oak leaves are the size of a squirrel's ear, or petals fall from apple tree blossoms
tomatoes	lily-of-the-valley enters full bloom
tomatoes, early corn	dogwoods enter full bloom
tomatoes, peppers	daylilies begin blooming
fall cabbage, broccoli	catalpas and mock orange bloom

Create your own crop calendar. Planting your own vegetable garden sounds great, but that plan can backfire if you fail to stagger the harvests. Sow crops that all ripen at the same time, and you'll be hard-pressed to pick them fast enough. Plan your harvest with this clever calendar. List the vegetables you want to plant this year, then mark the month you need to plant them and the month or months they will ripen. Going on vacation in July? Plant only vegetables that won't need picking while you're gone.

Sample Crop Calendar

Vegetable	March	April	May	June	July	August
green peas	P		H	H		
spinach	P	H	H			
carrots		P		H	H	
tomatoes			P		H	H
cucumbers			P		H	

P = month to plant   H = month to harvest

Schedule soil test for greatest growth. Testing your soil for missing nutrients gives you a leg up on mother nature. Just be sure to get your tests done in late fall or early spring. You'll have plenty of time to work in amendments, like fertilizer, before it's time to plant.

Follow folk sayings for planting and pruning. Those phenology folk sayings also apply to perennials. The key is temperature. When you see a certain flower bloom, or a particular plant put out leaves, you know the temperature is warm enough to sow seeds, prune, or transplant. Give this old-fashioned advice a try in your own garden beds.

Do this	When
prune roses	crocuses bloom
start planting perennials	maple leaves begin unfolding
sow morning glory seeds	maple leaves reach full size
plant cool-weather flowers such as pansies and snapdragons	aspen and chokecherry trees put out leaves

Best time to treat pests. Pay attention to the plants in your yard, and they'll tell you the best time to kill particular pests.

Start controlling	When
eastern tent caterpillars	crabapple and wild plum buds begin to bloom
adult apple maggots	Canadian thistle blooms
squash vine borer	the first chicory flowers open
gypsy moths	shadbush blooms
Japanese beetles	morning glory vines begin climbing
pine needle scale crawlers	horse chestnut blooms

Trick tells when soil is ready to work. There is no set date for when you can begin working the soil in spring, but it's best not to start too early. Wait at least until winter rains and snow have passed. Working wet soil destroys its structure, or tilth. Once damaged, it can take years to recover. Walking on wet dirt can also compact it. Rather than relying on the calendar, let the soil itself tell you when it's ready. Pick up a handful and squeeze. Does it crumble easily? Then it's ready to dig. If it sticks together and keeps its shape, then it is still too wet.

Magnolia helps keep bugs in check. Consider yourself lucky if you have a saucer magnolia in your yard. This beautiful tree is one of the best pest-control clocks. Each phase of blooming tells you when to treat for different bugs.

When the magnolia	Start controlling for
sets pink buds	eriophyid mites on hemlock and spruce, European pine shoot moth, pine bark adelgid, spruce needle miner, Cooley and eastern spruce gall adelgid
transitions into early bloom	eastern tent caterpillar, leaf crumpler, spruce spider mite, and Zimmerman pine moth
blooms	Juniper webworm, Fletcher scale, ash plant bug, and spring and fall cankerworm
drops its petals	gypsy moth, hawthorn mealybug, willow aphid, European sawfly, honey locust pod gall, and spruce budworm

Free timing tips from the experts. Plant your flowers too early, or too late, and you'll get nothing for your money. So consult the real experts — for free. Pay attention to when landscaping crews at shopping malls, parks, and local businesses put in plants, then follow their lead in your yard. These professionals know their stuff. It's a sneaky but successful trick for determining the exact right time to plant.

Guide to gardening through the seasons

Spring

- Prepare beds and borders for new plants by mixing in 1 to 3 inches of compost.
- Put fresh mulch in flower beds and around shrubs and trees.
- Lightly fertilize lawn. Aerate, dethatch, and overseed if needed.
- Apply a pre-emergent herbicide to kill crabgrass and other lawn weeds.
- Plant your summer-flowering bulbs and perennials.
- Divide perennials that have grown too large.
- Prune spring-flowering shrubs and climbers that have already bloomed.
- Prune rose bushes, butterfly bushes, and deciduous shrubs and climbers that flower in late summer.
- Fertilize established shrubs, including roses.
- Plant evergreen trees and shrubs.
- Prune away dead, broken, or diseased branches. These become easier to spot as plants leaf out in spring.

Summer

- Rebuild your compost pile, and water it to keep it moist.
- Mow the lawn regularly, but let grass grow a little taller during the hottest months.
- Mulch any garden beds you missed in spring with grass clippings or compost to keep weeds down and water from evaporating.
- Water lawns when nature doesn't provide enough rain. Grass needs 1 inch of water per week, rain and sprinklers combined.
- Water new trees and shrubs each week, with enough water to reach 1 foot deep.
- Prune the last of spring-flowering shrubs and climbers.
- Trim fast-growing hedges after their spring flush of growth. Wait until late summer to trim evergreen and conifer hedges.
- Divide cluttered clumps of irises and primroses after flowering.
- Deadhead flowers.

(Summer continued)

- Prune herbaceous plants and rambling roses once they bloom. You may get a second round of blossoms.
- Plant daffodil bulbs in late summer.
- Prune back fruiting shrubs.
- Prepare cold frames for fall vegetables.

Fall

- Rake leaves off the lawn, and add them to the compost pile.
- Add a layer of leaves over beds to crowd out weeds and feed the soil.
- Plant (or transplant) trees, shrubs, and certain perennials to give them a head start come spring. If they are deciduous, wait until after their leaves have fallen.
- Prune the roots of any shrubs and trees you hope to transplant in spring.
- Cut back flowering perennials, including rose bushes, to prepare them for winter.
- Divide cluttered clumps of hardy perennials, and replant them.
- Turn off and drain outdoor water lines and sprinkler systems.
- Store hoses and sprinklers for the winter.
- Clean up overgrowth in your yard, and add it to your compost pile.
- Fertilize the lawn again, and top-dress with a layer of compost. Overseed thin spots.
- Get spring-flowering bulbs like tulips into the ground.
- Dig up and store cannas, dahlias, and gladiolus after the first frost, in cold climates.
- Remove rotten fruit from the ground around fruit trees to discourage disease.
- Apply compost to vegetable beds.

Winter

- Begin planning next year's garden and landscape. Pre-order plants and seeds.
- Check your stored bulbs, and toss out any that are soft with rot.
- Prune woody shrubs and trees, especially fruit trees, while they are dormant. But don't prune plum and cherry trees.
- Plant bare-root roses.
- Apply a light scattering of nitrogen fertilizer to green winter lawns.
- Knock snow off tree limbs and hedges to guard against broken branches.
- Coppice shrubs in late winter, if you like the unique look.
- Keep adding kitchen scraps and leaves to your compost pile.

TROUBLE-FREE BORDERS & BEDS

Save big with beds and borders. They aren't just for looks. They can save a bundle of money and cut down on yard work. People in the United States spend about $40 billion each year on their lawns. Stop being one of them. Shrink your lawn and fatten your wallet by creating more beds and borders. You'll spend less on fertilizer, irrigation, herbicides, and seed or sod, not to mention less time mowing.

No-dig way to turn lawn into bed. Transform your lawn into a rich planting bed without heavy digging. Lay overlapping cardboard over the grassy area you want to convert, and wet it down with a water hose. Next, pile several inches of mulch, like grass clippings or chopped leaves, atop the cardboard. Give the cardboard a few weeks to begin breaking down, then plant or transplant directly through it into the dirt below.

Ease your workload with black plastic. There is no easier way to transform turf into an ornamental bed. In late fall, outline the area you want to convert with spray paint or a water hose. Spread thick, black plastic over the grass and secure the edges with rocks or landscape fabric pins. Leave it down over winter to completely kill the grass and weeds. Come spring, pull back the plastic and start planting.

Grow acid-loving plants in alkaline soil. Don't give up on growing azaleas in your alkaline beds. You can lower the pH in a garden bed gradually, and naturally, by mulching it with the right materials. Apply bark, leaves, pine needles, cottonseed meal, or composted sawdust to bring down the soil's alkalinity. These mulches work slowly, but the effects last a long time.

Move annuals annually to beat disease. Plant rotation protects garden vegetables from pest and disease. It can do the same for ornamental beauties in your beds and borders, too. Avoid planting the same annuals and bulbs in the same places year after year. Move them around, or put in different types of plants each year. Rotation naturally keeps pests and disease from getting a foothold in your garden.

Best blooms for evening enjoyment. Colorful red, orange, and blue blooms don't do any good after dark, because they don't show

Make your yard even more appealing by building beds that naturally look balanced and well-proportioned.

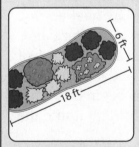

Lay out beds three times as long as they are wide.

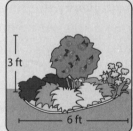

Don't put in plants that will get taller than half the width of the bed.

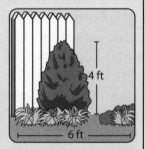

Plants in borders can be a little bigger, up to two-thirds as tall as the border is wide.

up well at nighttime. Plant white, yellow, or pink flowers near patios and porches where you like to sit in the evening. These colors shine once the sun goes down. They also show up better under outside lights.

Discourage dogs from digging up beds. Nothing can make you see red like the neighbor's dog digging up your newly planted petunias. Let him know he's not welcome by putting down a layer of finely shredded bark or hardwood mulch. Avoid fertilizing beds with bloodmeal, bonemeal, or fish meal. The smell will tempt even the best-behaved pooch.

Simple secret for designing beds. Outline the edges of planned beds and borders with a line of powdered lime or flour. Both show up easily and will break down naturally. Try living with the marked-off beds for a few days or weeks before you start digging. This way, you can tweak the boundaries before tearing up the grass.

Take the pain out of gardening

Build raised flower beds, and you'll do less stooping, kneeling, and bending. You may even want to spend more time in the garden. Build beds so plants are at knee or waist height for the most comfort. Top the bed walls with flat stones, blocks, or planks where you can sit while weeding or digging. They can also double as a place to set tools, pots, and soil while you work.

Tough plants that thrive beneath trees. Plant perennials, not annuals, under the trees in your yard. Tree roots don't like to be disturbed by digging, something you would have to do at least once a year to replace annuals. Trees tend to hog both sunlight and water, so choose drought-tolerant, shade-loving perennials. Wild geranium (*Geranium maculatum*), coral bells (*Heuchera 'Fireworks'*), phlox, Johnny Jump-up (*Viola labradorica*), and wild petunia (*Ruellia caroliniensis*) are all good options.

Don't add dirt under trees. It's tempting to build beds under trees by bringing in more soil, instead of digging down through all those roots. It's also a deadly mistake. Piling soil on top of tree roots can slowly cut off their water and oxygen. Eventually, the tree may die. Building up the soil around the trunk is a bad idea, too. This encourages rot to set in and roots to grow around the trunk, girdling it. Resign yourself to under-planting the hard way. In the end, it's the only way.

Let height be your guide. Height will help you decide which plants to put under a tree.

- Measure the distance between the tree's lowest branches and the ground.

- Check this against the mature heights listed on plant labels, and choose only plants that will stay well below the lower branches. Otherwise, the bed will look crowded.

- Place the tallest plants closest to the trunk.

Dial before you dig

Take five minutes to dial 811 before you do any kind of digging, whether you're putting in a new garden bed or planting a tree or shrub. This phone number will connect you to your local One Call Center, no matter where you live. Tell the operator what kind of work you want to do and where you want to do it. A few days later, the utility companies will stop by and mark any underground pipes, lines, and cables in that area.

The cheapest way to build a raised bed. You can make a raised bed out of almost anything, but some materials will last longer than others. Stone has the longest life span and won't warp or decay the way wood will. Still, it can be expensive. Find free rocks, instead. Check your local newspaper, or a website like Craigslist.org, for giveaway chunks of concrete. Someone may have torn out an old patio and need to get rid of the broken pieces. For the cost of hauling it home, you'll get a raised bed that will last for decades.

Build an instant raised bed from an old dresser

Remove the drawers and pry off the bottoms. Lay them out in a grid pattern, with enough room to walk and kneel between them.

To make beds higher, stack multiple bottomless drawers on top of each other until you reach the height you like. Fill with rich soil and start planting.

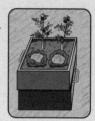

Fill up bed with free soil. Try this super-simple solution when you don't have enough dirt to fill a raised bed. Dig a shallow trench around the edge of the bed you want to build, and toss the dirt onto the bed itself. Pile on enough to bring it up a foot or so above ground level. Add a couple more inches of compost on top and rake smooth. Fill the ditch you've dug with a layer of straw to keep weeds and mud to a minimum and the soil inside the bed moist.

Quick check to catch big problem. Good drainage is a must in any garden — and that includes raised beds. Test the drainage in yours.

- Dig a hole 12-inches wide and as deep as the bed is high.

- Fill it with water, let it drain, and fill it again.

- Time how long it takes the water to drain out the second time. If under one hour, your drainage is fine. If longer, amend the soil to improve drainage.

Simple trick keeps sandy soil moist. Sandy soil poses a special challenge in raised beds. These beds dry out fast anyway.

Sandy soil makes them dry even faster. Plants can easily die from thirst, unless you use this trick. Instead of mounding dirt in a cone shape around the base of plants, do the reverse. Dig a slight pit around each plant, so water drains toward it when it rains.

Border planning made simple. Save yourself a lot of stress with this tip from the experts. Draw out your border on a piece of paper. Divide it into three or four parts, roughly the same size. Pick the plants and plan the layout for one section, then simply repeat it for the others. Far from looking boring, the repetition will tie your border together neatly, not to mention slash the design time.

10 tricks for jaw-dropping borders

- Divide the border into sections when planning it. Design one section, then repeat that design in each of the others.

- Plan a few large, bold curves in your border rather than many small curves.

- Design borders to curve in at corners.

- Choose flower colors next to each other on the color wheel for a serene, calm feeling.

- Combine opposite colors on the color wheel for bright, striking contrast.

- Add variety to one-color flower borders with a mixture of foliage and textures.

- Interplant bulbs among perennials to hide bulbs' dying foliage.

- Lay strips of cardboard around bed edges and cover with mulch to eliminate weed eating.

- Edge borders with creative materials like seashells.

- Mass containers together to create a potted plant border if you have poor or no ground to grow in.

Create moods with colorful blooms. Make your beds colorful without being garish or gaudy.

- For a serene, restful feeling, combine colors beside each other on the color wheel, like blue and indigo, or yellow and reddish yellow. Since they are so closely related, your eyes will move over them smoothly without feeling jarred.

- For more drama and excitement, pair colors from opposite sides of the wheel, like yellow and violet.

- Too spicy? Tone it down without taking away the zing by pairing near opposites, such as yellow with red-violet or blue-violet.

Liven up boring borders. One-color borders can work if you add interest with foliage and texture. An ocean of yellow blooms can look boring and monotonous. Try these tricks to liven it up.

- Toss in plants with different textures, like a coarse-textured plume poppy or a fine artemisia.

- Use the greens and blues of foliage to offset a one-color wall of flowers. Add swathes of pale green and dark green as well as silvers and blue.

Add excitement by tweaking height. You know the rule — short plants go at the front of the border, tall plants in the back. Some rules, though, are meant to be broken. Shake things up by scattering a few tall, slender see-through plants, like gauzy grasses or delicate-stemmed flowers, in the middle. They'll make the border more interesting without hiding the plants behind them.

Lay out curves for more curb appeal. Straight borders with sharp turns work well in a formal garden but not an informal one. Plan sweeping curves to lead the eye from one focal point to another.

- The deeper the curve, the slower the eye will move along it. A few large, bold curves will look better than lots of small, shallow ones.

- Make the border no less than 3 feet wide at its narrowest part.

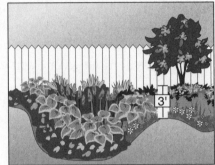

- Have the border curve inward at corners, so plants in the corner grab the limelight.

- Place finely textured shrubs behind the flowers along inward curves. Plants with large, course texture should go behind the flowers along outcurves.

Never trim bed edges again. Save yourself the headache of weed-eating. Set flat stones or bricks flush with the dirt all along the edges of beds and borders. You'll be able to mow around this hardscape without ruining your blade. To temporarily block weeds and grass, lay strips of cardboard around bed edges and cover with a layer of mulch.

Bring beauty to curbside beds. Don't settle for bland borders around curbs. Dress them up with hard-to-kill prairie flowers. Plants like garden phlox, ox-eye daisy, bee balm, switchgrass, and purple coneflower are made for tough-to-grow areas — like the space between the sidewalk and curb. They thrive in poor, compacted dirt with lots of sun and little rain. Pick plants that have nice foliage as well as beautiful blooms, so they'll look lovely even when not in flower. Talk to your city about planting restrictions before you start digging. It may limit the height of what you can grow here.

EARTHY MATTERS

MAKING THE MOST
OF YOUR SOIL

SECRETS TO BUILDING BETTER SOIL

Create the garden of your dreams. Gardening is not rocket science, but it helps to know the basics. Following these four steps will almost guarantee you gorgeous color in your garden.

- Prepare the soil, perhaps using compost, fertilizer, or other soil amendments. No matter what crop you want to grow, it all begins with great soil.

- Select the right plant for the site. Study the available sun, soil type, amount of drainage, and other key factors. Then pick plants that enjoy these conditions, and you create less work for yourself.

- Start with healthy plants. Check for signs of pests or disease before you bring a new bulb, shrub, or plant into the yard.

- Nurture with just the right amount of water. Plants need moisture to keep their stems upright, transport nutrients, and assist in chemical reactions inside their cells. But too much water can kill as surely as not enough.

Get perfect topsoil the lazy way. Turn rock-hard soil into soft, rich earth in one season — without exhausting yourself. There's no need to till when you let time do the work of breaking up the soil. Follow this no-dig plan for garden prep, and you'll also avoid pulling weeds later on.

- Put down a layer of newspapers about 10 sheets deep in the area where you want the garden. Use regular newspaper — not the glossy colorful sections. Don't bother digging, removing sod, or pulling weeds first.

- Water the newspapers well, then cover with a thick layer of compost and soil. Some gardeners like to add another layer of newspapers and organic material, watering it all well.

- Leave the layers for weeks or months, and weeds will rot while hard dirt softens up. By planting time you will find a thick layer of rich topsoil that plants will love.

Patience pays off in spades

How long do you have to wait for soil to be ready for planting in a no-dig garden? Some gardening experts say to wait six weeks, others recommend two or three months, while still others suggest letting your layers sit for six months or an entire season. The idea is to wait as long as it takes for the newspaper to break down, weeds to die off, earthworms to do their job, and nice rich soil to develop. The longer you can wait, the better your soil.

Save strength with autumn tilling. Get a head start on your spring gardening. Tackle the tough chore of tilling up a new bed months early, and you'll save lots of work and have soft, fluffy soil. Tilling in the fall allows you to do a quick, rough job, then let winter weather break up any large clumps that remain. If you wait to till in the spring, you may have to push through compact, wet soil. Besides that, soil left exposed over the winter allows freezing temperatures, heavy rain, and birds to take care of weeds and pests for you.

Avoid beginner's digging error. It can be tempting to push your spade into the ground, pick up a scoopful of soil, then turn it over and plop it upside down. Following this method over and over can create an underground barrier of leaves, weeds, or other trash from the surface that blocks moisture and air. Instead, carefully set each scoopful of soil on its side, lined up like dominoes. You'll do less work, and your soil will drain properly.

The benefits of not rototilling

Some gardening experts say you do not need to rototill if you already have good garden soil that is rich and fluffy. You just need to keep working compost into your soil at planting time and during the growing season. Rototilling may contribute to soil compaction and help limit the amount of oxygen and water available to your plants.

Of course, you may still need to rototill when breaking new ground or when you incorporate green manure into the soil. But as long as your garden soil is in good condition, your garden may do just fine without an annual rototilling every year.

Let plants till up the hard soil. If your soil is too hard and compacted to work with, don't break your back trying to till it. Plant a crop that will do the tilling for you. That's why farmers plant what is known as a cover crop — a plant grown just for the purpose of improving soil in some way. Good choices of plants that grow quickly and break up hard soil include alfalfa, buckwheat, clover, and winter rye. Some cover crops also provide benefits like adding nitrogen back to the soil and preventing erosion. Plant the cover crop in the fall, then till it under before springtime planting.

Easy way to prep straw. Before you spread a bale of alfalfa straw over your garden in the fall, loosen up the bale and run the lawn mower over it. Chopping up the straw will speed decomposition and encourage nitrogen release into the soil.

Create top-notch topsoil

All loads of dirt labeled "topsoil" are not created equal. Dirt sold as topsoil typically comes from the top 2 inches of the ground, but it may not be good quality soil for your garden. It may be low in organic matter or high in weed seeds, depending on where it came from.

When buying topsoil in bulk, ask about the source and whether it's been tested for nutrient levels, acidity, and contamination by herbicides or other chemicals. Then plan to mix in some compost with your new topsoil before you plant in it.

Give your soil the squeeze test. Want to know what's in your soil? Just reach down and give it a squeeze. That's how experts test the texture of soil to see if it's mostly clay, sand, or silt.

- Pick up a handful of soil and spray it with a bit of water.

- Knead the soil in your fingers, then try to squeeze it into a ball. If it's gritty and won't hold its shape, you have sandy soil.

- Try to form a ribbon by squeezing the soil between your thumb and forefinger. A longer ribbon means a larger amount of clay in the soil.

- Silty soil feels smooth and powdery when it's dry, but silky when you add water.

Try a simple drainage test. You don't need to send a soil sample off to the lab to figure out how much irrigation your garden needs. All you need is a shovel. Wait for the soil to dry out, then dig a hole about 1 foot deep and 1 foot across. Pour a bucket of water into the hole, and check the results.

- Good drainage. Water fills the hole then drains out completely within a few minutes.

- Sandy soil. Water seeps into the soil almost as fast as you can pour it into the hole. You'll need to water often to keep plants from drying out.

- Poor drainage. As you pour water into the hole, it quickly fills up. To keep plant roots from sitting in a swamp, consider amending the soil with compost or sphagnum peat moss. You may also try a raised bed system using an easy-draining soil.

Collect a soil sample you can trust. You will need about two cups of soil for a lab to do testing. Gather small samples from about eight places in the garden. Be sure to brush away plants or debris from the locations first, then dig a hole about 6 inches deep. Scrape a small handful of soil from the side of the hole. Leave the soil out on a piece of plastic to dry, then mix it well and place in a clean container.

Dirt cheap soil analysis

Get a soil analysis done by experts in your area for less than $20. You can find your local cooperative extension office through the U.S. Department of Agriculture website, *www.csrees.usda.gov/Extension*. A soil analysis will let you know if you should add lime, ash, or other nutrients to improve your garden. Experts say to have it done every three to five years.

Shake up a sample for simple testing. Sand or silt, clay or loam. Figure out the consistency of your soil so you'll know what amendments to add. Take a handful of soil and sift out rocks and stems. Fill a glass jar about one-third full with the soil, then add an inch or so of water and three teaspoons of detergent. Screw on the jar's lid, and shake it well. Let the jar sit overnight, then examine the contents. You should find layers with water in the middle, solids on the bottom, and possibly organic material floating on top.

- Cloudy water with bits of dirt floating means your soil is silty loam.

- Clear water with all matter settled out means the soil is sandy.

- A well-defined line of clay at the top of the settled material means you have clay soil.

Pantry tests give clues about soil. Most plants in the garden would love to grow in a soil that is just a bit acidic, with a pH between 6.0 and 6.5. Grab items from the pantry and do a rough pH test. Collect a soil sample and divide it in half. Add a few drops of cider vinegar to one sample. It if fizzes, the soil is alkaline. Wet the other sample, then add a pinch of baking soda. If this sample fizzes, the soil may be on the acidic side. That gives you a basic idea, but check with your county cooperative extension agency for a more accurate test.

Cook up a home soil pH test. Find out just what your soil needs to grow the best garden ever with a homemade pH test. Shred red cabbage leaves, then boil them until the water turns light red. Meanwhile, get a soil sample from the garden and place in a white bowl. Pour some of the cabbage water over the soil, then watch the color of the water in the bowl.

- If the water turns a deeper red color, the soil is acidic.

- If the water turns blue or purplish, the soil is alkaline.

- If the water stays the same color, the soil is neutral.

No-sweat tricks to attract earthworms. These helpful little creatures improve the nutrient content and texture of dirt, turning stubborn bare spots into rich soil. Attract earthworms to the part of your garden where you need them by hiding

fruit and vegetable scraps under straw. You can also try a couple
pieces of old bread, a bit of manure, or small pieces of cardboard
soaked in vegetable oil placed under a pile of straw or soil.

Save your worms from untimely tillage. Digging in the garden
is important to break up compacted soil and prepare a bed
for planting. But it's a hazard for the earthworms living
there. Do as little damage as possible to your wrigglers.

- A couple days before you till, lure worms away from
  the danger zone by placing a pile of damp hay or fresh
  grass clippings nearby.

- Till in the heat of midday, when worms have dug down
  deep to avoid the heat.

- Use a digging fork rather than a spade or rototiller.

- Till as shallowly as possible, preferably between 3 and
  6 inches deep.

Don't overdo soil treatments

Skip the weekend warrior method of gardening, and spread out your soil
treatments. Wait at least a week in between adding soil amendments,
fertilizers, or pH modifiers like sulfur or lime. Doing just one addition at
a time lets your soil get the greatest benefits from each treatment.

Rock solid way to boost your roots. Blending rock dust into your
garden soil is a great way to provide a mineral boost for roses,
veggies, trees, and grass. You can get it from your garden center
or a nearby quarry. Minerals in rock dust, including calcium,
iron, and phosphorus, improve soil's ability to hold water, plus
they provide important nutrients plants need. But for this kind
of inorganic mineral source to do much good at spring planting
time, you need to add it in the fall. If you don't have that much

time to wait, use a plant- or animal-based amendment like compost tea or seaweed.

Save money on garden minerals. Leftover drywall scraps from a home-improvement project can boost your soil. Chop up the scraps and add to your compost pile, or toss them on the soil and let rain, wind, and time break them down. Just like the gypsum you can buy in garden centers, plain sheetrock adds calcium and sulfur to the soil, and it helps break up tough clay so roots can get through easily. But avoid using sheetrock that has been painted, treated to make it water-resistant, or labeled as Type X. Those products can add chemicals into your soil.

Seaweed turns your garden green. Organic gardeners know the value of chemical-free fertilizers, including "green manure." Seaweed is a great natural choice to mix into the soil or use as a mulch, and you don't even have to buy it. Collect it fresh on the beach, then rinse it off before you use it to remove excess salt. Seaweed, or kelp, provides some of the main three minerals plants need — nitrogen, phosphorus, and potassium — along with other trace elements like magnesium and zinc. You can also add it to your compost pile, or chop it up and put it in the planting hole before you put in new plants. Along with adding nutrients to the soil, seaweed also helps ward off slugs. Be sure to follow local rules on gathering seaweed.

Dispense with drainage woes. Clay soil holds water — not a good thing when plant roots are left soaking in swampy ground. You may have heard you should break up the heavy clay soil in your garden by mixing in sand or vermiculite. Both are bad choices. When blended with clay they can create a cement-like mixture plants will hate. Instead, mix in organic material like compost, manure, or straw. Aim for one part organic material mixed with two parts native soil for a great garden blend.

Boil up hand-scouring pumice soap. Save money by making your own gritty, super-cleaning soap to take that tough layer of garden dirt off your hands. You need just a few ingredients.

- 2 tablespoons fine sand

- one-quarter bar Fels-Naptha laundry soap

- 1 cup water

Mix together soap and water in a saucepan over low heat, letting it melt together. Let the mixture cool, then add sand and blend. Store your gritty soap in a small butter tub, and dig out a portion to use when your hands get grimy. Fels-Naptha soap is made to use in the laundry, not on your skin, so don't use it as your everyday hand soap.

Skip the free beach sand

Don't be tempted to pick up sand from the beach during your next vacation to use in the garden. Ocean sand contains lots of salt, which may harm your plants. It's also unscreened, so the sand particles will vary greatly in size. Your best bet is coarse sand — not fine — to benefit your garden's soil structure. Look for a deal on a bulk purchase from a home-improvement store.

Explore peat moss substitutes. Peat moss is endangered in some places, and it's very slow-growing. If you're creating a seed-starting mix, you'll probably need to include some. Otherwise, try these to get similar soil benefits. Many of them are free.

- sulfur or pine needles to lower soil pH

- compost, shredded leaves, or green manures to help soil hold water

- coconut fiber or aged pine bark to add bulk to potting mix without adding much weight

- vermiculite, packing peanuts, or shredded newspaper to store summer bulbs in the winter

Give your wheelbarrow a rain hat. You don't want to spend time unloading soil, compost, or mulch from the wheelbarrow if you don't use it all in one day. But you sure don't want to deal with a wet, sloppy mess if the load gets rained on overnight. The solution is a simple cover that fits over the whole wheelbarrow, load and all. Find a waterproof grill cover at the hardware store that fits your wheelbarrow, or dig out an old one from the shed. If you're handy with a sewing machine, you can even make a cover from weather-proof canvas. The shape is just a simple three-dimensional envelope, similar to making a toaster cover. And the "rain hat" doesn't have to fit perfectly to do the job.

"Skate" your way to a lighter load. It's not easy to move a 40-pound bag of soil or mulch from your car to the shed, then out to the garden plot. Don't spend money on a wheelbarrow or garden cart when you already have a set of wheels. Borrow your grandson's old skateboard, and balance the heavy bags on it while you pull them to their final destination. Even if the bags topple off, they're only a few inches from the ground. An old children's wagon also works great to lug heavy items around the yard.

Take a hint from your weed crop. Don't spend money and time amending soil to improve drainage if you don't need to. Take note of the weeds growing naturally in the area planned for your garden. If you see pigweed, purslane, or ground ivy, the soil is probably already rich and ready to plant. But if you notice a healthy crop of curly dock, sheep sorrel, or hedge bindweed, the soil probably doesn't drain well. Add compost or consider building raised beds for best results.

COMPOSTING
A PICK-ME-UP FOR YOUR PLOT

Build 2 for prime composting. A compost pile is great, but you really need two — one heap of material that's been aging and rotting down for a while, and the other that you can constantly add to. That's because organic material — leaves, grass, wood chips, kitchen scraps — have to be broken down by bacteria before being put on your garden. If you put it directly on the garden soil, you risk drawing nitrogen from the soil and away from your plants. Your plants could end up starving for nitrogen for the next year. A two-pile system lets you add to one pile while you use compost from the finished heap.

Save the browns, balance the greens. Composting works best if you include the right mix of organic material. Certain raw ingredients, known as "brown" matter, provide carbon to the microorganisms that break down waste into compost. Others — "green" matter — provide nitrogen to the mix. Most gardeners end up with lots of green material, like grass clippings, kitchen scraps, garden waste, and manure, during the spring and summer. That's OK, except that the pile needs about three times as much carbon as nitrogen to process. An easy solution is to save up your brown matter — dry leaves, shredded newspapers, wood chips, and cardboard — to add in layers during the warm months.

Free help from composting connoisseurs

Get the straight scoop on recycling yard and kitchen waste into compost at *www.mastercomposter.com*. You'll learn how to build a bin, what materials to include, how to involve worms, where to use your finished compost, and much more. There is even a message board for your compost-related questions.

Fill your bin for free. Turn lousy soil into a gardener's dream for free. When you run out of compost materials from your kitchen and yard, check out these sources of prime organic material to get your compost pile humming.

- Local breweries. Spent hops are a residue from the brewing industry, and you may be able to pick up some for free. It's such a good soil conditioner, however, that farmers buy it in bulk.

- Supermarkets. Talk to the produce manager about old produce he'll need to get rid of at closing time.

- Golf courses or football fields. Grooming acres of grass produces mounds of grass cuttings.

- Beaches. Pick up kelp — seaweed — that has washed up, and add this high-potassium ingredient to the pile. Check local rules about gathering seaweed.

Thicken up soupy compost. Slime in the compost bin? That can happen if you put in too much green material, like fresh grass clippings, without enough coarser material. Create a good mix by including dry shredded newspaper, straw, or shredded cotton rags. The dry material will soak up extra moisture, then break down into nice compost. A good ratio is one part dry material to four parts grass clippings.

Toss in the sunflower seeds

You may have been told not to put sunflower seeds or their hulls into the compost pile. The fear is that sunflower seeds contain allelopathic — plant-killing — substances that can harm whatever plants you put the compost on. Don't worry. It's true that sunflowers contain these natural chemicals, but they will be broken down and harmless after the composting process.

Save money, skip the activator. Beginning composters may think they need to buy a product to add to the compost pile to help heat it up and start decomposition. Or sometimes cool weather slows down the process, and you may feel it needs an extra boost. But if you include enough greens and browns and provide air circulation and moisture, nature will take it from there. Toss in some extra grass clippings or used coffee grounds for a boost of nitrogen, and you can save the cost of buying activator.

Boost nitrogen with a personal contribution. Clean out your hairbrush — or your dog's brush — and toss the hair into your compost bin. This great source of nitrogen counts as green matter. Be sure the hair hasn't been chemically treated with color or a perm, and wet the pile after you add hair.

Balance the blend for speed. If you've been putting lots of acidic materials — coffee grounds, apple peels — into your compost pile, it may benefit from a bit of balancing. Add in something on the alkaline end of the pH scale. A sprinkling of fireplace ashes or lime will do the trick, speeding up the composting process.

Beware the dangers of killer compost

Organic matter can do great things for your garden. But if the ingredients you put in your compost bin are contaminated, you could end up killing your plants. Some herbicides used to kill weeds don't get broken down in the composting process. Even low concentrations can harm your tomatoes, lettuce, or carrots. Here's where it can come from.

- Hay that is contaminated with long-lasting herbicides, known as pyralids. Farmers sometimes use these on their fields, and the chemicals stay potent for years.
- Manure from animals that have grazed on herbicide-sprayed pastureland.
- Your own lawn clippings if you had the grass treated with a weed-killing chemical. Some experts say to wait at least three cuttings after herbicide treatment before putting the clippings in your compost.

Know the source of everything you put on the pile so you can avoid these dangers.

Keep away critters by careful sorting. Not everything from your kitchen can go into the compost pile. A reputation for being smelly and attracting wild animals comes from piles filled with the wrong items. The worst offenders include meat, bones, and other animal byproducts that decay and smell bad. Fence in the pile if raccoons or mice are still attracted. Also keep these other items out of the compost pile.

- Roots of hardy weeds, like bindweed and couch grass. Burn these so they don't multiply in the compost heap.

- Man-made fabrics, carpeting, and dryer lint, since synthetic textiles won't break down. But you can include natural fibers like cotton and linen.

- Rose canes and prunings from other woody plants, which don't break down quickly.

- Eucalyptus and walnut leaves. These may harm other plants.

- Leaves from a potato crop, which are likely contaminated with potato blight spores.

Brew a batch of compost tea. Sometimes you don't want to dig out the shovel to give your plants a bite to eat. You can make your own fertilizer with almost no work by mixing up compost tea. This concentrated source of organic goodness gives a boost to struggling or stressed plants, adds nutrients to a large area of lawn, and improves the soil in an entire garden plot. Just put a cloth sack of finished compost into a large bucket filled with water, and cover it. Let it steep for a few days, then remove the "tea bag." Add water until the color is like weak tea, so it won't burn your plants' leaves.

Perfect compost in a hole. Prepare the ground for your rose bush by composting in the hole where you plan to plant it next year. Layer the main ingredients in 4-inch bands of brown, dried organic matter; soil; green grass clippings or weeds; soil; manure; and a final layer of soil. In between, sprinkle a couple of light dustings of fertilizer, limestone, or compost activator.

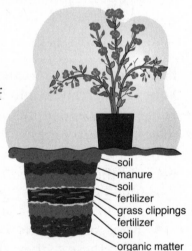

soil
manure
soil
fertilizer
grass clippings
fertilizer
soil
organic matter

Save with homemade tumbler. For a cheap and easy way to start composting, try recycling your waste in a trash can tumbler. It's ideal if you have an old leaky plastic or metal garbage can — just add a few more holes for drainage. You can also drill large holes in the sides and bottom of a new garbage can. Be sure the lid fits because you'll need to roll it, and you don't want anything spilling out. For insurance, use a bungee cord or rope tied through the handles to secure the top. Tip over your homemade tumbler about once a week, and roll several times to mix your compost ingredients.

Slow-cook straw for easy compost. Pick up a couple bales of straw, set them in a forgotten corner of your yard, and let nature do the work of making compost. All you need to add is water — and occasionally whatever leaves, yard waste, or manure is handy. Just pull apart the bales, keep the pile wet, and in a year or so bacteria will turn the straw into a great amendment for clay soil.

Free wood makes handy bin. Some 80 percent of yard waste ends up in landfills, according to the U.S. Environmental Protection Agency. That's 26 million tons of grass and leaves that could be improving garden soil. Do your small part by recycling waste in a bin you make from old pallets. These wooden platforms used to help forklifts move packages are like ready-made fencing. Stand up four on their sides, holding them upright with wire or rope, and you have a compost bin ready for use. The walls even allow for proper air circulation.

2 ways to snuff out weed seeds. Treat weeds properly, and you can compost them without worry of spreading these garden enemies in the spring.

- Pretreat weeds before they go in the bin by letting them rot. Put them in a covered bucket of water, and let them sit until they turn black. Then add the harmless mushy stems, roots, seeds, and all to your compost bin.

- It's not too late if weeds are already in the compost. Put an old slow cooker in your mud room, fill it with batches of compost, and turn it on low. Most seeds in the compost will be dead after about three hours at 160 degrees Fahrenheit. After it's cooked, let the compost cure for a few weeks with a few earthworms to bring back the compost's organic punch.

Red worms to the rescue. Get help from worms — red wigglers, not your everyday garden earthworms or night crawlers — to start an easy composting project. Only red worms like the crowded conditions and rich organic material that vermicomposting requires.

- Pull out an old plastic bin with a lid. If it's leaky, great. If not, drill holes in the bottom, sides, and top for drainage and air. Be sure the bin blocks out light.

- Fill it with shredded paper that has been watered down. Also put in kitchen scraps, like vegetable peels, coffee grounds, and eggshells.

- Release your red worms into the bin. You can buy these through a gardening catalog or website, or barter for free worms from a local gardening friend.

You'll end up with lots of vermicompost, or dark, rich, loamy material that plants will love.

Don't overdo compost layer

Some people say you can never have too much compost. That's not quite true. As with anything else, too much of a good thing is not good. If you overdo the organic matter in your garden, soil can become spongy, and plants can suffer from pests and disease. Stick with a 4-inch layer of compost.

3 tips to help worms survive the winter. Red wigglers prefer moderate temperatures of 55 to 85 degrees Fahrenheit. Much colder than that, and they won't do their best work digesting garbage in your compost pile. Help them survive a cold winter.

- Move your worm composter into the basement or garage if the temperature drops too much.

- Don't think simply adding more bedding will help them survive the cold. More than 10 to 12 inches of bedding in a bin can cut the oxygen supply these worms need.

- Feed your worms right, avoiding salty foods, citrus rinds, seeds, and cabbage-family scraps. Worms thrive on coffee grounds, bread and pasta, eggshells, and cooked vegetables.

Sniff out finished compost. The decomposition process in your compost bin can take weeks or months. Check out these clues to help you know when your "black gold" is ready.

- Put a bit of the compost in a bucket, and take its temperature. If the temperature changes noticeably over about four days, it may still be heating up and processing. Give it more time.

- Take a sample and seal it in a plastic bag. Wait a couple of days, then open the bag and take a sniff. If you smell ammonia or another unpleasant odor, it's not ready. Finished compost will give off a pleasant, earthy smell.

Freeze kitchen scraps for faster turnover. Before you dump those limp veggies, overripe bananas, and potato peelings onto the compost pile, give them a couple of days in the deep freeze. Cold temperatures cause cell walls to burst, so the produce will turn into mush that helps along the composting bacteria. You can even give the thawed produce a whirl in the blender to really hasten the process.

3 ways to speed up your compost. Some like it hot. Bacteria, for instance. To speed up the compost process, help the pile heat up, and allow those helpful little critters to work faster. These easy tricks can encourage a hot compost pile.

- Add manure. The pile needs both green and brown matter, but damp organic matter will cause it to heat up and speed up.

- Chop up yard waste. Put dry leaves into a barrel, insert a string trimmer, and turn on your giant blender. Shredding leaves increases their surface area, giving the process a big head start. Besides that, it cuts down their volume.

- Keep it moist. A dry pile won't heat up, so you may need to spray it down.

Put buried treasure where plants will find it. Create a honey hole, or small underground area of compost, in the middle of the garden. Plants with shallow roots, like tomatoes and blueberries, will appreciate a nearby source of organic material and moisture. There is no need to fuss with containers or messy piles, since you just bury the compostable items and forget about them. Just pick a spot in the middle of your bed, then dig a small hole about 2 feet deep. Toss in the usual yard waste and kitchen scraps in layers, then plant your garden around it. Whenever you water your plants, water the honey hole also.

Take a hint from little critters

If ants seem to have taken over your compost pile, you know it's getting too dry. Add water to the pile to get it back to the proper conditions for decomposition, and the ants will scurry away.

Put water right where you need it. Watering a compost pile can seem like a waste during a drought. Get water to the heart of the pile without losing a drop.

- Insert a leaky bucket into a depression in the top of the pile. Fill the bucket with water in the evening, and watch it seep down into the pile.

- Tie newspapers into tight rolls and place them into the pile to serve as wicks. Pour water on the end of the wick, and it will be drawn into the inside of the pile.

- Before you complete your compost pile, build a chimney. First drill tiny holes into the sides of a 3-inch diameter PVC pipe, then insert the pipe straight down into the pile. When it's time to irrigate, just insert a plastic bottle of water into the pipe, and let it drain down into the compost.

Save steps with "walking" compost pile. Kill two birds with one stone by moving compost while you mix it. Start your compost pile about 15 feet from the place in your garden where you will use it. Then every time you turn and mix the pile, move it a couple of steps closer to that location. Plan for four or more sessions of mixing and moving a few weeks apart. When it's finished, the pile should have gradually moved right to where you need it.

Easy way to get air into compost. Your compost pile needs air — all the way to the bottom. The helpful bacteria that break down waste can't do their job without oxygen. Plan ahead and you can provide air without having to turn the pile. Build chimneys when you're first creating the pile by inserting several 4-inch perforated PVC pipes upright in the pile. Hold them up with bricks until the pile grows. The pipes should be about a foot taller than you expect the pile to end up.

FERTILIZER
QUICK & EASY PLANT
FOOD FIXES

Rotate fertilizers for top-blooming roses. You can buy fertilizers labeled for use on rose bushes, but you'll need to change what you use over the course of a season. Pay attention to the numbers. Roses need a different blend of the three main nutrients — nitrogen, phosphorus, and potassium, or N-P-K — at different times of the year. Early in the season, when roses want to put out leafy growth after they've been pruned, give them lots of nitrogen. That means selecting a fertilizer with roughly equal amounts of N-P-K, like one that says 7-7-7 or 10-10-10 on the label. But later in the summer, when it's time to put out lots of flowers, give your rose bushes a boost of phosphorus to encourage flower growth. Pick one with a high middle number, say 9-27-15.

Don't overpay for N-P-K

Fertilizer bags list how much nitrogen, phosphorus, and potassium, or N-P-K, they contain. Basically, they refer to the percentage of total weight in the bag that each nutrient takes up, so a fertilizer listed as 10-15-20 contains 10 percent nitrogen.

The numbers are most useful as ratios, so you'll know if you are buying a fertilizer that's balanced — say, 10-10-10 — or one higher in phosphorus, like 10-25-10. Also, pay attention to price per pound of nitrogen. Stay away from high-priced bags with lower numbers, like 5-5-5.

Old-fashioned fertilizer for free. Have gardens as beautiful and bountiful as Jefferson did at Monticello by using his favorite natural fertilizer — manure. Animal waste contains minerals plants need, including nitrogen, potassium, and phosphorus. The nitrogen in manure is released more slowly than other forms, so it's still benefiting the soil years after you apply it. Manure also can reduce soil erosion and runoff while it makes your garden more productive. You can probably find manure available cheap or free at these types of locations nearby.

- pet stores and animal breeders
- elementary classrooms with pets
- zoos, petting zoos, and circuses
- cow or goat dairy farms
- your local county extension service
- horse stables and racetracks
- online swap sites like *www.craigslist.org* and *www.freecycle.org*

Fertilize with 10-cent kitchen wonder. Don't pay for expensive fertilizer when you can grab that bottle of ammonia from under the kitchen sink. Household ammonia contains nitrogen, a major ingredient in commercial fertilizers. Some gardeners suggest using around one-quarter cup of ammonia with some liquid hand soap in a 20-gallon hose-end sprayer. That might work, but you need to check three things first.

- Calibration of your sprayer. Be sure it's set to deliver a diluted mixture of ammonia and water so you don't burn your plants.

- Tap water pH. If it's higher than 7.0 — on the alkaline end of the scale — your plants may be harmed by toxic aqueous ammonia from the solution. But if your water has a pH lower than 7.0 — acidic — then ammonium ions will be released to plants. They'll consider that a treat.

- Soil pH. If it's alkaline, skip using ammonia to avoid the risk of toxic aqueous ammonia.

> ## *Go low-budget for great results.*
>
> Epsom salts contain magnesium and sulfur — two nutrients plants need. Mix one tablespoon of Epsom salts in a gallon of water, and treat your plants to a healthy feast. It's a great homemade fertilizer for roses, vegetables, and houseplants.

Feed your plants with throwaways. Used coffee grounds can go into the compost bin, but you can also use them straight out of the filter. They're a great source of nitrogen, potassium, and magnesium, and they're easily processed by soil-improving earthworms. Many gardeners warn of adding too much acidity to your soil by sprinkling coffee grounds. However, research has found the pH of coffee grounds is not always acidic, so you may not need to worry about it. To avoid a bad smell in the garden, dry coffee grounds before use. Simply spread several days' worth of used coffee grounds on a cookie sheet that's lined with newspaper, and leave them to dry overnight. They're ready to work into your garden soil.

Steer clear of beer

You may have heard it's a good idea to pour out leftover beer around plants, providing them a nice boost of minerals and other nutrients. Don't risk it. Beer, like other alcoholic beverages, contains ethanol. This form of alcohol can burn plants and even kill them. It's best to stick to water.

Prep eggshells for happy plants. Don't toss the shells next time you cook up an omelet. Let them dry, then save them until you have enough to pulverize in a blender. Sprinkle the eggshell powder in your garden to give plants a boost of calcium, along with magnesium, potassium, and phosphorus. It's like five-star dining to your plants.

Pickle your posies for fabulous flowers. Don't dump out the juice left in the jar after you eat the last of the pickles. Mix it with water, and pour it around your flowering gardenia and azalea bushes. These acid-loving plants will appreciate a slightly lower pH from the vinegar in pickle juice. But keep the solution weak to avoid doing any damage to your prize bloomers.

Share a banana with your bromeliad. Place small bits of banana peel into the cup of a bromeliad plant, and the plant will grow and bloom. Minerals from the banana peel enter the plant through water in its cup.

Feed plants a sip of buttermilk. Don't toss that buttermilk in your fridge that's ready to expire. Mix it up — one part buttermilk with four parts water — and spray on the leaves of plants that need a fertilizer boost. Buttermilk may be too pricey to use as your regular foliar fertilizer, but it will do the trick in a pinch.

3 secrets for successful foliar feeding. Plant food that you apply directly to the leaves can give plants a quick boost of nutrients. It's easy to use, since you just combine a bit of foliar food with water in a spray bottle. Ensure success with these tricks.

- Mix in a spoonful of vegetable oil to the food and water mix. The oil will help the food stick to leaves so it can do your plants some good.

- Spray directly on leaves early in the day to let it dry before the sun gets high.

- Use once a month or even more often during the growing season.

Evergreens flourish with shot of iron. If your broadleaf evergreens — like holly or magnolia bushes — are sporting yellowish leaves with dark veins, they may need a shot of iron. Give them a boost with an iron cocktail. Just toss some old scrap iron, like nails, wire, or anything else that rusts, into a bucket of water. Let this sit until it looks rusty. Add one-quarter cup to a gallon of water, and give your bushes a dose.

Rose fertilizer offers long-lasting nitrogen. Foliage plants with yellow leaves are probably low in nitrogen rather than iron. You can give plants nitrogen from a variety of sources, from fish emulsion to packaged chemical fertilizer — any kind will work. The main difference between the various types of fertilizer is how quickly the nitrogen is available for plants to use. For a dose of nitrogen that lasts a long time, splurge for a premium rose fertilizer like Miracle-Gro rose food or Osmocote.

Solve growth problem with ashes. Stunted, dark-green leaves with purplish veins or stems may be a sign plants need more phosphorus. Late blooming and fruit production also tell the tale of phosphorus deficiency. You can solve the problem by using a fertilizer with a high phosphorus number — the middle number of the N-P-K listing — of 9-27-15. But a simpler and cheaper solution may be to sprinkle wood ashes around the base of the plant.

Be light-handed with fertilizer

If you've heard the advice to give your perennials lots of fertilizer, don't follow it. Too much fertilizer may actually be bad for your perennials, encouraging them to become leggy with fewer flowers and stunted roots. Give new plants a tiny bit of quick-release fertilizer, then let them get on with growing.

Follow your neighbor's lead. Ashes from a wood-burning stove can give acidic soil a more neutral pH. Your plants may need that change if you live in the eastern part of the United States. But if you live in the West, your soil may already be plenty alkaline. Ashes would be the last thing the soil needs. Check with your county cooperative extension agency about soil testing, or ask your neighbors with lovely gardens. They already know the soil.

Give shrubs a break before winter. Make sure your controlled-release fertilizer is all used up at least six weeks before the first frost. Trees and shrubs need to harden off their new growth before cold weather arrives.

Plan ahead for great spring growth. Your garden may look empty and tired in the fall, but that's not the time to stay inside and rest. Add some lime to the soil after the growth season, and you'll get a bonanza of blooms in the spring. Lime takes about three months to alter your soil. It's an alkaline ingredient, a natural "soil sweetener" for ground that's too acidic. Lime blends more easily with dry soil, so wait for a dry spell, then mix it into the top 10 inches of your soil.

Pantry cure for lime-dry skin

Even dedicated gardeners who don't mind the thought of dirt under their fingernails hate what garden chemicals can do to skin. Lime, in particular, is a harshly alkaline powder that can leave skin dry and leathery. After you handle lime, treat your hands to a rinse with vinegar, an acidic solution that can neutralize the lime. You'll get back your soft, supple skin in no time.

Recycle medicine cup for just-right fertilizing. Fast-acting fertilizers work great — but only if you measure accurately before you dissolve them in water. Get it wrong, and your plants can end up burned. You can use a teaspoon from the kitchen to measure, but you won't want to eat with that spoon again. Save the little plastic cup from a cough syrup bottle, and designate it your fertilizer measuring cup. It's marked to let you measure accurately.

Create multi-use watering can. Rinse out an empty plastic milk or juice container, and make it into a watering and fertilizing jug. Save several lids that fit the container, and drill each with more or fewer holes. Pick the lid that allows faster or slower spray depending on how much food you want to dispense.

Homemade funnel keeps leaves safe. Keep liquid fertilizer off the leaves of your large, bushy plants with a length of PVC pipe. Place one end at the base of the plant, then pour fertilizer into the top end, using it like a funnel. No more burned leaves.

Easy way to figure weight. When instructions say to spread 1 1/2 pounds of fertilizer over a 100-square-foot garden, how do you measure that amount from the bag? A simple trick is to fill a 1-pound coffee can with fertilizer. It actually comes out to about 1 1/2 pounds of fertilizer — just the right amount.

Mulch magic
THE MULTI-PURPOSE
COVER-UP

Let "living mulch" choke out weeds. Farmers sometimes plant what's called a "cover crop" to avoid leaving bare ground between rows of the main crop. Typically a clover, alfalfa, or rye grass, this type of groundcover prevents erosion, crowds out weeds, gives nutrients back to the soil, and keeps soil nitrogen in balance. You can get the same benefits in your vegetable garden as long as you pick a living mulch plant that doesn't compete. Here's how to make it work.

- Be sure your garden is free of weeds before you begin.

- Plant the main crop, and let it become established for about five weeks.

- Sow the seeds of your living mulch carefully between the rows of the main crop.

- Plan to plow the living mulch under at the end of the season to boost the soil's nutrient content.

2 tricks to figure soil amendment. You don't need to be a math whiz to buy the right amount of mulch, compost, or peat moss for your garden project. Just remember these two tricks.

- Get the units right. Before you calculate, convert all the numbers to the same units — either inches and cubic inches, feet and cubic feet, or yards and cubic yards. If you try to multiply feet by cubic yards, you'll never get the right answer.

- Round up. If you figure you need 15.5 cubic feet of peat moss, and it's sold in bales that are 4 cubic feet, go ahead and buy 16 cubic feet — four bales. If you round down, you won't bring home enough to finish the job.

Easy spreading with flip of the wrist

Spread a light, even layer of mulch by using a flying disc like a Frisbee. Just pick up a handful of mulching material on an upside-down disc, then flip your wrist to toss it evenly. No need to pour mulch from a heavy bag.

Get an unlimited supply of free mulch. Don't spend a fortune on mulch for your garden when you can get it for free. Ask your neighbors or call around locally to find a tree-trimming company or municipal utility that will deliver loads of wood chips at no cost. They're happy to get rid of ground-up brush and trees, and wood chips make a great organic mulch under shrubs. This kind of yard waste has a lot in common with rich compost, so it feeds the soil while it decomposes. But that also means you may have to replace the mulch sooner than you would with purchased bark chips.

Keep it light to beat the heat

Don't over-mulch, especially if you live in a hot, dry place. Too much mulch can soak up vital water from rain and sprinklers before it gets to the roots of plants. Excess mulch may also attract slugs looking for a cool refuge. Woody shrubs with shallow roots, like azaleas and rhododendrons, suffer the most from too much mulch.

3 secrets to using grass clippings. Every time you mow the lawn you have to dispose of cut grass. Lawn clippings can make a great mulch but only if you follow these three rules.

- Don't use clippings from a lawn that has recently been treated with weedkiller. Wait at least three cuttings after the treatment to be sure all the chemicals are gone.

- Be sure clippings are dry, then spread a 2-inch layer. Fresh green grass clippings can give off heat and bad smells as they break down.

- Don't use clippings that are full of weeds and weed seeds. Applying these as mulch will simply spread around your weed problem.

Smart mulching prevents pests and mildew. Make your yard look like a million bucks when you learn to mulch like a pro. Don't heap mulch around tree trunks, creating a volcano appearance. Instead, pull the mulch back from the trunk about 3 inches, leaving a donut of breathing room around the tree. Mulch piled up around trees and shrubs keeps the plants from getting acclimated to winter temperatures, plus it retains moisture that can cause mildew damage and attract pests.

Prepare bed with a good soaking. Mulch is great for keeping weeds at bay in your garden. But be sure to water the ground before you lay it down, or you could be doing your plants more harm than good. Once the mulch is in place, rain water will have a harder time getting through to the soil. That's why it's best to start with damp ground — for both organic and inorganic types of mulch. Be sure to water again once the mulch is down to keep small pieces from blowing away.

Mix it up for fluffier leaf mulch. Big, flat leaves like maple leaves don't always make the best mulch. They tend to mat down into a solid mass, creating a barrier that keeps air from reaching the soil. Mix in oak or beech with maple leaves to create an airy mulch that allows for ventilation.

Prepping leaves is a piece of cake. Take the bag off your lawn mower, and use the mower to chop up fallen leaves to make mulch. Walk in a circular pattern from the outside to the inside of the circle, directing the cuttings toward the center. When you get to the center, you'll have a tidy pile of shredded leaves.

Avoid dangers of black walnut. Some plants just don't get along. That's the case with black walnut trees, which give off a natural chemical that stops other plants from growing. Don't mulch with black walnut leaves or wood chips, and compost their leaves for at least a year before using them in the garden.

Keep your house safe from flammable mulch. Don't turn your yard into a firetrap. If you live in the country or any fire-prone area, choose fire-resistant materials to mulch your beds.

Researchers at The Ohio State University found organic materials including cocoa hulls, hardwood bark, and medium-size pine bark chunks, along with stone, are the best choices to avoid accidental fire. They also suggest using mulch with large chunks rather than shredded pieces and avoiding rubber mulch. It's also important to leave a space of at least 18 inches between a mulched bed and anything that may catch fire, like wood siding on your home. But don't skip mulch altogether, since excess weeds can also spread fire.

Myth: mulch attracts termites

You might think organic mulches would be a magnet for termites, but it's not true. Some woods used as mulch actually produce natural chemicals that repel termites and other pests. Any termite with a choice would prefer munching on a cardboard box to nibbling your wood chips.

But place only a thin 2-inch layer of mulch near the foundation of your house. That will allow soil to dry out in that area and prevent a bridge that termites can cross without touching your treated soil.

Let organic mulch blend with soil. Don't bother using landscape fabric underneath organic mulches, like wood chips and pine straw. These mulches are meant to decompose and mix in with the soil over the years, and a barrier layer would keep that from happening. Besides that, putting down landscape fabric is time consuming and costly if you don't need it.

Don't let straw grab all your nitrogen. When you mulch with straw, you can count on improving the texture of your soil as the straw breaks down. That's a great thing for heavy clay soils.

But the microorganisms that decompose straw also rob nitrogen from the soil, leaving it less fertile. Avoid starving your plants by adding nitrogen to the soil before you put down straw. You can use a commercial lawn fertilizer, or simply till in some manure to boost the nitrogen level.

Put pine where it's appreciated. Mulching with pine straw works great around acid-loving plants, like azaleas and hydrangeas. But don't spread this acidic mulch around plants that prefer alkaline soils, including forsythia, lilacs, and clematis. Instead use an inorganic mulch like crushed stone.

Turn winter reading into springtime spread. After you finish with the daily newspaper, staple it to the one from yesterday. Connect the papers until the strip is as long as your garden row, then roll it up and store it. You'll have lengths of newspaper mulch ready when you need them. And don't worry about lead from the ink leaching into the soil and contaminating the ground. That's not a problem nowadays, since black ink used to print newspapers no longer contains lead. Colored ink may still be a problem, so avoid using colored newsprint as mulch.

Mulching trick for speedy produce

Get tasty tomatoes and beautiful flowers sooner by using foil as mulch. Just spread aluminum foil between the rows of plants, and let reflected light encourage quicker ripening by up to two weeks. The foil can also ward off thrips and aphids.

But leaving foil on the ground for long periods can allow aluminum to leach into the soil. Instead, use black plastic mulch sprayed with reflective aluminum paint if you plan to leave it down long-term.

Harvest more vegetables with colored mulches. You can pick up to 30 percent more tomatoes from the same plants if you place red plastic mulch around them, but other vegetables also benefit from colored plastic mulches.

- Green. May produce more squash and melons where summers are cool. Dark green is particularly effective with melons.

- Dark blue. May lead to nearly one-third more cucumbers.

- Silver. May pump up your pepper plant production and help fight thrips.

You can find these plastic mulches in gardening centers or online. For best results, place soaker hoses beneath the mulch except where drainage is poor, install the mulch during the warmest part of the day, bury the edges, and cut holes for planting. Remember that all plastic mulches warm the soil, so avoid using them with plants that cannot handle the heat.

Modify mulch for summer cooling. Plastic mulch can trap heat in the summer, injuring roots and making your plants suffer. Make your plastic mulch work through the summer with one of these modifications.

- Spray black plastic mulch with white latex paint to reflect the sun. Be sure to avoid spraying plant leaves in the process.

- Cover the plastic with a layer of organic mulch, like pine straw or wood chips. You should be able to easily remove the organic layer after the weather cools down.

3 perks of pebbles. Stone mulch is heavy to work with and difficult to keep clean. But it beats out other types of mulch in certain situations.

- If you need to mulch a sloped area or around a downspout. Organic mulches can wash away, but stones will stay in place.

- When you want to use a landscape fabric under the mulch. Don't use unbreathable plastic under stone.

- In high-visibility areas. Stone mulch is available in a variety of colors, so you can use it to dress up your yard.

Go big for lasting impact. With organic mulch materials, generally those with larger pieces last the longest. That's because bigger chunks tend to take longer to decompose. So pick large pine bark nuggets over shredded cypress if longevity is your main goal. But no mulch lasts forever, so plan on adding more in two or three years.

SHARPEN YOUR YOUR GARDENING SKILLS

HORTICULTURAL HABITS THAT SAVE TIME & MONEY

Easy way to show what's planted where. Emerging seedlings sometimes all look alike. Take out the guesswork with signs to show what you've planted. Include planting dates on the back of the signs for quick reference. Save money and make signs from throwaway items.

- Dig out mismatched forks from your flatware drawer and use them to hold index card signs. You can laminate the cards at a copy shop so they stand up to the elements, or do your own laminating using clear packing tape.

- Pick up plastic spatulas and wooden spoons at yard sales, and write plant names on them with a permanent marker. Use clear nail polish over the marker to keep it from fading.

- Reuse plastic sign holders. If you or your neighbors use a lawn-care company to apply fertilizer, the company leaves a sign staked in the yard after each treatment. Save the stakes, and use them to hold your row labels.

Never forget where you buried your bulbs. Try this 5-cent trick to remind you not to dig up your bulb bed. Rinse off popsicle sticks after your grandchildren are done with them, then paint the sticks the colors of the flowers you planted. Use nail polish in the colors you need, since it won't wash off or fade. The bright colors make these markers easy to find in the spring, and you can use them again year after year.

New use for an old apron. Keep an old kitchen or barbecue apron handy to use in the garden. Besides keeping your clothes clean as you work, an apron with pockets keeps your hands free. Stock it with small tools, packets of seeds, even a little notebook and pencil to record planting and pruning dates.

File seeds in planting order. Sort seed packets according to when they need to be planted, whether early, middle, or late in the season. Then file them away in a divided box, perhaps a shoe box or an old recipe card box. When it's time to start planting, just go to that section of your filed seeds and grab the correct packets.

Take note of this nifty scheduling idea. Create a gardening journal or calendar to track the dates you plant, fertilize, prune, and harvest. It's important to keep records so you can avoid overfertilizing some plants or skipping others. And don't toss your journal after the growing season. Save it from year to year so you can track trends, note expenses, and plan for long-term projects.

Stop sticky seeds from sticking to you. Sandburs and seed pods just love to take a ride on your cotton and wool gardening clothes. Foil their plans by wearing a nylon jacket when you clean up your garden in the fall. Nylon and similar slick fabrics don't offer sticky pods and burs a chance to hang on, so you won't drag them around the yard and into your house.

Create an outdoor hanging place. Install a coat hook or over-the-door towel rack on a fence near your garden. It's a convenient place to hang your sweater, hat, or gardening gloves while you work among the plants. The point is to make a space that's designated for items that need to come back inside. Then you'll never leave your jacket lying out in your yard again.

Smart suggestion for new gardeners. Don't go blindly into gardening if it's a new activity for you. Find a local mentor, talk to people at your nursery, or contact your county agricultural extension service for help. You'll need answers to some basic questions to avoid a big-time blunder.

- When does the major planting season begin?

- What's the date of the earliest frost and the last?

- Are there common periods of drought?

- Which USDA plant hardiness zone am I in?

- Does local soil have specific needs when it comes to adding amendments?

- Is the soil acidic or alkaline? Is it made of clay, sand, or loam?

- Which vegetables or flowers grow best in this area?

- What common pests do I need to look out for?

Team up for an enriching experience. When you garden in a group, you can share advice, split expenses, collaborate on soil-improvement projects, take turns with weeding and other tedious tasks, and meet your neighbors. If your apartment or condominium complex has unused common space on the ground or rooftop, see about organizing a group flower or vegetable garden. If that's not an option, look for a local community garden, sometimes located on vacant lots in cities or public land in the country.

TECHNIQUES TO KEEP TIP-TOP TOOLS

Stop losing your tools in the grass. Golfers finally got smart and started playing with brightly colored balls. Now they can search for a fluorescent orange ball in a field of long, rough grass rather than having to pick out a tiny white blip. The same idea can work with your garden tools to make them more noticeable when you leave them lying outside.

- Mark a spot or stripe on the handle of your shovel or hoe with fluorescent spray paint.

- Tie a length of shiny holiday ribbon on the handle. Use curling ribbon so it really stands out.

- Attach an unused brightly colored luggage tag to the handle.

Great garden tools on the cheap. Don't spend a fortune on tools for your garden. Secondhand tools are often made of better-quality steel than some newer ones, plus they're a great deal. Check out these sources.

- Flea markets and yard sales.

- Pawn shops, thrift stores, and consignment stores. Look for a Goodwill store or Habitat-for-Humanity ReStore in your area.

- Estate sales in rural areas.

- Internet exchange sites, such as *www.craigslist.com* and *www.freecycle.org*.

- Tool lending libraries. Some are open only to churches and community groups, but a source like *www.neighborgoods.net* offers all kinds of tools and gadgets for loan.

- Your gardening-expert neighbor, who may be willing to lend you a tool — along with good advice.

Pick a trick to clean pine pitch. Sticky pine sap can really gum up the blades and handles of your pruning tools. Clean it off using one of these home remedies.

- Dip a rag in vegetable oil. Rub off the sap, then continue rubbing to lubricate the wood on your tool and protect the metal.

- Mix up a paste of baking soda and water, and scrub off the sap. This method also works to get sap off your hands.

- Use a dab of turpentine on a rag to cut through the sap.

Plan ahead to avoid cleanup mess. Use cooking spray to make gardening easier. Spray your pruner blades, shovel, and hoe before you start working in the garden so dirt and sap don't stick to the tools. The metal won't rust, and cleanup will be a breeze.

TLC for wooden handles. Take special care of the part of your garden tools you touch — the handles — before you put them away for the winter.

- Scrub off dirt with soapy water and a stiff brush.

- Sand down wooden handles to remove splinters. You can use an orbital sander for large areas, then switch to sandpaper for hard-to-reach spots.

- Wipe down the wood with a rag dipped in boiled linseed oil. After the oil soaks in, wipe off the excess.

- Replace wooden handles if they split to avoid injuring your hand.

Give your hands a beauty treatment. Coat your hands with a generous layer of your favorite hand lotion before you put on gardening gloves. The lotion will act as a barrier, keeping garden dirt from sticking to your skin or getting under your nails. After you take off the gloves and rinse off the lotion, your hands will be clean and smooth.

Easy way to haul yard waste. Don't toss out that hard plastic baby pool after it starts to leak. Drill a couple of holes near the rim, run some rope through the holes to make a handle, and place it where you're weeding or pruning. You can fill the pool with leaves and sticks, yet still be able to drag it to your compost bin easily.

Old mailbox keeps tools within reach. Set up a post in the corner of your garden, and install an old mailbox on it. You can store small hand tools, gardening gloves, a ball of twine, a notebook and pencil — all those little things you tend to forget when you go out to play in the dirt. A mailbox with a door or lid will keep items fairly safe from the weather, and you can stop trudging back to the house for that forgotten tool.

Gardening tools you never thought you'd need. Look beyond typical gardening tools to other items that come in handy when you're working with plants.

- A handheld magnifying glass lets you inspect plants for signs of disease and small pests. A 10-power lens is strong enough to do the job.

- One or more hand trucks or moving dollies can help you move heavy containers or large bags of mulch or soil with ease.

- Gloves of all varieties keep your hands safe while you do specific jobs. Look for heavy-duty leather gloves with extended arm protectors for pruning roses, pyracantha, or other shrubs with thorns. But use rubber gloves if you are mixing or spraying pesticides or other chemicals.

- A steel fence post, wooden 2 x 4, or car axle makes a sturdy lever when it's time to move a heavy rock or pry up a tree root.

Make tool handles easier to hold

Give your garden tools cushioned handle grips by wrapping handles with foam pipe insulation or rubber shelf liner. Use duct tape or electrical tape to secure the padding. Your shovel and rake will be easier to hold and won't cause blisters on your hands.

Rolling caddy makes quick work of hauling. Save that old rolling backpack or suitcase that's too damaged to use when you travel. It's a great helper in the garden, letting you trundle tools and supplies between garden beds without lifting a thing.

Prepare power tools for storage. Your outdoor power tools that use gasoline — a snow blower in the winter and a chain saw and lawn mower in the summer — need a little TLC before you put them away in the off-season. Experts say to drain the gasoline from the fuel tank to be sure the engine starts up again when you need it. Use an old turkey baster to remove all the gas you can, then run the engine until it stalls. You can even put the drained gas into your car. Check your tool's owner's manual, which you can probably find on the Internet, to see about these other maintenance steps.

- Change spark plugs and oil, and inflate tires.

- Lubricate fittings and other parts.

- Inspect for worn belts, frayed cables, and loose bolts.

- Look for wear on skid plates and other parts.

- Sharpen mower's blades.

Keep your boots spider-free. Stretch a pair of old pantyhose or tights over the tops of your gardening boots when you leave them in the shed overnight. They'll keep spiders, scorpions, and other creepy-crawlies out of your galoshes.

Handy trick protects your hands. Save a clothespin or binder clip, and use it to fasten your gardening gloves when you're not using them. Clip the pair of gloves to the hem of your favorite gardening jacket so they are always at hand.

Never untangle twine again. Save a plastic flower pot that's just the right size to hold a ball of twine. Thread the end of the twine through a drainage hole in the bottom of the pot, and place duct tape across the top of the pot to keep the twine in place. No more chasing a rolling, tangling ball of twine.

Say hello to your new best friend. Talk about a tool that's worth its weight in usefulness. Hold on to that five-gallon bucket that came free with your last batch of pool chemicals, paint, or floor cleaner. You may also get one free from restaurants, which get supplies delivered in these buckets. They're lightweight, all-purpose garden helpers with many uses.

- Hold weeds while you're working, then carry them to your compost pile.

- Haul tools and supplies around your garden.

- Store kitchen scraps to be used in your compost bin.

- Turn upside down to use as a seat while you're gardening.

- Plant tomatoes on your deck or patio. Drill drainage holes in the bottom of the bucket first. Be sure to choose buckets that didn't contain chemicals, paint, or cleaners when planting fruits or veggies.

Make your yard safe for kids

Never leave even a small amount of water in a five-gallon bucket where children can get to it. The U.S. Consumer Product Safety Commission reports that close to 300 young children have drowned in buckets since 1984. Because the buckets remain stable even with weight on top, a curious toddler can easily topple in headfirst and be unable to get back out.

Vital reason to keep your tools clean. A surgeon uses a scalpel that's been sterilized to avoid infecting patients with germs. Do the same thing with your tools. A fungus called black leg can infect geraniums, impatiens, poinsettias, and petunias. It's common in greenhouses, and infected cutting tools can spread it from plant to plant. To avoid a black leg epidemic, always use new potting soil, clean pots, and a clean knife to take cuttings. Clean your gardening tools by washing them after each use, or use a blowtorch to get the metal hot enough to kill germs. Always let the tools cool down before you use them again.

What to do before you pick up a rake

The U.S. Consumer Product Safety Commission reported that some 28,000 people needed medical treatment in 2009 for injuries related to using nonpowered garden tools. Follow these raking rules to avoid injury.

- Stretch the muscles of your arms and legs before you begin — just like you do for any other exercise.
- Don protective gear, including gloves, closed-toe shoes or boots, long pants, and sun protection.
- Use the right rake for the job. A light, fan-shaped rake is great for gathering up leaves, while a flat-headed, metal rake might work better for smoothing a surface.
- Pick a rake that fits you, avoiding one that's too heavy or too large to handle comfortably.
- Change positions as you work, alternating which hand and foot are in the front.
- Never set a rake down with the teeth pointing up.

Comfort tools take away the pain. Don't let advancing years or joint pain keep you from playing in the dirt. Tools that work with your body can help you stay active.

- Lightweight tools keep you from maneuvering extra pounds. Look for good-quality varieties, labeled as "lady's," "border," or "flower" — but not flimsy options.

- Long-handled spades, shovels, and shears let you reach the ground without bending. They also give you leverage to make the work easier.

- Ratchet-cut pruners and shears help you make a cut without putting strain on your hands.

- Small blades encourage you to take small cuts and shorter strokes.

- Shovels and spades with Y-D-shaped handles transfer less force to your hands than old-fashioned T-shaped handles.

- A watering can with a handle big enough to fit your hand keeps the weight of all that water from pulling on your fingers.

Rolling cooler does double duty. Put your large, rolling ice chest to use during picnic off-season as a portable potting bench. Store a bag of potting soil, gloves, and a small hand trowel in the cooler so the soil doesn't freeze in the garage over the winter. You can easily roll the whole collection into the house to repot a houseplant or start some seeds. If your cooler comes equipped with a drainage hole in the bottom, it will be easy to hose off and drain out next summer when you want to use it to keep food cold. Or you can invest in a full-time gardening cooler for about $20.

4 tricks to sidestep rust. Keep rust off your metal tools by using one of these thrifty methods.

- Place a piece of sidewalk chalk in your toolbox to absorb moisture. You can also use a charcoal briquette.

- Apply a little WD-40 lubricant, that great household item that costs less than a dime per squirt, to prevent rust and keep soil from gumming up your tools.

- Stuff an old sock with sand, tie the open end into a knot, then dip it in vegetable oil. Squeeze out the excess oil, and rub down the metal parts of your tools with the oil sock.

- Fill a large pail with sand, then saturate the sand with motor oil or vegetable oil. After you rinse off your tools, plunge them a few times in this oil dip. While the sand gently scours the metal, a light coating of oil keeps off rust.

Buy tools that won't rust. When some metals meet air and water, rust forms. That can happen with carbon steel tools. Pay a bit more for stainless steel, and you can skip worrying about rusting.

Pantry potion takes off rust

Don't throw away an old rusty garden tool. Soak it overnight in a pan of undiluted white vinegar and watch the rust dissolve away. The acetic acid in vinegar is powerful enough to take care of the rust without damaging your tools — as long as you rinse it off when you're done.

Put citrus wonder to the test. Clean rusty garden tools in no time flat. Just add enough salt to a tablespoon of lemon juice to make a thick paste. Apply it to the rusted areas of your tool with a dry cloth and rub. The combination of gritty salt and acidic lemon juice gets rid of the rust. Rinse off the paste when you're done.

2 clever uses for a broken rake. Don't just toss out that old landscape rake after it breaks. Pull it apart and put the head and the handle to good use.

- Attach the rake head to the wall in your tool shed, teeth at the bottom and facing out. Use it to hang hand tools.

- Use the wooden handle to support a tall plant, or cut into smaller sections for staking trees.

Organize long-handled tools in a snap. Splurge for a new clothes hamper, and make a tool organizer with your old wooden or wicker hamper. Just cut several round holes, about 2 inches across, in the lid. Space them so your tools won't knock into each other. Place a couple of bricks in the bottom of the hamper for stability, and slide your long-handled tools into the holes in the lid, handles first. Tools stay neat and won't damage each other.

Unusual way to keep tools off the floor. Create wall storage that works like a peg board to hold small tools where you can find them. Take a length of unused, vinyl-covered chain-link fencing and nail it to the wall in your gardening shed. Make it loose enough so you can push the handles of small hand tools through the mesh to hang them up. Use bent wire coat hangers to make hooks to hold tools that won't fit into the mesh.

Repurpose sewing room castoffs. Recycle empty thread spools into a handy tool hanger in your shed. Just pick two spools that are the same size, either wooden or plastic. Slide a long nail through the center hole of one spool and nail it to the wall. Two nails will make the hanger sturdier. Do the same for the second spool, placing it level with the first one and a few inches to the side. The spools create enough depth to hold flat tools like a rake or small shovel.

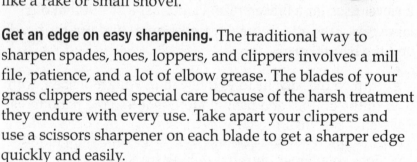

Get an edge on easy sharpening. The traditional way to sharpen spades, hoes, loppers, and clippers involves a mill file, patience, and a lot of elbow grease. The blades of your grass clippers need special care because of the harsh treatment they endure with every use. Take apart your clippers and use a scissors sharpener on each blade to get a sharper edge quickly and easily.

Hands-free gardening. Recycle an old men's leather belt into a tool holder you can wear around your yard. Just slide individual tool pockets onto the belt and use them as holsters for your shears, trowel, soil knife — everything you need when you work in the dirt. You can also use an old carpenter's apron with pockets.

SUPER-SIMPLE SEED STARTERS

Free seeds for the swapping. Give your garden some variety without buying seeds or plants when you join a seed swap. These informal gatherings, usually held in the spring, let gardeners trade surplus seeds and growing tips. If you don't know a local gardening group, find a seed swap online at *www.seedswaps.com*. Be sure you've saved seeds from last year's garden so you'll have something to offer. You can trade for free flower seeds, as well as vegetable seeds to grow a garden that will help cut your grocery bills.

The "dirt" on budget seed. Skip the sales on last year's seed at the discount store. Seeds lose their growing power as they age, so older seeds may not sprout. Paying full price for fresh new seed each season is well worth your pennies and will save you time fiddling with second attempts at germination.

Shaker solution for tiny seeds. Some of the spices in your cabinet look an awful lot like seeds. Take a hint and save empty spice containers to store your smallest seeds for next year. Be sure to rinse and dry the containers first, then add a label so you'll remember what's inside. When it's time to plant, use the shaker top to get just the right amount of seeds where you want them.

4 secrets to saving seeds. Keep the seeds you harvested from your garden fresh and ready to plant come springtime with these seed-saving secrets to success.

- Dry your fresh seeds by laying them out on a tray for several weeks in a warm, dry place out of direct sunlight.

- Remove dirt or chaff by straining through a kitchen sieve with tiny holes. You can also blow across the seeds to remove chaff.

- Store seeds in an airtight container in a cool, dry place.

- Label each seed container, including type of plant, variety, special traits, and date and place where you collected the seeds.

Simple way to test old seeds for success

It's possible old seeds may still grow — but then again, they may not. Test old seeds before it's time to plant. Take a damp paper towel and lay out 10 seeds. Roll it up, seal in a plastic bag, and leave in a warm place. Wait the recommended time of germination — check the seed packet — then count the number of seeds that have sprouted. If it's below 50 percent, toss the old seeds and get some new ones.

Keep seeds to a ripe old age. Store your seeds in the refrigerator, and they'll last up to 10 times as long as those stored at room temperature. In fact, some types of seeds require a period of cold before they will sprout. For alpine plants and flowering varieties like columbine, globeflower, lavender, primrose, and violets, put the seeds in your refrigerator for a three-month chill before sowing. Or sow them outside in the fall to enjoy winter temperatures.

Save flower seeds from wind and critters. Don't let your impatiens, sunflowers, or foxglove go to seed before you get a chance to save that bounty for next year's planting. Winds can take off with tiny seeds, while birds are happy to make a meal from your sunflower seeds. Here's what to do.

- Pay close attention so you'll know when the seeds are nearly ripe.

- Tie a lightweight fabric bag or ventilated paper bag around the flower heads. The bags will catch the seeds before they can scatter or provide dinner for the crows. Your garden may look odd for a while, but you'll be rewarded with free seeds for next year.

- Another option is to place a bag around the seed heads and shake off the mature seeds, catching them in the bag.

Clean azalea seeds with ease. Don't wear out your hands and wear down your pliers cracking open azalea seed pods. Try one of these tricks to get the seeds out so you can store them or plant them.

- Leave seed pods on the plant until they mature in autumn. Collect them and place in a glass jar. Cover the top with cotton cloth held by a rubber band, and set the jar on your kitchen counter. Leave it there for days or weeks, gently shaking the jar every so often. Pods will split open on their own, spilling out the seed.

- Place mature pods on a hard surface and roll over them repeatedly with a pencil, rolling pin, or other similar item. Pods will split open easily, so be ready to capture the seeds.

Identify your garden's superstars. Pay attention to which plants in your garden produce the biggest and best flowers. Tag these with a bright piece of yarn or ribbon so you'll remember to let them set seed heads. You can deadhead the poor performers and collect seed from the stars.

Pick heirloom over hybrid. If you want next year's crop to be similar to this year's, save the seeds from heirloom or open-pollinated varieties only. You can save and plant seeds from your hybrid plants, but they won't be just like their parent plants. Instead, they will have a mix of traits from previous generations — a real surprise. Catalogs should specify if seeds are "hybrid" or "OP" for open-pollinated.

Trade heirloom seeds with expert growers

For just $25 a year for seniors, you can trade heirloom seeds from your garden to get vegetable and fruit seeds from around the world. Join the Seed Savers Exchange (SSE) and start sharing seeds with other gardeners and farmers for just the price of postage. You'll help preserve heirloom plants while you expand the variety of plants in your garden. See the SSE online at *www.seedsavers.org*.

No-fuss way to keep seeds dry. Keep your seeds from molding in storage with a little household drying agent. Take a couple of tablespoons of powdered milk and place on a paper napkin. Fold and roll up the napkin into a small packet, sealing the ends with tape. Place your homemade desiccant pack into the container with your seeds and seal. After six months, put in a fresh pack of powdered milk so it will continue to absorb moisture.

Plant seeds in a safe zone. You know you planted your seeds in a certain part of your garden, but those new sprouts look a lot like weeds. Avoid the seedling mix-up by cutting empty toilet paper rolls into thirds to create tiny fences. Place them where you want to plant, then sprinkle seeds inside the fences and lightly cover with soil. To start seeds in your house, cut four slits in the bottom of the roll and fold toward the center to make a tiny pot. Use it to start seeds. When it's time to transplant, open the bottom of the roll and plant outside with the tube still on.

Protect baby plants with Bubble Wrap

Protect your young seedlings from cold nights by placing tomato cages around the young plants, then wrapping the cages in Bubble Wrap. The seedlings benefit from light streaming through the clear plastic, but it keeps out the wind and cold. If you don't have spare Bubble Wrap, cover tender plants with a brown paper bag on cold nights, making sure to remove it in the morning.

2 uses for an old shower cap. Save the free plastic shower caps from your next hotel visit, and use them to give seedlings a good start.

- Stretch a cap across the top of a pot with seeds germinating to make an easy mini greenhouse. Your seeds will flourish in the moist environment.

- Before you give your sprouts a good watering, stretch a cap around the bottom of the pot to catch any drips.

Keep your eyes peeled for junkyard gems. Don't pay good money for seed-starting flats when you can pick up these great sturdy options for free or next to nothing.

- automobile tire rims

- cat litter boxes

- refrigerator crisper drawers

- large cookie tins

- plastic dishpans

- wooden dresser drawers

Be sure to drill a few small drainage holes in your free seed flats before you plant.

Save seedlings with a dash of cinnamon

Sprinkle cinnamon on the surface of soil when you start plants from seed. This spice is a natural fungicide, so it helps prevent damping off, a disease that kills tender, young seedlings.

Create a gentle watering tool. Don't blast your seedlings out of the soil with powerful pressure from a hose. Give them a gentle sprinkle from a watering can made from an old ketchup bottle, soy sauce bottle, or mustard squeeze bottle. You can drill holes in a large lid, or leave in the plastic pouring insert for slower flow. Be sure to rinse out the condiment bottle before you fill it with water. Always let water sit to reach room temperature, since seedlings may not grow well if they suffer the shock of cold water.

Water seedlings with cheap "starter solution." Give your precious garden babies a jump-start on growth. Mix a teaspoon of baby shampoo into a quart of water and use it to water trays of newly planted seedlings. The mild soap prevents a tough crust from forming on the soil surface.

Kitchen scraps give seeds a great start. Save rinds, peels, and other natural food coverings, and you'll have a bonanza of biodegradable seed starters. Plan ahead so you can cut grapefruit or avocados in half to create nicely shaped cups. Eggshells also work for very small plants. Be sure to punch several small holes in the bottom of the "pots" for drainage, then fill with potting soil and plant a few seeds in each. Line them up in a clear plastic deli container to sprout. When it's time to plant outside, put the natural pots in the ground to avoid disrupting the roots and to give the soil a bit of extra fertilizer.

4 ways to make a mini-greenhouse. While you're waiting over the long winter to start gardening again in the spring, seek out free items to use as little greenhouses for seedlings. With a clear lid to let sunlight in, these tiny houses help regulate temperature and humidity. Try these items.

- Clear plastic supermarket containers with lids used to hold strawberries and blueberries.

- Large plastic cups with domed lids that come filled with slushies at the corner market.

- Zippered clear plastic storage bags that are sold with a set of sheets or drapes. Use wooden craft sticks or chopsticks in the corners to prop up the top.

- Gallon-size plastic storage bags. Pop one of these over a little pot with seeds growing, and you can easily remove it later.

Turn seed-starting into home decor. Repurpose an old muffin or popover pan into a cute seedling nursery you will want to display on your dinner table. First, drill some small holes in the bottoms of each cup in the pan, then fill with potting mix and plant a few seeds in each cup. Place the pan on a baking sheet to catch drips. If you use a popover pan, dress it up by tying a ribbon around each cup.

More sunlight for indoor plants. Windows give your seeds the greatest amount of light, but it all comes from one direction. Keep your seedlings from leaning over as they reach for the sun with a reflecting box. Simply line the inside of a large cardboard box with foil, so light is reflected in all directions. Place the box on its side with the seedlings inside, and they'll think they're in a field of sunshine.

Save money with homemade seed tape. Buying enough seed tape — biodegradable paper studded with seeds at planting intervals — to plant your entire garden could cost you hundreds of dollars. Make it yourself and still get those tiny seeds planted evenly.

- Tear newspaper or paper towels into long strips about an inch wide.

- Mix a little flour and water to make a paste, and apply dots of paste along the paper strips using a pencil or chopstick. Follow the suggested spacing on the seed packet.

- Carefully place one seed on each flour dot, and let the tape dry.

You can roll up the tape and store until planting time, but it's usually best to use it soon so the seeds don't fall off the tape.

Combo tool lets you plant with ease

The back of the seed packet tells you how deep to plant your crop. But you don't want to measure each planting hole with a ruler before you drop in a seed. Make a simple depth gauge by wrapping a rubber washer or rubber band around a length of thick dowel at the specified planting depth. It's a measuring tool and dibble all in one.

Simple way to space seeds. Make a seed guide bar to help you plant seeds at even intervals. Find an old piece of 2-by-2-inch wood, maybe a foot or two long. Pound long nails into the wood, spacing them evenly at the intervals you want your plants growing. Your guide will look like a giant comb. When you're ready to plant seeds, press the guide, nail-side down, onto the soil to make small holes. Place a seed in each hole, then cover with soil based on seed size. That means covering large seeds with a couple of inches of soil, and tiny seeds with almost none at all.

Relief for your aching back. Stop the backbreaking routine of bending over to make holes for seeds using a short-handled dibble. A walking stick with a metal tip works great to make holes in your garden without missing a step.

Sow your fall garden sooner. You've learned to wait to plant in the spring until the soil warms enough for seeds to germinate. But what can you do in midsummer, when the soil is hot but you want to plant your fall garden? Give your soil the cooling treatment.

- Moisten the soil the day before planting, since damp soil is cooler.

- Plant larger seeds, like beans and peas, a little deeper than the seed package suggests. Soil is cooler farther from the surface.

- Shade the area where you plant with shade cloth, cardboard, or even a thin layer of grass clippings. Be sure to remove the cover once your seeds germinate.

You don't need to splurge for a fancy soil thermometer. Inexpensive outdoor thermometers are accurate enough.

Give seedlings a hot bed for free. If you don't have soil heating coils to protect seedlings from a spring cold snap, use the heat put off by microorganisms in decaying manure.

- Break up soil in your garden and cover with a 10-inch layer of fresh horse manure with straw in it.

- Cover with several inches of soil and dust with lime.

- Spread two more layers of manure, separating with another layer of soil and lime in between.

- Dig out several small holes around your hot bed and fill with compost. Spread a bit more soil on top.

- Transplant seedlings into the compost-filled holes, where warmth from the manure will keep their roots cozy.

For a more permanent hot bed, surround with a wooden frame and cover with glass or plastic to capture warmth from the sun. It's an all-natural way to keep seedlings warm.

Don't make seedlings compete for life. Do you know how those giant redwood trees grow so tall? They get an edge on other plants nearby by producing a natural chemical that blocks growth. That's why you should avoid using redwood mulch or compost near your seedlings. In fact, don't use any kind of mulch around seedlings until they're at least 5 inches high and growing well.

"Free" soil not worth the risks. You hate to pay through the nose for bags of fancy potting mix, but you won't really save by using dirt from your yard to start seeds.

- Native yard soil is more dense than potting soil, so seeds may not get the oxygen they need.

- Soil-borne problems like fungus or insect eggs can do damage to your young plants.

- Weed seeds may be lying dormant in the soil, ready to sprout under the ideal growing conditions you will provide.

If you get a bigger yield without having to spend money on weed and insect solutions later on, you may actually save money buying a potting mix.

Put an end to transplant shock. Plan ahead for an easy transition from indoor sprouting to outdoor planting for delicate seedlings like melons and squash. Line plastic mesh berry baskets with a sheet of newspaper, fill with potting mix, and sow a handful of seeds in each. Thin to two plants per container once they sprout. When it's warm enough to transplant outdoors, plant the baskets, covering the plastic and newspaper with soil. Roots easily grow through the mesh, so there's no loss of plants to transplant shock.

Transplant seedlings damage-free. The first pair of leaves most plants put out are "false leaves," part of the plant's embryo. Don't transplant your tiny seedlings when you see those. Wait until the plant produces the first true leaves, usually the second set of leaves. Handle the seedlings by these leaves rather than by the stems, which are easily damaged. The plant can grow new leaves, but it can't spare its delicate stem.

Hardening off doesn't need to be hard. The traditional method of hardening off seedlings to make the transition from indoors to outdoors involves a week or two of daily moves. Outdoors during the day to get used to the sun and wind, then back inside at night. Skip the hassle of all that moving by placing your seedlings in a transitional place, like a covered porch or along the east side of your house protected from the wind and sun. Assuming the weather is mild, you can leave them here for the days and nights of hardening off, then move them straight to your garden.

Plant expertise
Buy for less, select the best

4 signs you're buying a hearty plant. Leave the unhealthy perennials at the garden center and take home only the gems that are sure to thrive in your garden. Look for these signs you're buying a strong perennial.

- You see a compact form rather than a leggy mess.

- The plant is in proportion to its pot.

- Leaves are free of white spots or insects underneath.

- The plant is stocky in form with tough, substantial leaves.

What retailers know about "bargain" plants. Next time you're shopping for plants, just say "no" to plants that look like they need a little too much TLC. These deals may not be worth the trouble or expense if the plant shows certain signs of ill health.

- Dead leaves. These can signal disease, neglect, or both.

- Spots or odd growths on leaves. If the plant is carrying a disease, it might spread to your entire garden.

- Roots that have grown into a solid mass, filling the pot. The plant may not grow well even when planted in the ground.

- Weeds growing in the pot. They're a sure sign of neglect.

- Large gaps between leaves. Another sign of neglect.

- Soil with a hard, crusty surface. This plant has been in the pot for a long time.

Look for hidden treasures when buying plants

Peek under the leaves for extra baby plants in the soil next to the main stem when buying a potted plant at your garden center. You can separate these hidden treasures when you transplant, allowing the seedlings more room to grow. Best of all, you just bought two or three plants for the price of one.

Signs a dormant plant is a bargain. You can save up to 50 percent buying shrubs and trees in the winter, then either planting them immediately if the ground is not frozen or saving them in a cold frame until spring. But check to be sure your bargain is dormant rather than dead.

- Scratch the bark of a woody plant to be sure you see green underneath the outer bark.

- Pull the plant out of the pot and look for roots that are healthy and firm — not black, moldy, or crumbling.

- Check the leaves and stems of evergreens to see if they're healthy and supple rather than brittle and brown.

Wait until spring to fertilize a dormant plant to avoid waking it up too soon.

Beat the rush for best selection. Plan ahead for your weekend projects, and shop for plants at the garden center on Thursdays and Fridays. You'll find a better selection after weekday restocking and avoid having to settle for picked-over plants.

5 signs of a root-bound plant. Buying a plant that's too large for its pot is not a good choice. That's because pot-bound plants are stunted, typically slow to start vigorous growth once they're set free. But you can't always pull a plant out of the pot at the store to check the roots. Look for these signs the plant is root-bound.

- The plant is too large for the pot.

- Roots are protruding above the soil line.

- You see dead branches in the crowded pot.

- The plant looks leggy and spindly.

- Roots have grown through the pot's drainage holes.

If you get your plant home and find it's root-bound, take a soil knife and cut a slit in the root mass about one-third up from the bottom.

Don't invite disaster into your plot

Inspect any new plant before you introduce it into your home or garden. Even if you don't see signs of disease or insects on a new plant, that's no guarantee it's perfectly healthy. Some pests and problems, like cyclamen mites, spider mites, and certain bacteria, are difficult or impossible to spot. Quarantine a new plant for at least a few weeks to be sure it doesn't spread disease to your other plants. That means keeping it a safe distance from plants of the same variety and other types.

Bare-root gives best value. Trees and shrubs don't mind being shipped and sold without pots. And you shouldn't mind buying bare-root plants, since you can enjoy their benefits. Bare-root plants have well-developed roots and adapt quickly to the soil in your garden. Hundreds of rare varieties are available without a pot. Plus, you can save up to 70 percent buying bare-root.

It's best to put bare-root plants in the ground as quickly as possible. If you can't do that, place the plant in a shallow hole and cover the roots with damp soil or sawdust.

Give baby trees a good start. Whether you buy trees with bare roots or balled-and-burlapped, give their roots a good soaking for a day or so before you plant them. Just set the tree's roots in a bucket of water or mud overnight, then plant as usual.

Buy the perfect tree for your yard. A new tree is a big investment. Make the right choice by paying attention to these tree-buying details.

- Check the ratio between a nursery tree's height and its caliper, or trunk diameter. Avoid trees that seem too tall in relation to their caliper, since they may not survive being transplanted.

- When buying fruit trees, find out whether the tree is self-fertile or if you'll need a second tree to act as a pollinator. Otherwise, no fruit.

- The age of tree you buy is really a matter of choice and patience. If you don't mind waiting a couple of years, a two- or three-year-old tree will quickly outpace an older specimen.

- Look for multiple-trunk trees whose trunks separate near the base rather than farther up. This goes for trees like sweet bay magnolia, crape myrtle, redbud, and Japanese ligustrum.

Buy disease-resistant plants. After a garden epidemic of disease or pest infestation, repopulate your plants with varieties that have been bred to avoid the problem. Look for these label abbreviations: N — vegetables resistant to nematodes; V — tomatoes resistant to verticillium fungus; F — tomatoes resistant to fusarium fungus; BCMV — beans resistant to bean common mosaic virus; TMV — vegetables resistant to tobacco mosaic virus.

> ## *'Dwarf' plant surprise*
>
> That small potted hibiscus with large flowers may appear to be a dwarf variety — but beware. These plants are usually treated with a growth retardant to keep them small in the store. The chemical will wear off after the plant has been in your home for a month or two. Then it could grow to be 6 feet tall.

Pick the perfect rose. Select a rose variety based on growing conditions in your yard — not merely by the color of blooms you like. If your garden gets sun for only part of the day, you'll have more success with one of the varieties that flower just once a season. Try Constance Spry, Alba Semi-plena, or American Pillar.

Get your yard landscaped for free. Don't spend a dime at the garden center on plants. There's plenty of greenery looking for a good home — if you're not too picky about using a certain variety. Try these sources of free plants.

- Swap plants with other gardeners, or check online swap sites like *www.freecycle.org* and *www.craigslist.org*.

- Call a funeral home and offer to pick up plants left by families. You'll be doing the funeral director a favor.

- Stop by your local nursery and ask if you can carry away tired, sad plants that haven't been sold.

- When you see landscaping crews at work along the road or in a retail display, offer to cart away the plants being removed.

- Look for baby plants that sprout up in the garden all on their own that you can transplant.

Become plant swap savvy. Follow these basic rules at a plant or produce swap so other gardeners will be happy to share with you again next time.

- Alert the swap organizer that you are planning to come so she can make space.

- Find out if the swap has basic rules for participation. Some groups assign monetary values to different types of plants or produce to encourage fair trades.

- Prepare plants by potting them and labeling with genus and species names.

- Feel free to bring seeds, bulbs, and tubers to trade, but be sure they're in plastic bags with labels.

- Avoid taking plant cuttings to offer, since they can be difficult to transport.

- Bring your own reusable bags or boxes to carry all your items home.

- Don't remove plants from another gardener's table-without asking if he would like to make a trade.

Rules for foraging free plants. Native plants, or the varieties that grow wild in your area, have a good chance of surviving a move to your yard. But follow these rules for foraging when you gather free-growing plants. Ask before you take plants or seeds from private property, even if it's clear the plants are being removed for construction. Don't take an entire group of wild plants. Leave a few so they can grow back. Never take a rare or endangered species. If you're gathering wildflower seeds, spread a few where you found them so they can continue growing. Finally, be sure you have the knowledge to transplant successfully. If you don't know how to deal with a certain variety, you may kill it rather than save it.

Propagation
FREE PLANTS FOR LIFE

Several plants for the price of one. Never buy multiples of the same houseplant. Instead, pick one good specimen, then take it home and plunder it for stem cuttings. Be sure to use a pasteurized rooting medium like vermiculite, sand, or perlite to ensure success. Keep your cuttings moist and warm, say on the top of your refrigerator or clothes dryer, until they grow roots. This works great for a variety of plants, including geraniums, coleus — pretty much anything with a distinct stem.

Grow an African violet from a cutting. You can grow a new African violet plant from a healthy leaf cutting, but don't expect it quickly. Trim the leaf stem to about 1 1/2 inches, then push it into a small hole in a vermiculite-sand growing medium. Roots should start to appear within a month, and new leaves in another month. You probably won't see blossoms for the first six to nine months.

2 ways to multiply clematis. To get more of your favorite variety of clematis montana, you'll need to buy seeds. Otherwise these hybrids won't grow true to species. But you have two options.

- Buy seeds and plant them. Mix seeds into a moist blend of half peat moss and half sand or vermiculite. Seal it all into a plastic bag and keep in your refrigerator for three months. Then sow the seeds into a shallow container filled with the same peat moss-sand mixture, and let them germinate with bright light but no direct sun. Keep the soil moist, and seedlings should sprout in a few months.

- Ground layer. This method lets you grow more of the variety you already have. Simply layer long shoots directly into the soil, then wait while new roots form.

The secret to ground layering. You can multiply plants like hydrangea, forsythia, and clematis by ground layering, or burying a branch that's still attached to the plant. You'll need to strip off the leaves from the branch, be sure there's a leaf node on the buried section, and hold it down with a brick or stone. But include this final step for more success. Even after you think a new baby plant is ready to survive on its own, cut it off from the mother plant and leave it in the ground for a few weeks. Then you can transplant it and be sure it will thrive.

Find rooting hormone in your pantry

Some gardeners swear by using honey instead of purchased rooting hormone. You can spread honey directly on the cutting, or make a dip for cuttings by adding a tablespoon of honey to two cups of boiling water. After the honey dip cools, keep it in a sealed container away from light.

Multiply your favorite woody plants. There's no need to buy more bushes. Create more of the ones you have by taking hardwood cuttings. Here's how.

- Pick a stem with at least three leaf nodes.

- Cut the stem just below a leaf node at an angle. An angled cut leaves more surface area for roots to grow.

- Remove all the leaves from the cutting.

- Dip the cut end in rooting hormone, but don't waste it by using too much. Use just a dab, and tap off the excess.

- Plant the cuttings, several to a pot. They'll soon grow roots and leaves.

Save suckers for free crape myrtle

Next time you're cleaning up and pruning your crape myrtle, don't just pull out and toss the little suckers that pop up around the roots of the tree. Instead, dig them up with a handful of roots and plant them in a pot. They'll grow slowly and bloom contentedly with lots of sun, a little fertilizer, and some water. Bring the pots into a shed or garage when it gets close to freezing.

Spread daylilies all over your yard. Bulbs like daylilies and daffodils love to multiply, creating more plants each year. But they can get crowded after a few years' growth. Divide large clumps to spread the beauty, and you'll keep these plants healthier. Dig up clumps late in summer, after they're done blooming and the leaves die back. Use two garden forks inserted straight down to divide the root ball, gently pulling it apart. Plant your 'new' bulbs right away.

Sidestep iris rot. You can divide iris rhizomes anytime from just after they're done blooming to right before a hard frost. They like to be divided about every four years, so use the presidential election schedule as a reminder. Just be sure to leave the rhizomes uncovered for 24 hours after you divide them to avoid rotting and insect problems.

> ## *Get timing right for dividing success*
> The best time to divide perennials is soon after they finish blooming, but not too late in the fall. Give your new little plants enough time to become established before they feel the cold of winter.

Good news for begonia lovers. Save the tubers from tuberous begonias, and you can enjoy them as indoor container plants. Store tubers in a cool, dark place, then plant them cut-side up in a pot of well-drained soil. You'll need to provide extra light if indoor begonias don't get any sun. Use two 40-watt fluorescent tubes or a combination of one standard cool white and one daylight tube placed about a foot above the rim of the pots. For the most blooms, shower them with light for 18 hours a day. You can also take stem cuttings to grow new begonia plants.

Peat pot caution. The salesman at the garden center said you can put your vegetable seedlings in the ground, peat pots and all. That may work with small plants, but larger peat pots may not break down so easily, forcing roots to work themselves free. Here's how to get your money's worth from your peat pots and keep your plants growing happily.

- When it's time to move seedlings outside, soak the peat pots in water until they're soggy.

- Tear away the tops and bottoms of the peat pots to help them decay more quickly and allow roots to stay moist.

- No matter the size of the pot, if roots have grown into the peat container, don't try to remove it. You're likely to damage the plant.

Prevent top cause of graft failure. To grow a new apple tree of a certain variety, you can't just plant a seed. Instead, you'll need to graft, or join scionwood — a cutting from the kind of tree you want to grow — with rootstock. Experts use several types of grafts to join new and old wood, depending on the size of each piece and time of year. But sometimes grafts don't take, and the main reason is letting air dry out the wood. Keep this from happening by using a sealing compound to coat all cracks and the cut end of the grafting stick.

Small batches save cuttings from disaster. Don't put all your eggs in one basket. Plant stem cuttings in small batches in separate boxes to avoid losing the entire crop in case of disease or a watering mishap. You're more likely to end up with a nice batch of lupines or chrysanthemums after all your hard work. Recycle plastic shoe boxes, shallow dishpans, or plastic storage bins for this purpose.

Speedy way to make moss spread. Get that vintage moss-covered look on your patio stones or outdoor pots by mixing up a mossy milkshake.

- Gather moss from surfaces similar to the one where you want it to grow — wood, stone, or soil. Take only small patches an inch or two in diameter.

- Make a slurry of moss and a thick liquid in a blender. Yogurt or buttermilk work well, since they are thick and acidic. The blended mixture should be about the consistency of thin pudding. Add more moss or liquid to get it right.

- Dampen the surface where you want to grow moss, then spread on the slurry using a spoon or paintbrush.

- Keep the growing moss wet by misting it at least once a day. In about six weeks you'll see thin fingers of moss growing.

PRUNE & GROOM
TOUGH LOVE FOR BETTER PLANTS

Secrets to successful pruning. Experts say to spread drastic pruning of overgrown shrubs over two to three years, but some can handle more cutting. You can prune up to 50 percent of a hawthorn or beech bush at one time. Do it late in the winter, before new leaves sprout. Cut back the top and one side of the bush one year, then the other side the next. After a hard pruning, be sure to water and fertilize your shrubs, then spread mulch. For more information on how to do serious hard-pruning of shrubs, see *3-stage plan for hard-pruning shrubs* in the *Sure-fire success strategies for shrubs* chapter.

Prune pines without stunting their growth. If you prune away the terminal bud on a new pine branch, it can't grow back. That's because pines have buds only at the branch tips. So prune pines in early summer before the needle bundles open. You'll get a more compact tree shape, but your pine tree can keep growing next year.

Simple rule of thumb for right-time pruning. The best time to trim your trees and flowering shrubs depends on when they bloom. Follow this rule for the most abundant blooms ever.

- Shrubs that bloom in the spring, such as azaleas and rhododendrons, flower on old growth. Prune them just after their flowers fade.

- Shrubs that bloom in the summer and fall, like rose of Sharon, flower on new growth. Prune them in the early spring when they are still dormant from winter.

- Deciduous trees, including elms and oaks, do best when pruned late in the winter.

Following this schedule lets shrubs recover from pruning before it's time to bloom again.

Pruning myth debunked

If you've been told pruning at the wrong time will kill a plant, don't believe it. Pruning a flowering shrub at a less-then-ideal time of year may cause it to lose a season of blooms, but it won't harm the shrub in the long run. Same thing with maples, birch, and other trees that bleed. They may make a mess with sap, but they won't die. So if you don't get a chance to prune at the right time, never fear. Your plants will survive.

When to prune deciduous trees. The best time to prune most deciduous trees is late winter or very early spring, when they're still dormant but just before the buds open. But that's not the case for trees that "bleed" sap heavily in the spring, including maples and birch trees. Instead, prune these in winter when they are completely dormant, or do it in late summer or early fall. At least they will bleed less at that time of year.

Skip pruning during drought. You may have heard pruning your shrubs will make them need less water. That's a bad method of getting through a dry season, say experts at the

University of Georgia. Instead, pruning plants will send them into a growth spurt, so they need even more water than usual. You would have to cut back at least half of a tree's foliage to force it to use less water, and that much pruning might kill it in difficult conditions. Wait for the wet season to prune.

To cut or not to cut

Prune a tree's limbs for one of three reasons — first to ensure safety, second for the health of the tree, and third to make it look beautiful. Next time you do maintenance pruning on a tree, use this branch-size decision guide to figure out what to cut off.

- For a branch less than 2 inches in diameter, go ahead and cut.
- Between 2 and 4 inches in diameter, think twice before you cut.
- More than 4 inches in diameter, be sure there's a good reason to cut.

Make pruning cleanup a breeze. Stop raking up those leaves and limbs after you prune your shrubs. Save time and work by spreading an old shower curtain liner under shrubs and trees to catch cuttings while you prune. When you're done, just gather up the corners and carry the clippings to the trash or compost pile. You can also use an old sheet, tarp, or vinyl tablecloth.

Give yourself a third hand. Use that extra TV tray stand next time you need to rake up and bag leaves or grass clippings. Set up the stand as a frame to hold open your large plastic trash bag. Place the open bag on its side, and sweep the yard waste straight into the bag. No helper required.

Harness the power of your strongest muscles. No matter how strong your arms are, sometimes they'll meet up with a sapling that's tougher. Next time you need to cut through a large woody stem at ground level, use your legs. Position the blades of your lopper around the stem you want to cut and hold in place. Then bend your knees, placing your thighs next to your arms, and squeeze. As you use pressure from both your arms and legs at once, the thick stem should be no match for your muscles. Don't try this method for more-precise pruning.

Triple cut gets big limbs down safely. A heavy tree limb can start to fall before you're done cutting it, tearing away the tree's precious bark. Avoid that damaging mistake by using this three-step method to cut limbs that are larger than 1 1/2 inches thick.

- Cut a shallow notch on the underneath side of the branch about 6 to 12 inches away from the branch collar. This protective cut is key to avoiding bark damage.

- Make a second cut from the top, about 3 inches farther out on the branch and all the way through the branch. The limb is gone, but you're not quite done.

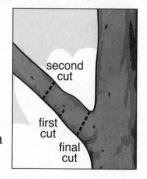

- Cut off the remaining stub of branch just outside of the branch collar.

It's also best to support the heavy branch with a rope so it doesn't cause damage or injury below when it falls.

Trick for straighter hedge lines. Give yourself a guide to follow while you trim the flat tops of hedges. Place bamboo stakes at both ends of the hedge, and run a string between the stakes. Check the string with a level, then follow the string as you prune.

Pick easy-care shapes for shrubs. When your square shrub with military-style corners gets overgrown and ragged, it's pretty easy to notice. But new growth is less obvious on a shrub with curved edges. Aim for round designs, and you can get away with less-frequent pruning.

Train shrubs with castoffs. Getting shrubs into shape sometimes requires training along with pruning. Hold stems or vines in place by tying them to a stake with an old pair of pantyhose. These handy ties are sturdy and flexible.

Get winter preview of planned pruning. With little digging or harvesting to do in the winter months, spend time planning garden jobs for later. While the leaves are off your trees and you can see their skeletons, tie ribbons around limbs you are considering removing. Leave the ribbons for a few days or weeks, so you can take your time thinking about the final result.

Save that stem. You may be able to salvage a stem that's been broken by a pruning accident but is still attached to the plant. Use wooden toothpicks and tape to make a splint. With any luck, it'll heal itself.

Shearing trick for fuller hedges. Avoid letting your hedges get thin and spindly at the bottom by trimming them to let in light. Leave the base of the hedge wider than the top so lower branches are not shaded from the sun. It's also best to prune hedges regularly, at least twice a year, to help them grow more bushy and full.

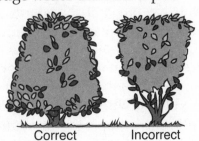

Correct   Incorrect

Pick right pruner for the job.
When it's time to cut branches from trees or large bushes, pick a cutting tool based on the size of the limb so you don't damage the plant or ruin your tool.

- Hand pruners work for branches less than one-half inch in diameter.

- Lopping shears are best for branches between one-half inch and 1-inch thick.

- A pruning saw is ideal for branches larger than 1 inch in diameter.

If you need to make a cut on a branch high off the ground, look for a pole pruner with a lightweight fiberglass pole.

Neat way to prune a rubber plant

Protect your hands and nearby surfaces from the sticky sap that oozes out when you prune a rubber plant. The best way to do this is to wear gloves and seal the pruning cut quickly using wood ashes or powdered rooting hormone. Rubber plants often need repeated pruning to achieve an even form, so you may need to do this several times a year.

Little-known way to keep plants healthy. Needles and scalpels can spread disease from person to person, and pruning tools can do the same with plants. Don't spread disease from one tree to another through fresh wounds created when you prune. Keep harmful bacteria, viruses, and fungi from attacking your plants by cleaning pruning tools properly.

- Before you cut a branch, sanitize the cutting blades. You can use either 70-percent rubbing alcohol or bleach diluted with water, one part bleach to nine parts water. Immerse tools in the solution for up to two minutes.

- Wipe off any visible wood particles from the cutting surfaces of the tools.

- After you finish pruning, clean the blades with soap and water to avoid leaving corrosive bleach on the metal.

Easy trimming with less mess. Trimming shrubs and grasses is the easy part — then comes the cleanup. Avoid the mess by putting a bungee cord to use before you make the first cut.

- Wrap a bungee cord around tall ornamental grasses, securing it above where you plan to cut. Trim the grass near the base while it's held secure by the cord, and you have a neatly wrapped bundle to carry to the trash.

- Make the bungee cord into a third hand by using it to pull the lower branches of a shrub out of the way. Then you can trim, mulch, and rake thoroughly underneath without having branches get in your way — possibly being cut in the process.

You can substitute a length of rope or duct tape for either of these jobs if you don't have a bungee cord.

Thorn-free flower cutting

Save your fingers from the prickly part of cutting roses with the help of a clothespin, binder clip, or sturdy chip clip. Use the clip like an extension of your hand — one that won't feel the sting. Then focus on keeping your cutting hand safe.

Simple way to keep boxwoods under control. If you don't prune a boxwood for years, it can become massive but with new growth only on the outside. Then a severe pruning might kill it. Keep boxwoods in check by cutting them back at least by the time new growth reaches a foot. But don't use shears on your boxwood. Use a hand pruner, reaching inside the hedge to clip individual stems at the next crotch. Doing this regularly — called "plucking" — allows light and air inside the plant to encourage new growth. It also keeps your boxwood neatly shaped and tidy.

Free stakes from your garden. Look at each twig and branch you prune to see if it will work as a support stake. Straight twigs make great flower stakes that blend in to the environment, and branches with a V at the tip can be used as supports for leaning stems. You can also lash together three or more small branches to form a triangle-shaped trellis for vines to climb. You save the cost of buying metal or plastic stakes, plus your garden looks more natural.

Grow an endless stake supply. Pick the right variety of bamboo, and you can raise bamboo stakes in your own backyard. But avoid planting an invasive species by asking your local nursery for a clumping variety of bamboo, like *Phyllostachys*. These "bamboos that behave" don't send out aggressive rhizomes like traveling bamboo. You may need to invest in a fine-tooth pruning saw or reciprocating saw to cut the stakes.

Steer clear of cord-cutting danger. Drape the power cord of your electric trimmer over your shoulder while you trim, letting it drag behind you as you move. This will keep you from accidentally slicing through the cord while you're pruning.

TAP INTO WISE WATERING TIPS

Easy ways to cut watering in half. Up to 80 percent of home water use occurs outdoors. Take three simple steps to cut your water bill in half.

- Convert half of your lawn to beds or a natural area. Giving an inch of water to 1,000 square feet of lawn uses 624 gallons — more than two days of indoor water use for a family of four. Mulch over part of your lawn and plant through it, arranging paths through the beds and leaving just a patch of grass.

- Plant drought-tolerant native plants. According to the Los Angeles County Water District, switching to these varieties can cut your outdoor water use in half.

- Collect rainwater in barrels. Just one-half inch of rain falling on your roof will fill a 50-gallon barrel. Set up a row of barrels in the right places, and you can gather many times that over a rainy week.

Look to your "indicator plants" for advice. You don't need to check on every single plant in your garden to see if it's time to water. By watching certain plants, you can tell the perfect time to get out your watering can. In your vegetable garden, keep an eye on how your squash or melon plants look. When their big leaves start to droop, it's probably a sign to water everything. And if you plant impatiens or coleus in the root zones of a tree, look to these little indicator plants to know when the tree is getting thirsty. You'll notice their wilting leaves long before the tree shows signs it needs water.

Double-check droopy plants

It's just as bad for plants to get too much water as it is to get too little. Take out the guesswork by checking them twice. If plants look sad and saggy in the evening, you can wait overnight. Check again in the morning to see if they still seem thirsty. Then give them a drink.

Don't be a slave to the clock. You can use an automatic timed controller to water your plants, but don't follow it strictly. Changing weather may mean yesterday's water is still standing in pools or has been soaked up by the sun. It's a waste of money and harmful to your plants to water when they don't need it. Check out the soil, and adjust watering as needed.

Time watering to banish fungus. Leaving water on plant leaves overnight can make them prime targets for fungus. Yet you don't want to run your sprinkler in the heat of the afternoon, since up to 40 percent of the water can be lost to evaporation. If you want to use a sprinkler, do it in the early morning before temperatures heat up. This will also give the leaves time to dry off before evening. You can water in the evening if you use a soaker hose or drip irrigation system. These methods apply water directly to the roots, so leaves don't get wet.

Clever way to check soil moisture. It's usually time to water when half the moisture the soil can hold has dried out. Here's a way to check soil moisture without getting your hands dirty. Insert wooden dipsticks at several places in your garden, and leave them there for an hour or more. Then pull each one out and check to see if the bottom is damp. If not, it's probably time to water. Use wooden paint stir sticks, craft sticks, or other light-colored wooden sticks to do the testing.

Drip your way to big savings. A lawn sprinkler sends out up to 480 gallons of water in an hour, but a 100-foot drip irrigation hose releases only about 60 gallons in that time. Even better, all the water from a drip system goes straight to the roots of your plants. And since you usually run a drip or trickle irrigation system for just 15 minutes at a time, releasing water all along the length of the hose, you won't see water running down the street. This method can easily help you cut your garden water bill by up to 60 percent compared to using a sprinkler.

Put an end to water runoff

Watering a sloping or terraced yard is tricky, since water insists on running downhill. Consider these hints to keep water where you want it.

- Don't follow the same timing rules as you would on flat ground. You may need to spread out watering into shorter irrigation times to avoid losing excess down the slope. Water for no more than 10 minutes per hour.
- Put in a soaker hose or drip irrigation system rather than using a sprinkler. This encourages water to soak into the ground instead of running downhill.

Water your plants while you're away. You can vacation without worry when you train your plants to water themselves. Set up a self-watering system using a plastic soda bottle.

- Heat a thick needle or tiny nail over a candle, and poke a small hole in the bottle's plastic lid.

- Fill the bottle with water and screw on the cap.

- Turn the bottle upside down and check the water flow. It should stay in the bottle for a minute, then slowly begin to drip out the hole. If no water comes out, loosen the cap slightly to release the vacuum.

- Place the bottle upside down into the top of the soil near the plant you want to water. Depending on the size of the bottle, you can be sure your plant is getting a slow stream of water for up to several weeks.

You can also use a clean, plastic milk jug. Poke a small hole in the side of the jug, near the bottom. Hold a finger over the hole as you fill the jug with water. Position the hole near the stem of your plant. Tighten or loosen the cap to adjust the flow.

Myth: all plants hate wet leaves

Actually, plants in the cabbage family enjoy having water on their leaves. You can water them from above without doing any damage. But use a watering wand on most other plants in your garden, including tomatoes, squash, and peas, to avoid mildew and rotting.

Prep pots for watering. Your large pots of flowers live on the back deck, but somehow the rain never makes it to the soil. You'll need to water them by hand — preferably twice. First, pour on a little water like you're moistening a dry sponge. Wait a few minutes, and then water them again. This method lets soil soak up the water rather than having it pool on top or run straight through the pot.

Give water-loving plants a watering hole. If you live in a fairly dry part of the country but you really want to grow plants that need lots of moisture, here's your solution. Dig a planting hole, lining it with a large, heavy-duty plastic bag. Then plant as usual. The liner will hold moisture around the plant's roots, cutting the need for extra watering. Your elephant ears will enjoy this bathtub effect.

Make a giant watering can for free. Turn that empty, jumbo laundry detergent bottle into a watering can that will hold enough for an entire flower bed. Rinse the container well, then drill several tiny holes in the cap and a half-inch hole just above the handle. Water will flow smoothly without spilling.

Best strategy for gathering rain. Place small buckets and plastic bowls around your yard to catch rain and runoff. Notice where water runs off a porch roof or collects under a patio table, and collect it to water your plants later. You won't need to lug around heavy containers, and you'll put clean rainwater to great use.

Save money on a rain barrel. You can easily pay $150 or more for a prefab rain barrel system. Make your own and collect free water from your roof every time it rains.

- Contact a hospital or school cafeteria and ask for a used 55-gallon food container. Rinse the barrel well before you use it.

- Put to use that old plastic trash can with a fitted lid — the one you've been saving since the city delivered rolling bins. Be sure it doesn't leak.

- Contact your water company or local government to see if they offer free rain barrels or kits.

Elevate your container on a stack of bricks next to your house, cut a hole in the lid, and fit the downspout into the hole. Drill another hole near the base of the barrel and attach a water spigot. After the barrel fills, connect a hose and water your garden.

Turn functional into fantastic. Dress up a drab rain barrel by turning it into a planter.

- Wrap coarse netting or chicken wire around the barrel, securing it in the back with twist ties.

- Plant clematis or morning glories at the base, and let them grow up through the netting. Soon your flowering vines will hide the barrel.

- Keep the vines in check so they don't block the downspout.

3 ways to salvage a leaky hose. That leaky garden hose is not ruined. Repair it yourself, or put it to another use.

- To fix a small leak in a rubber hose, apply a layer of plastic rubber compound. Let it dry, then sand lightly with fine sandpaper. Use a second coat covering a slightly larger area to be sure the repair lasts.

- Use a plastic adhesive to repair a plastic hose. Reinforce it with plastic tape or a plastic patch. Then add a second layer of plastic adhesive. Let it dry overnight before using.

- Convert it into a soaker hose by puncturing the underside at even intervals with a hot ice pick. Then lay it in your garden bed between the rows, and attach it to your new hose. Plug the other end with a plastic end cap. Turn on the water and give your flowers a good soak.

Take the challenges out of watering. It's as certain as death and taxes — watering your garden. Yet this important task can be a challenge if you have trouble walking or lack the strength of your younger days. Consider which of these tools can make the job easier for you.

- An extra faucet installed near your vegetable garden means you don't have to lug a long hose across your yard.

- Drip irrigation systems or soaker hoses can let you do the job by flipping a switch.

- Lever faucets are easier to turn off and on than those with round handles.

- Hose-end shutoff valves keep you from wasting water while you move to a new part of the yard.

- A long-handled watering wand lets you put water where you want it without bending.

Don't waste money on a short hose

Measure the distance from your outdoor water faucet to the farthest plant in your garden. Add about 10 feet to give you some wriggle room. That's the minimum length of garden hose you should buy.

Save delicate plants from toxic water. Fluoride in drinking water may be good for your teeth, but some plants can't take it. Palms, spider plants, and other varieties with long, slender leaves are sensitive to fluoride in water. The mineral tends to build up in the tips of these leaves, turning them brown and dry. Collect rainwater for these plants instead.

4 ways to cut minerals from tap water. Minerals in water can damage plants and make the soil crusty. Certain plants, including orchids, avocado, and citrus, are especially sensitive to the calcium and magnesium in softened water. Here's how to reduce mineral content.

- Filter your tap water by using a countertop filter, like the Brita system.

- Be sure pots drain well so excess minerals can be flushed away.

- If you have a water softener to treat water that feeds

indoor faucets, get water for plants from an outdoor line that is not connected. Rainwater is also a good option.

- When it's time to recharge your water softener, use potassium chloride instead of the typical sodium chloride.

Simple trick removes chlorine. Chlorinated tap water probably won't harm your houseplants. But if you can smell it or taste it from your faucet, consider aging your tap water before giving it to your plants. Just draw water into a wide-mouth container and let it sit on your counter for 24 hours. Chlorine escapes into the air just that fast.

Look for signs of underwatering. Your houseplant will tell you whether to water or wait. Symptoms that it's getting too much water, like yellow leaves, rotting roots, and soft patches, don't show up for a while. You'll notice the following signs when it's time to water.

- Tips of leaves wilt and turn brown.

- Flowers and leaves drop too soon.

- Lower leaves begin to curl and turn yellow.

- Leaves start to look translucent.

Don't wait until you see the stem wilt or the soil pull away from the side of the pot. This causes stress on the plant.

Pamper your plants while you're away

Prepare houseplants before you leave for a long vacation. First, check them for bugs or disease and water thoroughly. Then place each plant in an individual clear plastic bag and close loosely. Place your plants in medium or low light, and let them enjoy the moist environment in their individual greenhouses.

THE FLOWER GARDEN

BEST BETS FOR
BOUNTIFUL BLOOMS

AMAZING ANNUALS

Beat spring rush with fall seed planting. Spread out the gardening chores by putting your annual seeds in the ground in the fall — same time as you plant bulbs. Aim to sow seeds just before the rainy season in a warm climate, or right after the first killing frost in a colder area. You'll enjoy a colorful surprise in the spring when it's sprouting time. Annual poppies, pansies, and larkspur are good candidates for fall sowing.

Save money with self-seeding annuals. You don't buy new bushes for your yard every year. Why spend money for new flowers? You can enjoy long-lasting, colorful flowers year after year when you pick annuals that seed themselves. Choose popular varieties like bachelor's button, zinnias, and impatiens, and you'll get blooms anew next year — with hardly any effort on your part.

- Let the generous self-sowers drop their seeds, and you'll find a clump of flowers near the original plant next year.

- You can also transplant any volunteer seedlings to a new location once they develop three sets of leaves.

- Or collect the seeds hiding behind fading flowers. Keep them in an envelope in the refrigerator until planting time.

Plant your annuals where water will not wash the seeds away, and water them gently. Mark the area so you will not accidentally clean it up or mow it down.

Give budget wildflowers best chance for success. Seed packets claim you can create a lush field of flowers with a quick scattering. Wildflower seeds can save money over buying pricey annual flowers. But sow them right so you get more than unsightly weeds.

- First, be sure your wildflower mix is right for your region and your use, such as a dry area.

- Next, prepare your seeds by soaking them in water overnight to speed up germination.

- Clear weeds or grass from small patches of ground, loosen up the soil, and press seeds into it. Use twice the amount of seed the package recommends.

- Finally, water your seeds just like you would other young flowers.

Your field of wildflowers will be less spectacular next year because some of the annuals won't come back, but you can repeat the steps if you like the results.

Plant vintage treasures among the blooms. Get that cottage garden feel without spending a dime on a new gazing ball or pricey iron sculpture. The key is to select interesting vintage items and place them in your garden so the plants appear to be growing around them. Try an old metal sign planted among your impatiens, or petunias growing up through a cracked crock. Even a broken spice cabinet looks great when zinnias are sprouting from the drawers.

Get good seeds for next to nothing

Join the American Horticultural Society (AHS), and you can request free seeds from the group's annual seed exchange. Seeds are collected by other members every year from home gardens and cataloged to share with others. You pay just a small donation to cover the cost of shipping. The $35 annual membership fee also gets you other AHS benefits, including a subscription to *The American Gardener* magazine and discounts at public gardens. You can join online at *www.ahs.org*, or call 800-777-7931.

Flowering herbs do double duty. Your flower garden turns into a functional kitchen garden when you mix in lovely culinary herbs like rosemary, chives, lavender, and German chamomile. Flowering herbs fit so well among the other blooms, you may forget to pick them when it's time. Just be careful with flowering annuals like basil, dill, cilantro, and chervil. Once these herbs start making flowers, leaf production slows down or stops. Harvest them often to enjoy their fragrant leaves and delay flowering.

Annuals add variety to perennial beds. Who says you can't mix annual and perennial flowers? A blend of various types of plants brings some zing to flower beds.

- Mix unusual potted annuals in your perennial bed, changing them with the seasons. Move the pots around to meet changing water or lighting needs of each flower.

- Plant annuals in the ground among the perennials. A variety of plants mixed together — called polyculture — helps all the plants thrive because they don't compete for identical nutrients. Plus, they're less likely to share the same diseases. So your zinnias may enjoy greater health if you plant them next to your hostas.

- Use annual flowers that won't spread or grow above 10 inches to fill in the spaces between newly planted shrubs or ground cover. These compact plants can camouflage bare spots while the permanent residents reach maturity.

Give tiny seeds a chance at life. Follow the package directions when you plant flowers that come from tiny seeds. California poppies, columbine, shasta daisies, and similar flowers need light to begin germination. If you bury the seeds too deep, they won't make it out of the ground.

Work in the dirt with clean fingernails. Try this simple trick to keep from getting dirt under your nails. Scrape your fingernails over a bar of soap and smooth on some hand lotion before you go out to play in the dirt. Cleaning up will be much easier.

Mr. Smarty Plants to the rescue

Get gardening help from the experts at the Ladybird Johnson Wildflower Center in Texas. Mr. Smarty Plants is a free online service offering advice on all things related to native plants. You can even get help with plant identification if you send a digital picture of your mystery plant. Navigate to *www.wildflower.org/expert* to find answers to all your gardening questions.

Give impatiens their own sun shade. Provide temporary shade for sun-fearing flowers like impatiens, amethyst, and Persian violets with an old umbrella. You can "plant" it in your garden where you need it or make an umbrella-shaded pot for a sunny deck.

- Find a large, heavy container to use as a pot, and dig out a big umbrella — possibly an old golf umbrella or canvas market umbrella.

- Keep the umbrella upright in the pot by wedging bricks around it or placing it inside a short length of PVC pipe.

- Add a layer of sand to the pot, then potting soil.

- Place your plants so that the tallest grow near the umbrella at the center of the pot. You may want to do the planting with the container in its final location since it will be heavy.

Clever trick locates shady spot. Your shade-loving impatiens, violets, and columbine are counting on you to put them in a spot where the light is just right. But the changing seasons can mean shadows move across your yard in ways you don't expect. Check the shadows made by a full moon at midnight in January. These dark areas, created by shadows of buildings and trees, should be the same places where the sun will cast a shadow at noon six months later. That means they're safe places to plant flowers that can't handle lots of direct sun.

Help beautify your neighborhood

The America the Beautiful Fund provides flower, herb, or vegetable seeds to community groups for just the cost of shipping. All you do is complete an application and include a short description of your planned community garden or neighborhood beautification project. If your project is accepted, you'll get up to 6,000 seed packets from Operation Green Planet. See *www.america-the-beautiful.org* for details.

Prompt petunias to bloom twice. Freshen up your flowering plants and encourage a second bloom with a midsummer makeover. Many annuals, even the more forgiving varieties like petunias, can become leggy and tired by the middle of the growing season. Give them a good pruning, and top-dress the soil with about one-half inch of vermicompost — compost helped along by worms. Then water thoroughly to help nutrients reach the roots. Sit back and wait for a new show of flowers from your refreshed bloomers.

Just-in-time transplanting keeps flowers safe. Strike the right balance in timing your transplanting. Move flowers too early in the spring, and a surprise freeze could put a chill on your efforts. But wait too late, and your annuals won't have enough time in the warm soil to do their best blooming.

Easy watering cue

Figure out which flower bed dries out first and which holds the most water. Then use these as your cues to know when to water all your plants. There's no need to check every bed or flower once you decide which area works as the canary in your coal mine.

Pick free party favors from your garden. Next time you host a dinner or baby shower, look to your garden for free gifts to send home with your guests. Take cuttings of your geranium plant and place in tiny water-filled bottles. If your garden is overflowing with marigolds, pot up some small samples. Whatever you have in abundance, use it to create table decorations that guests can take home and enjoy. They may seem small to you, but healthy seedlings, cuttings, or flowers are a bonanza to someone who doesn't share your green thumb.

Get perennial color from annuals. Save money by keeping this year's annuals for next year's garden. Dig up your healthiest begonias or geraniums in the fall, put them in pots, and store them in a garage or cool basement. Water them monthly, then plant them in the yard come springtime. You can also try keeping geraniums by shaking the dirt from their roots and hanging them upside down in the basement. Another option is to keep them in their original nursery pot and insert them into another pot that has been planted in the ground. At the first threat of frost, simply remove the original pot and bring the plant indoors.

Sprinkle grounds to bring out the blooms. Save old coffee grounds to sprinkle around your flowers. The extra nitrogen in coffee gives a nutritional boost to the plants, encouraging a flourish of flowers. Adding coffee grounds will raise the soil's acidity, so try rinsing them first to help balance the pH. You can also try composted manure if coffee is not your thing.

Better soil can't be rushed. Don't give up hope. Your flowers need good soil, but it may take up to five years for soil improvements to show up in the form of better flowers in your yard. Be patient and keep adding amendments every year. For faster improvement, create a raised bed and fill it with a blend of good topsoil and leaf compost. Your flowers will enjoy an instant rush of nutrition.

Give your cosmos the support they crave. Recycle twigs and twine to create a support structure for your top-heavy flowers, like cosmos and mums. Once the plants reach about one-third their full size, place sticks at four corners in a square formation around each one. Then crisscross twine around the tops of the twigs, leaving large spaces for flowers to poke their heads through as they grow. Keep an eye on the plants, and tuck the stems into the structure as needed.

Time flower cutting for best-kept blossoms. Cut flowers from your garden either early in the morning or in the cool of the evening — not in the heat of midday. Cutting them when the stems are full of moisture and the plant has plenty of stored food helps keep flowers looking fresh longer.

Douse stems quickly for perkier blooms. Carry a bucket half-filled with water when you cut flowers from your yard. The idea is to get the stems into the water as quickly as possible to reduce the amount of air that enters the stems. Use water that is room temperature, since colder water can shock your flowers into drooping. Also, be sure your cutting shears are sharp to avoid tearing the plants.

Outwit pesky sunflower thieves. Save sunflowers from insects by cutting them before they're fully open. As soon as you see petals beginning to pull away from the center of the flower, get out your shears and get cutting, then bring them indoors to enjoy. Wait any longer, and pests like cucumber beetles will chew their way through your blooms.

Keep cut flowers happy

Put your cut flowers into water quickly with a portable water station. Start with a small, light wooden table that's large enough to hold a bucket.

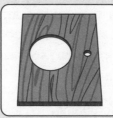

| Measure the circumference of the bucket just below its handles by wrapping a string around it, then measuring the string with a yardstick. | Draw a circle on the table top the same size, and cut out the circle carefully. Also cut a hole big enough for a pipe that fits a standard three-quarter-inch garden hose. | Place the bucket in the hole you cut. Then connect the pipe to a hose and spigot. Solder the spigot valve to the pipe if needed. |

Arrange cutting garden for best use. If you love having fresh flowers in your home, reserve a spot in your garden especially for flowers you plan to cut. This area doesn't need fabulous design. It's more important that you can easily reach the plants for thinning, fertilizing, and cutting blooms to take into the house. That's why a simple arrangement of rows — like a traditional vegetable garden — works great for your cutting garden. Leave space between the rows, and group together plants of the same type, height, and with similar light and moisture needs.

Get a second life from drying packets

Save the silica gel packets from boxes of new shoes and pill bottles. You can use them to dry cut flowers without losing the beautiful natural colors of the blooms. Simply pour them into a container, place the flowers inside, then sprinkle more gel on top. Drying can take anywhere from two to six days. Make sure the silica gel is not coarse or it can damage the flowers.

Recycle twigs for lovely floral arrangements. Don't waste money buying florist tape to keep your flowers in place. Cut trimmed forsythia or willow twigs to about the same height as your flower vase. Put enough in the vase to use up about one-third the space. Then add flowers, placing them so the sticks hold the stems upright and loosely arranged.

Clean out a vase with no scrubbing. To clean the inside of a flower vase, fill it with hot water and add a handful of sand or clay kitty litter. Shake it up, and watch the dirt disappear from the glass.

Protect buds while they dry. Place daisies face down when you dry them in silica gel. Same thing goes for other flowers that are open and flat with strong petals. But place complex, three-dimensional buds like dahlias face up in the gel so they keep their shape. When drying flowers like roses or hydrangeas, be sure to support the blossoms so the petals aren't crushed.

Overpick flowers for dried bouquets. Pick double the volume of flowers you think you may need if you plan to create a dried arrangement. Flowers tend to shrink in the drying process, so more blooms will help fill out the bouquet. And avoid using flowers that will likely turn black when dried, such as dark red or purple blossoms. Instead, go for pink or yellow varieties.

Branch out for dried flower creations. Annuals like strawflower, globe amaranth, and bells of Ireland make great dried flower arrangements. But don't feel confined to using only these traditional blooms. Mix in some unexpected items from your garden, like garlic, chilies, or corn. If you can find it outdoors and dry it, it's fair game.

Turn faulty flowers into potpourri. If your flowers don't look perfect when it's time to cut, skip the vase. Dry your blooms and make up a batch of fragrant potpourri. Place petals in a single layer on a cookie sheet in a 180-degree oven with the door ajar. Remove after a few hours, and let them stand overnight to finish drying. Mix with your favorite essential oil, and store in a cool, dark place for several weeks.

BEAUTIFUL BULBS

Give potted bulbs a fighting chance. If you want to enjoy pots of bulbs on your deck, select a hardy variety. With just a smidgen of soil surrounding bulbs in pots, they get little protection from cold weather. Play it safe by picking a variety listed as hardy to at least one zone colder than where you live. For example, if you live in Dallas, classified as zone 8, select bulbs that are hardy to at least zone 7, like in Oklahoma City. That way your bulbs are sure to do better in pots. Another way to help your bulbs beat the cold is to move the pots into a cool basement or garage in the winter. Or wrap the entire pot in burlap, and bury it in the ground until springtime.

Take planting cue from nurseries. Spring-flowering bulbs, summer-flowering bulbs — different varieties of bulbs grow and bloom at different times of the year. How do you know when to plant them? Companies that sell bulbs take out the guesswork. They typically offer bulbs for sale near the time of year they should be planted. So if you see tulip bulbs offered for sale and that's the flower you want, buy them now and plant them soon.

Hedge your bets with odd-looking tubers. Most bulbs have an obvious top and bottom. With tubers, it's not so clear. If you can't tell heads from tails, plant a tuber sideways. The plant will use up some energy pulling itself right with its contractile roots, but it can successfully make the move.

Trees and bulbs team up for healthy garden. In a good marriage, each partner gives as well as receives. That's what happens when you plant early bulbs under the trees in your yard. The trees are happy, since you won't bother them much once the bulbs are planted. Meanwhile, the bulbs appreciate sun filtering through the trees early in the season followed by hot-weather shade later on. Besides that, they get a free layer of natural mulch when the trees lose their leaves. Try winter aconites or snowdrops under the trees for a happy garden "marriage."

Blend soil for better growth

You may have been told to add a layer of sand in the bottom of a planting hole for bulbs. Don't bother. It's true that most bulbs need well-drained soil to thrive, but a layer of sand won't help if the ground beneath it is hard. Instead, amend heavy clay with sand or loose soil blended in before you plant.

Avoid rotting lilies with easy planting trick. Let gravity do the work to keep scaly bulbs like lilies from rotting in wet, poorly draining soil. Plant scaly bulbs on their sides so moisture won't accumulate between scales before the bulbs get a chance to sprout.

Give bulbs space to breathe. Plant bulbs at least 1 foot away from the house. This allows your tulips to enjoy the rain without having it blocked by the roof overhang. The space also keeps your plants from being baked in the summer by sunlight reflecting off the house.

Banish bugs from glad corms. Thrips love to spend the winter on your gladiolus corms. Kill these pests before you plant your glads. Mix a few teaspoons of Lysol or another disinfectant into a gallon of water. Soak the corms for several hours, then let them dry.

Protect your skin from hyacinths

Touching hyacinth bulbs can leave your skin itchy and red. You're especially at risk if you're allergic to garlic and other members of the lily family. Wear gloves when you plant these bulbs to avoid a reaction.

Give hybrid tulips a longer life. Most bulbs thrive if you follow this general rule — plant a bulb three time as deep as its width. For example, you only need to dig down 6 inches to plant a 2-inch bulb. But if you break that rule you can turn hybrid tulips, which typically bloom only once, into perennials that bloom year after year. Plant hybrids deeper, about 10 inches down. The color you'll enjoy for several years will be well worth the extra digging.

Speed-plant daffodils for less digging. Skip the tedious chore of planting bulbs one by one. You can get all your tulips or daffodils in the ground in less than an hour with this quick method. It's as simple as digging a few large communal holes and tossing in your bulbs. Then just turn them pointed end up and cover with dirt. Figure four large bulbs per square foot you dig. That means you can plant about 100 bulbs in a 5 x 5-foot bed.

Keep tubers intact by staking early. When you plant dahlia tubers, or other tall flowers from bulbs, plant a stake at the same time. These tall plants will need support to help them stay upright when they're in full bloom. But if you wait until the stems reach their full height, you risk piercing and damaging the tuber with the stake. Even better, the stakes serve as guides so you'll know exactly where your flowers will emerge.

Knock out disease with one simple step. Crop rotation, or moving the location of plants from year to year, keeps bulbs healthy. When you plant bulbs in a new area, you keep last year's soil-borne diseases and pesky insects from returning this season. So replant summer bulbs like gladiolus and begonias that you lifted last fall in a new place this spring.

Leave a bread-crumb trail to your buried bulbs. It's easy to forget where last year's bulbs are buried. Mark the spot when you plant bulbs in the fall so you'll know where to expect color in the spring. Place Popsicle sticks, golf tees, or plastic skewers in the ground above where the bulbs are buried, or mark the spot with a handful of crushed oyster shells or colored stones. No more springtime tulip surprise.

Go natural for fuss-free bulbs. Make your bulbs look like they planted themselves. A naturalized bulb garden is a display that avoids straight lines or perfect symmetry in arrangement. Get the look by following two rules:

- Include only one or two species of bulbs in an area.

- Toss out bulbs, then plant them where they fall.

Take a break from mowing for bulb success. When naturalizing bulbs in a grassy area, you'll need to give the plants a chance to get started. That means you can't mow the grass near the bulbs for about six weeks after they flower. Wait until the leaves ripen and turn yellow. Choose daffodils, snowdrops, or crocuses for best success.

Scare varmints away from planted bulbs. Arm your bulbs with the horrid scent of turpentine before you plant them, and squirrels and chipmunks will look elsewhere for a snack. Prepare the bulbs for planting by putting them in a paper sack, adding a few drops of turpentine, and shaking the bag gently for 60 seconds. Then leave the bulbs in the bag overnight to soak up the aroma.

Use natural defense against rodents

Keep pesky squirrels from making a dinner out of your newly planted bulbs. Plant a clove of garlic along with each bulb. Squirrels hate the scent of this Mediterranean seasoning, so they'll look elsewhere for a snack. You can also try using hot pepper spray to deter bulb eaters. Your flowers will thank you.

Soapy solution to garden thievery. Get out your kitchen grater, take a bar of pungent soap, and sprinkle soap shavings on the soil after you plant bulbs. Stearic acid from the soap works to deter squirrels and other critters from digging down to eat your bulbs. The soap shavings should last several weeks. When you can't see them anymore, repeat the process.

Thorny trick wards off squirrels. Build a fence around your bulbs with canes pruned from your rose bush. Save up the thorniest canes you can find, then place them on the ground to enclose the area where you plant bulbs. Secure the canes with landscape pins or bent wires. Squirrels won't bother to cross the thorny barrier.

Take a hint from Dutch flower experts

Gardeners in charge of those fabulous fields of tulips in Holland know how to keep the squirrels away. They mix in plants like *Fritillaria imperialis*, or crown imperial plant, among the other bulbs. This lovely flower on a tall stem sends off a smell squirrels can't stand.

Keep elephant ears cozy at night. The large tuberous plant elephant ear can grow up to 3 feet tall in parts of the United States, and up to 8 feet tall in the tropics. But it won't reach those heights if a surprise frost kills it back. Protect elephant ears when the weather is questionable by covering the plants at night. Dig out an old blanket and a broomstick, and construct a tent over the plant in the evening.

Don't use shears on tired hyacinths. Deadhead your faded hyacinths by hand. Just knock off the small flowers by running your hand from the bottom of the flower cluster toward the tip. You want to leave the stem so it will help nurture the bulb.

Trick bulbs into blossoming. Spring-flowering bulbs, like tulips, hyacinths, and crocuses, need to lie dormant for a period of cold weather before they can grow and bloom. That's how these bulbs know to sprout and bloom during spring rather than in the middle of winter. It's a natural process called vernalization, and it's no problem if you live in a cold climate like Minnesota or Maine. But if you live in a mild climate like Florida or Texas, you can get brilliant blooms with this refrigerator secret.

- Pre-chill bulbs in the fridge at around 40 to 45 degrees Fahrenheit to make them think it's wintertime.

- Leave them there for eight to 15 weeks, depending on the variety of bulbs.

- Be sure to keep apples and other fruit away from the bulbs. Ethylene gas from ripening fruit will kill your flowers.

Give bulbs breath of fresh air. Store bulbs over the winter in a sack that gives ventilation. If you use airtight containers or plastic bags, your bulbs might come out damp and moldy. You can use mesh bags made for storing bulbs or substitute a paper bag. Old pantyhose also work great, since they let your bulbs breathe freely. Hang the bags in a cool, dry place like the basement.

Save money — skip the fertilizer

Don't waste money on fertilizer for your new bulbs. There's no need to fertilize bulbs when you plant them, since bulbs are ready-made storage units with all the food the plant needs for the first year. Besides that, fertilizer that touches plant roots can burn them.

Save bulbs from a moldy death. Don't toss out bulbs just because they have a coating of blue powdery mold. They have probably built up moisture, which resulted in a penicillin-type mold that is not serious. Wipe them off with a wet towel and plant them, and you may still get good results.

Help daffodils get their blooms back. Give your daffodils a new lease on life. If they seem to slow or stop producing flowers, a condition called "blindness," they may have grown too crowded. Daffodil bulbs split in two every couple of years, so they need to be thinned regularly. Relieve the pressure by dividing crowded clumps, and you can spread the wealth of flowers around your yard and help them bloom again. This remedy also works for overcrowded daylilies.

- As soon as the leaves turn yellow and die back, dig deep under a clump and lift it out.

- Shake off the soil and pull the bulbs apart. You can use a spray of water from the hose to get dirt off easily.

- Toss out any unhealthy bulbs, then plant the good ones at their original depth and spacing.

Beef up blooms with the right fertilizer. Planting larger bulbs usually means you'll get larger flowers later on. To help your bulbs bulk up for next year, apply a healthy dose of tomato fertilizer to the bulbs after they flower. This low-nitrogen treat will help your bulbs gain in size while they gather strength underground for next year's show.

Force your hyacinths to stand at attention. Save the cardboard rolls hyacinths to grow longer stems. Simply place a cardboard roll on the stem of the plant before it blooms. Your flowers will obediently stretch toward the sun, growing taller before they bloom. Then cut away the collars when they're the height you want.

Helpful site for iris lovers

If you've fallen in love with the beautiful, exotic-looking iris, check out the website of the American Iris Society (AIS) at *www.irises.org*. You can use the Iris Encyclopedia to select a particular type, get expert help with planting and growing, or find a local meeting of the AIS where you can mingle with experienced iris gardeners.

Smart choices for problem soil. Here's a tip for the lazy gardener. Pick species bulbs, like nonhybrid tulips, snowdrops, and irises, for areas of your garden that have poor soil. These varieties actually thrive in problem soil that is less fertile and not heavily composted. Save the soil improvement for where it's needed.

Plant bulbs you can't kill. Robert E. Lee mused that daylilies were the sign of a neglected garden. It's true that these hardy orange flowers tend to come back year after year, even outliving the people who planted them. Rumor is that RoundUp won't even kill them. Use daylilies to fill space or liven up an area with poor soil or too little sun.

Let bargain bulbs shine indoors. Take advantage of sale bulbs. Buy bulbs at the end of the growing season, then force them to grow inside for year-round blooms. Bulbs do best if you plant them soon after you buy them, so saving your bargain bulbs to plant outside next year may not be a great idea. Narcissus and paperwhite bulbs work especially well when grown indoors.

- Find a shallow container and fill it with gravel, or look for a vase made especially for forcing narcissus or hyacinth bulbs.

- Place the bulbs in the container, and add water so the base of the bulb stays moist.

- Keep the bulbs in a cool, dark place until you see roots, then move them into the light.

You can expect to see flowers within six weeks from the time you start the bulbs.

'Nip' paperwhites into shape. Healthy paperwhites tend to grow so tall that they flop over. Keep them short enough to support their blossoms with a change in water. Make a weak alcohol solution using whatever liquor you have around, like gin, vodka, whiskey, or tequila. Mix the solution one part liquor to seven parts water, and use it to water your paperwhites after the roots have appeared. The flowers will be just as big, yet stems will be one-third shorter.

Give yourself a bouquet of happiness

Cut flowers are not pure luxury. Research shows they can increase your happiness. Harvard University researcher Dr. Nancy Etcoff studied a group of people for one week, noting their moods and energy levels. Half the group had a bouquet of flowers at home, while the other half did not. Over the course of the week, people with flowers reported happier moods, less negativity, and more compassion for others. That's a nice reward — simply for bringing your garden into the house.

Make cut daffodils stand tall. Don't cut daffodils with scissors or a knife. Twist and snap the stalk with your fingers. This method retains the white part of the stem, so the flower will last longer in water.

Avoid the dreaded daffodil slime. Don't mix daffodils or narcissi with other types of flowers in a cut arrangement. The stems of these flowers give off a latex material when they're cut, known as "daffodil slime." Chemicals in the slime cause other flowers in the water to wilt quickly. You can avoid the problem by soaking daffodil stems in water for half a day, changing the water a couple times to drain off the slime. Then they're safe to mix.

PERFECT PERENNIALS

Clever way to find the best plants for your yard. You'll have more success if you plant perennials that are best for where you live. You can find out for sure which ones will do well in your yard by paying attention to the plants in your area — not by visiting a website. Look around town to see what plants are thriving in old graveyards, around neglected farm yards, or near old houses. Droughts, storms, and all manner of bad conditions — these flowers have seen it all. They have survived for years with little or no care, so they should stay healthy in your yard, too.

Create a moon garden to enjoy at night. Group several types of white flowers, like gardenia, jasmine, or sweet peas, and flowers that bloom at night, such as night jessamine and moonflowers, to create a moon garden. You'll enjoy wandering through your garden in the evening, when moonlight bounces off the white blossoms and night-blooming plants release their fragrance. As an added benefit, it's a fragrant garden that won't attract too many bees, since bees don't usually fly at night. A collection of all-white flowers is also striking during the daylight.

Plant flowers that care for themselves

Make your garden self-sufficient by picking virtually indestructible flowering plants. Best bets are plants that are suited to your climate and the conditions of your yard. Look for plants that don't need lots of pruning, staking, or dividing, and have some resistance to disease and pests. The ability to tolerate variations in temperature and humidity, as well as expected life spans of five years or more, also make them great choices. And be patient while your new plants are getting established. Before you head to the nursery, be sure to check out this list of the top 10 low-maintenance, garden-ready flowers.

- morning glories
- irises
- moonbeam coreopsis
- lavender
- impatiens

- marigolds
- daylilies
- peonies
- black-eyed Susans
- columbine

Simple way to keep your columbines pure. Plant only a single variety of columbine flowers in your yard if you want to keep their color the same every year. Planting more than one type — even at opposite ends of your yard — allows birds and bees to cross-pollinate them, and the colors won't stay true.

Easy trick helps tall flowers stand up. Metal or plastic chicken wire makes a great grow-through support for tall chrysanthemums or phlox. Cut a piece of chicken wire that's roughly the length and width of your planting bed. Prop it up with stakes horizontally a few feet above the ground. The stems will grow up through the holes, and the flowers will bloom above the level of the support. No more floppy flowers.

Closer look at 'edible' ferns

You may have heard your fiddlehead ferns are a springtime delicacy. Some people enjoy eating them, but the pleasure may not be worth the risk. Some similar-looking species can cause cancer, so be absolutely sure you have fiddleheads, or ostrich ferns. And cook them thoroughly so they don't cause an upset stomach.

Plant a stake that "grows" along with flowers. Recycle expandable curtain rods as stakes for tall perennials. Plants that grow tall fast, like delphiniums and monkshood, will benefit from a stake that keeps up with their height. Place the rod next to your flowers and carefully tie it to the stems, then extend the rod as the plant grows.

New twist on staking tall plants. Some very tall plants, such as lilies and delphinium, do best if each plant is staked individually. Avoid damaging the stems by twisting the tying string between each stem and its stake. Otherwise, the stake can cause the stem to break.

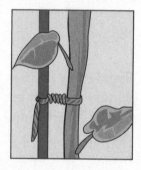

2 tricks to avoid a staking hassle. A little planning and pruning can let you avoid spending an afternoon staking up your asters one by one.

- Plant a support system around your asters of larkspur or other annuals with strong stems. These plants will help hold up the asters until their stems are strong and mature.

- Prune tall perennials when they are half-grown, and you can limit their eventual height. They may never need staking.

Change hydrangea color in one step. When it comes to hydrangeas, it's all about the large blossoms. Their color reveals the pH level of your soil. Blue flowers show the soil is acidic, while pink means it's alkaline. Certain varieties with white flowers are always white, no matter the pH. But you can change the color of many varieties by altering the pH of the soil, although the process may take several months. A word of caution — before you amend your soil, have the pH tested, and try to keep it between 5.0 and 6.5.

- Encourage blue flowers by mixing a cup of vinegar into a gallon of water and using it to water your hydrangeas. Be careful when mixing up your vinegar solution, since too much vinegar can kill plants.

- If you want pink flowers, make the soil more alkaline by adding lime or a phosphorus-rich fertilizer.

Rusty nails won't alter flower color

It's a myth that you can change the color of hydrangea blossoms by spiking the soil nearby with rusty nails. The iron you're adding to the soil won't change flower color. But if your plant's leaves are yellowing due to a lack of iron, rusty nails may just do the trick.

When not to divide perennials. It's best to divide perennials like coneflowers and black-eyed Susans in spring or early fall. But you'll do more harm than good if you try to divide them at these dangerous times.

- when the weather is very hot

- after a long drought

- in late fall, close to the first freeze

Plan ahead for springtime color. Make the most of your poppies and peonies by planting them in the fall. You can look forward to colorful blooms in the spring. If you wait until spring to plant, they may not flower the first year.

Quick trick brings out blooms in abundance. Get amazing flower displays on rhododendrons, lilacs, and butterfly bushes. All it takes is a pinch here and there. After the bush seems to be done blooming for the year, pinch prune the growing tips of limbs. This encourages the plant to grow more bushy side growth and more flowers next year. Skipping this step could cause your rhododendrons and lilacs to skip a year of blooms.

Lazy way to make your yard a bird haven

Skip the task of deadheading flowering plants if you want to attract beautiful birds to your yard all through the winter. Seed-eating birds like sparrows and chickadees will flock to gather seeds from the spent blooms of perennials.

Leave your coneflowers, coreopsis, asters, and sedums alone when they're done blooming, and they become a grand buffet for a variety of birds. You may also notice visits from hungry finches, cardinals, nuthatches, and many others.

Nudge perennials to extend the life of flowers. Your flowering perennials have a lot of work to do producing flowers, seeds, and possibly fruit. If it's flowers you want to see, let your plant know. Cut off the seed heads, removing the entire flower rather than only the petals, in summer and fall. The plant will then continue to put its energy into producing more flowers. You can twist off the blossoms of soft-stemmed perennials by hand, or use shears for woody stems. This process, referred to as "deadheading," keeps your garden looking fresh all the way into fall.

Save azaleas from a frozen death. Azaleas love a moderate winter, but an early or late freeze can injure the plant's buds or bark. When cold causes the bark to pull away from the stem, it's called bark split — damage you won't see until next spring. If the split goes all around the stem, the azalea can die. Help azaleas heal bark split by applying melted paraffin wax over the exposed area. Next fall, cut back on watering about a month before the first expected freeze, then surround your plants with mulch after the first frost.

Don't dig a deathtrap for azaleas. You can transplant an azalea into clay soil, but you'll have to dig out a large area and mix in soil that drains well. Simply digging a hole in the clay and filing it with rich soil won't do the trick. The heavy clay wall of the hole will hold in water, keeping the roots wet. Azalea roots need both water and oxygen, so they can't abide wet feet.

Shield roses from winter chills. The most fragile part of a rose bush is the bud union. You'll find it between the root system, or rootstock, and the branches, or canes. Protect it in the winter with insulation kept in place by a newspaper collar.

- Open a few sheets of a full-size newspaper, then fold the sheets in half to form a long section.

- Create another long section, then staple them together end to end.

- Prop the sheets around the base of your rose bush, and staple the ends to form a cylinder.

- Fill with insulating garden material like soil, compost, or shredded leaves.

Keep your bed of roses weed-free. Look forward to a season of weed-free, healthy roses that are easy to maintain with this simple newspaper trick. Before planting roses, lay down multiple layers of newspaper on the ground. Add a few inches of soil and compost mixture, then water the area. Wait six weeks or longer, then plant your rose bushes. Your plants will appreciate the rich soil, and you didn't have to pull a single weed.

> ## *Find fragrant varieties with expert help*
>
> Not all roses smell sweet. For help picking a variety that does, consider one awarded the American Rose Society's James Alexander Gamble Fragrance Award. Only a handful of rose varieties have been honored, including Angel Face, Crimson Glory, Fragrant Cloud, and Sweet Chariot. Winners also must be hardy, disease-resistant, and popular.

Train roses for abundant blooms. Skip the pruning and revive the lost art of pegging, or training roses horizontally to encourage flowering. This method works best with mature bushes that have canes around 6 feet long, like bourbons and some damask roses. Canes growing straight up tend to put out blooms at the top end, but they will bloom along the length of the cane when they grow horizontally. Just before the start of new growth, bend a long cane in an arc to the ground, and attach it with a small peg or hook. You can also use small wood or bamboo pieces, metal staples, or even hairpins to hold down the canes. Arrange the canes flat or in the shape of a dome for an interesting effect that gets the job done.

Pick pruning method for best effect. There's no way around it —
if you have rose bushes, they will need pruning. You may
need to prune a larger bush to keep it within bounds, and you
should remove rootstock suckers if they appear. These are easy
to recognize as light green and typically covered with lots of
thorns. A healthy bush can be pruned to a couple of feet from
the ground. Decide what results you want, then choose the
pruning method to produce a variety of brilliant blossoms.

- Light pruning will lead to lots of small flowers on
  short stems.

- Moderate pruning leaves more canes on the bush.

- Severe pruning will produce longer canes and a few
  larger flowers.

White glue helps heal rose cuts

After you prune a rose branch, seal the cuts with glue. You can use wood
glue or a white glue like Elmer's. This step protects the bush from insects
and disease, plus it cuts down on loss of the plant's nutritive sap.

One step battles two rose woes. Keep Japanese beetles from
eating your lovely floribunda and grandiflora roses this
summer, and block black spot disease while you're at it.
Just give your roses a good trim after they share their first
flowering in the late spring. Your roses will bloom again
by September — after beetle season is over. But don't try
this trick on climbers or other roses that bloom on old
wood. Midsummer trimming will prevent later blooms on
these plants.

Careful pruning brings second rose bloom. Deadhead roses before they go to seed, and you can entice another round of blooms. You can even spur repeat-bloomers to go ahead and set new buds. Cut stems that have finished flowering back to a bud with a full leaf, up to one-third of the way down the cane. This pruning prompts the rose to bloom again.

Discover the secret to award-winning roses. Know how growers get huge, perfect, lovely blooms that win at rose shows? It's all about disbudding, or removing all but one flower from each cluster of buds. Doing this tells your rose bush to put all its energy into the remaining flower. You can also try this trick to get oversized dahlias.

Find a friendly rosarian near you

Get the best advice on keeping your roses healthy from the American Rose Society. The group has branches across the country, so you're sure to meet an expert who can help. Or pay just $10 for a trial membership in the society. See the group's website at *www.ars.org*, or call 800-637-6534.

Quick trick thwarts black spot. Kill black spot fungus with the power of lactic acid. Mix a batch of half skim milk and half water, and spray it on rose leaves every two weeks. Lactic acid in the milk lowers the pH level on the leaves, so fungus can't survive.

Easy homemade spray protects roses. A treatment made from baking soda can protect your roses from mildew and black spot. It's a safe, effective alternative to chemicals and poisons in your garden. Mix a tablespoon of baking soda into a gallon of water, then add two tablespoons vegetable oil and one teaspoon liquid soap. Be sure to use unscented liquid hand soap like Ivory — not dishwashing detergent — to avoid damaging the leaves.

Spray the mixture on rose bushes as a preventive measure to keep mildew and fungus from getting started. The spray can't kill fungus once it takes hold.

Find the perfect way to water your roses. Roses need water, especially in the heat of summer. But getting the leaves wet and letting them stay that way overnight can make your rose bush a haven for fungus. Instead of spraying from the top with a garden hose, use a soaker hose to apply water directly to the roots. You'll get the soil saturated 12 to 18 inches deep, yet the leaves will stay dry. If you have to water your roses from the top, do it in the morning so the sun has time to dry the leaves. These methods can deter mildew, black spot, and other fungal diseases from attacking your roses.

Stop rose fungus without dangerous chemicals. Mix up a powerful fungicide with ingredients from your kitchen. Start with a gallon of water and add three tablespoons of apple cider vinegar. Stir in three teaspoons of molasses, and mix well. Put the mixture in a spray bottle, and spray your rose bush in early morning or late evening. Be sure to measure carefully, since strong vinegar can harm plants.

Crop rotation myth exposed

Don't believe the advice that you should plant new roses in a new location to avoid "rose replant disease." That's a myth. Because rose diseases live in the plant's leaves and stems rather than in the soil, you can put roses in the same place forever.

Just-in-time rose cutting. For a perfect table arrangement, cut your roses as soon as the second petal unfurls above a five-petal leaf.

Secret to long-lasting cut flowers. Don't let bacteria make your flower arrangement wilt. Be sure everything that comes into contact with your flowers, including the knife you cut them with, the vase, and the water, is clean. You can ensure this by adding a drop of bleach to the water in the vase. Also remove most of the leaves so they don't rot and dirty the water. Your cut flowers will last and last when you follow these florists' secrets.

Extend the life of cut flowers with conditioning. Before you display that vase of cut flowers, they need to be conditioned. It's a simple task that just means letting the flowers rest in lukewarm water in a dark place for several hours to absorb water. Also be sure to cut the flower stems at a slant under water, letting them draw up more water but fewer bubbles. And either use flower preservative in the water, or change the water every few days. Adding a few drops of vodka will also help your flowers stay perky.

Maintain a flower-friendly environment. Cut flowers need more than just the right water. They will fare best if kept out of direct sunlight, a drafty room, or high temperatures. And don't place a bowl of fruit near your flowers, since ethylene gas from ripening fruit will hasten the demise of your buds.

Help woody stems draw water. Split the stems of rhododendrons, lilacs, and other woody plants with sharp shears before you put them in a vase. They'll draw up more water.

THE KITCHEN GARDEN

EXCELLENT EDIBLES
FOR LESS

Fabulous Fruits

Beat apple coddling moths with cardboard. When midsummer arrives, bind strips of corrugated cardboard around the trunks of your apple trees starting at 12 to 18 inches above the ground. Tie the cardboard snugly against the tree, and make sure the corrugated side faces inward. The larvae of apple coddling moths like to nestle inside that corrugated surface for their long winter's nap. So pick a cold night in January, cut off the cardboard, and use it to start a bonfire. Do this every year, and you may never have to worry about coddling moths again.

Stick it to apple maggots. Tempt apple maggots into traps so they never get the chance to lay their eggs in your apples. Start collecting plastic, rubber, or wood balls now. You can even use old croquet balls if you have them. When June arrives, paint the balls red, and attach a screw eye or screw-in hook to each one. Cover the balls in a sticky coating designed to trap insects, and hang them in your tree. The apple maggots will think your balls are apples and latch on to them — permanently. Just remember to clean the balls and add a fresh coating of sticky stuff every few weeks, so you can keep fooling the maggots and keep the apples for yourself.

Outsmart worms with apple "footies." Try these nontoxic, no-spray tactics to help stop worms, coddling moths, and apple maggots right in their tracks — but be prepared to start early. When your apples are nearly the size of a penny, shield them with one of these.

- Slip a small paper lunch bag over each apple, and staple it shut across the top. Leave no gaps for bugs to sneak through.

- Gather a pile of stretchy little nylon footies, the kind some people use when trying on shoes. Slide a footie around and over each apple, and tie it around the top of the stem to enclose the apple.

These clever tactics may not be practical to try on tall apple trees, but they should work well on espaliers, semi-dwarf, and dwarf trees.

Rescue overloaded apple branches. You thinned your crop early in the season, but some of your apple branches have grown so heavily laden with fruit that you are afraid they will break. Give those branches a helping hand with a measuring tape and a roll of twine.

- Measure the distance from the center of the drooping branch to the trunk, and cut a length of string at least a foot longer.

- Wind one end of your twine around the center of the drooping branch several times, and tie it off. Wind the other end around the trunk.

Make sure the string between the branch and trunk does not sag or droop, and then tie off the trunk end securely. If your tree's trunk is too small to bear the extra weight, consider tying the branch to a trellis, fence, or stake instead.

Make a do-it-yourself high-rise apple picker

Cut the base off a 2-liter soda bottle, and use duct tape to attach a broom or old rake handle to the neck of the bottle.

Stuff small plastic grocery bags into another plastic bag, and pack them over and around the broom handle to give your apple a gentler landing.

To pick an apple from the tree, position the bottle around the apple, and jiggle the picker to dislodge the apple.

Enjoy more attractive bird protection. Instead of buying bird netting, purchase wedding tulle from the fabric store, and use that netting to keep birds out of your fruit. You will pay less, your yard will look better, and the tulle may not snag as much as regular bird netting does.

Protect strawberries with free winter mulch. Start shredding your newspaper every day, and save those long spaghetti-like strips of paper. If you do not have a shredder, ask friends and family for their newspaper shreddings. Office paper alone will not work. Keep boxes to collect these shreddings during warm-weather months. When you are ready to mulch your strawberries for winter, empty the boxes, and use your shreddings instead of paying for straw. Lay down 4 or 5 inches of shreddings between your plants to help protect them from cold, weeds, and disease.

Make your own pyramid for less. Dodge the high prices of the exorbitant strawberry pyramids in your garden catalogs. Save your money, and try this instead.

- Decide where your pyramid should live, and use 6-inch-tall corrugated lawn edging to frame a 6-foot-wide circle centered on that spot. Anchor the edging, and fill the circle with soil to the top of its rim. Each level of your pyramid needs 6 inches of soil for healthy plant growth.

- Make a second circle, 42 to 48 inches wide, centered on top of the first circle. Fill that with another 6 inches of soil.

- Center a third circle, 30 inches wide, on top of the second circle. Fill the last circle with soil, and you have a strawberry pyramid. For best results, plant everbearing strawberries, and water regularly.

Easy way to water your strawberry pyramid

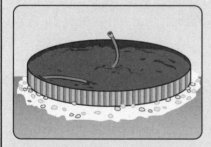

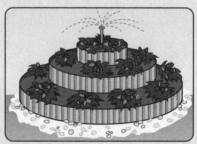

Run a hose from the nearest spigot, and bury part of that hose under the planned site of the pyramid, letting about 2 feet emerge at the center.

Place a sprinkler on top of the finished pyramid, and connect the hose to it for convenient watering.

Foil winged berry thieves. Before your strawberries appear, either unpack some miniature red Christmas balls, or coat large nuts or small, round rocks with red outdoor paint. To attract hungry birds, hang these red "strawberries" on your strawberry plants, or scatter them among the plants. After a few frustrating weeks of trying to peck at these fake berries, the birds may stop visiting your garden — leaving your true strawberries free to ripen untouched.

Smart way to get easier pickings. After you harvest this year's raspberries, cut back the canes that produced fruit. This increases the sunlight on the canes that will bear next year's fruit, helping them grow. Later, after these new canes lose their leaves, trim them back to five feet. They will produce just as many berries, but now those berries will grow at an easy height for picking.

Keep strawberry barrel plants from drowning. Waterlogged soil can kill plants in the bottom half of your strawberry barrel — unless you install a good drainage system. Fortunately, that is easy to do when you replace the plants in the barrel. Just try one of these before refilling the barrel with soil.

- Find a length of drainpipe, PVC pipe, or a wrapping paper tube as tall as your barrel. Place the pipe or tube in the center of the barrel, and fill with small rocks. As you add soil to the barrel, occasionally pull the bottom end of the pipe up to slightly below soil level. This will create a rock pipeline that quickly drains excess water from waterlogged soil.

- Use hardware cloth to make a narrow cylinder as tall as the barrel. Place the cylinder in the center of the barrel, fill with perlite, and surround with soil as you plant.

Build in bird protection for blueberries. Just after planting your berries, place a piece of tall garden art at each end of the row, build several decorative sapling or willow arches over the row, or place a pretty arbor over the berry plants. As long as they don't shade the plants too much, you'll have an attractive focal point while the blueberries grow. As soon as berries appear, use these focal points to support your bird netting.

Train your plants to make more blackberries. The way you arrange blackberry canes on your wire trellis can determine how many blackberries you har-
vest. To get the most, tie the newest canes — the ones that will not produce fruit this year — to the top-most wire, so they are vertical. Tie canes that will produce this year's fruit in a fan pattern. For example,
you would tie one fruiting cane to the left half of the top wire on your trellis, and another to the right half of that wire. A third fruiting cane would be tied to the left half of the second wire while a fourth cane would be tied to the right half. If you have additional wires, attach more fruiting canes to them in the same manner. Then remove any excess or dead canes.

Warning: don't plant raspberries here

Never plant raspberries where eggplant, peppers, potatoes, and tomatoes have been grown. These plants may carry diseases, like verticillium wilt, that can infect your raspberries.

Stretch blueberry season with bigger berries. Don't grow just one variety of blueberries. Grow one early-season variety, one midseason, and one late-season type. Not only will this add extra weeks of blueberry harvesting, but it also may help you grow bigger berries. Besides, you need more than one variety so your berries can cross-pollinate and set fruit in the first place. But remember to be careful with pesticides, especially around bloom time. Many pesticides are deadly to bees, and your bushes depend on bees to make cross-pollination — and blueberries — happen.

Repel birds with a "kool" spray. Grape Kool-Aid may seem yummy to most people, but it contains a grape compound birds hate with a purple passion. This compound is called methyl anthranilate, and it is so effective that it has been used in a commercial bird repellent. To make your own version at home, mix four packets of grape Kool-Aid into one gallon of water. Spray this on the plant and fruit of your blueberries, cherries, and grapes as soon as the fruit begins to show its color. In most cases, the birds will turn tail and hunt for food elsewhere. If the birds come back, use other bird-repelling tricks in addition to spraying.

Grow Juneberries to boost your health

Eat just 4 ounces of fresh Juneberries, and you have all the vitamin B2 you need for the day. You will also enjoy healthy servings of iron, manganese, calcium, antioxidants, and dietary fiber. Juneberries even taste delicious — like a cross between a dark cherry and a raisin. These nutrient-rich berries can grow in a wide range of soils, and they have few pest and disease problems. But you can only grow them if your area experiences at least three months of freezing temperatures every year. Contact your local cooperative extension agent for more information.

Trick your fruit tree into budding. Your tree shows no sign of buds this year even though it is mature enough to set fruit. So check its main limbs. If they are angled upward too steeply, they may be blocking sunlight and preventing buds from forming. Fortunately, with a little imagination, you can try this no-cost solution.

- Imagine the tree's trunk as the minute hand on a clock pointing to 12:00. The first few feet of each branch should point to 10:00 or 2:00.

- If any limbs point up to 11:00 and 1:00, fill old milk jugs with water or sand, and hang them from the limbs. This will pull the branches downward.

- If any sink too far, say to 9:00 or 3:00, empty water or sand out of that limb's jug until it points to the 10:00 or 2:00 position.

Avoid these 'berry' bad choices

You may have to take currants, gooseberries, or jostaberries off your planting list if you live in certain areas of the country. These berries are illegal in some counties and states because they can carry white pine blister rust *(Cronartium ribicola)*, a disease that kills white pines. Check your local and state regulations before planting. If the berries are still legal in your locale, play it safe. Choose blister-resistant varieties of the berry you like, and make sure no white pines are growing in your yard or neighborhood.

Easier way to force budding. If weighting the tree branches does not work — or if it seems like too much work — you can also try swatting the side of the tree a few times with a baseball bat. That will help spark its reproductive hormones.

Rejuvenate a low-producing apple tree. An apple tree that offers few apples may only need a makeover. Take these steps during late winter before buds appear.

- Remove any dead, weak, injured, or diseased branches and any suckers near the trunk's base. Then remove branches that grow downward, cross each other, or have limb angles forming a very narrow letter V with the trunk.

- Keep five lower "scaffold" branches. These should be evenly spaced around the tree but grow at different heights. Picture the trunk as a clock hand pointing at midnight, and only choose branches that point to 10:00 or 2:00.

- Retain an upward-pointing "leader" growing straight up from the tree's center. Then cut out the remaining branches that shade the tree's interior the most.

If this will result in severe cutting of the tree, either spread the pruning over three seasons, or do not fertilize the tree that spring.

Spread limbs to get extra apples and pears. Train the main limbs outward on apple and pear trees, so branches throughout the tree receive more sunlight and produce more fruit. During the first or second growing season, spread the limbs to a 60-degree angle from the trunk using nails and branch prunings.

- Choose sturdy prunings that fork at one end. Cut the pruned branch to an appropriate length, insert a galvanized nail in the unforked end, and cut off the nail head. If you would rather avoid nails, cut a wide notch in the unbranched end instead.

- Position the pruned branch so the nail or notched end faces the trunk and the forked end presses into the branch. Push or pull the limb downward, and wedge this limb spreader between the trunk and branch so the limb points to 10:00 or 2:00.

Prune your peach tree for more fruit. Keep your peach tree low and spreading so the inner branches get enough sunlight to set fruit. That means you must make sure no branches grow inward toward the tree's trunk. Fortunately, the buds for leaves and branches grow in the direction they face. So always prune back to an outward-facing bud and the resulting new branch will grow outward, too.

Give a new fruit tree a stronger start. That potted fruit tree lost some of its roots when it was dug up by the plant nursery. Pruning the tree's branches will keep them in balance with the roots plus help the tree put more energy into new root growth. Before leaving the nursery, ask if the tree was already pruned. If not, prune it right after planting. Reduce the tree's height to about 35 inches or to a height one foot higher than the mature height you would prefer for the lowest branches. If your tree already has branches, contact your cooperative extension agent for instructions on the best way to prune it after planting.

Sideswipe bud-suppressing hormone

Just like teenagers, fruit trees can have hormonal problems that leave you scratching your head. If you have a limb full of buds that refuse to grow into side branches, blame it on auxin, an inhibitor hormone that flows downward from the tip of the limb. This hormone may be keeping your buds dormant.

To prevent auxin from suppressing a bud during bloom time, cut a notch just above the bud, and make it deep enough to reach through the surface bark to the top of the interior wood. This notch causes auxin to flow around the bud as the hormone makes its way down the limb. Once the bud no longer receives auxin, it is free to produce a growing branch.

Turbocharge your vines for better grapes. You can train your grapevines to produce bigger harvests of higher-quality grapes. Use this strategy for American varieties on a two-wire trellis.

- During your first growing season, tie one shoot to the top wire. In late winter of the second year before buds appear, tie one cane to the left half of the lower wire and another to the right half. Using the same pattern, tie one cane to each half of the upper wire for a total of four canes on the trellis. Remove all other canes.

- Your vine also grows green shoots. Select the four healthiest shoots that are near the trunk, and cut them back to four buds. These "renewal spurs" will become next year's canes. Remove all other shoots.

- During late winter of the third year and all future years, remove old canes that have fruited, cut new canes back to 40 buds, and tie them to the wires like you did the second year. Cut four new shoots back to four buds, and remove all other shoots.

Ripen melons faster. Sink the open top of a coffee can into the soil near each melon shortly after it reaches baseball size. When it swells to softball size, move the melon up to rest on the top of the can. This keeps the melons away from insects and diseases that live at soil level. It also concentrates heat on the melons so they become sweeter and ripen more quickly.

Harvest pumpkins from a small space. You can grow watermelons, cantaloupes, and pumpkins on a tiny patch of land with this ingenious method. Train each vine on a large, sturdy trellis, and nestle each fruit in a sling made of pantyhose, an onion bag, cheesecloth, netting, or an old T-shirt. Use pantyhose slings for smaller varieties, but choose the stronger options for bigger fruits. Slip the melon or pumpkin into its sling when the fruit is small, tie off both ends to envelop the fruit, and tie those ends to the trellis. Be sure to hang your sling high enough to keep the melon or pumpkin off the ground, even after the fruit becomes full-grown.

Choose the right trellis for melons. Obviously an airy, willow twig trellis will not be right for pumpkins and melons. You need a trellis that can easily carry heavier weights. If possible, use wire fencing or livestock panels. Otherwise, choose a sturdy wood or metal trellis, and anchor it in wide buckets of concrete sunk into the ground. Another option is to tie it to thick wires that are firmly connected to a solid wall.

Harvest sweeter pumpkins safely. Leave pumpkins in the garden until their vines die completely, but be sure to harvest them before the first hard freeze. A light frost or two can lead to a sweeter pumpkin with a longer shelf life, but a hard freeze may rob you of your crop.

Grow exotic edibles

If you've always hankered to grow your own mango, check out the website *www.pitplants.com.* This site offers free information and inexpensive publications detailing how to grow mangos, pineapples, papaya, taro, tamarinds, malangas, and at least 40 other kinds of exotic edibles. It was created by the Rare Pit and Plant Council, which began growing fruits from the pits and seeds of supermarket produce more than 30 years ago.

Grow a tree from supermarket lemons. Collect seeds from three supermarket-bought lemons, and rinse them in warm water. Soak overnight, let dry, and choose three small containers with drainage holes. Fill each container with sterile potting mix, plant each seed one-half inch deep in its own container, and set the container in a dish. Water and cover the container with a clear plastic bag. Place the container where temperatures stay around 70 degrees and continue to water regularly. When plants appear, uncover the containers, and move them to a sunny spot. You must wait at least five years to find out whether your lemon tree will produce lemons, but it should make a lovely houseplant in the meantime.

Go natural for better-sprouting seeds. If your lemon seeds haven't sprouted after eight weeks, try again with fresh lemons from a natural foods market or farmer's market. According to the Rare Pit and Plant Council, many supermarket fruits are treated with tiny amounts of radiation. This radiation should not harm you, but it may prevent supermarket lemon seeds from sprouting.

Get gardening advice for free from a master

You can get free advice via telephone or email from a local master gardener. These volunteers have undergone many hours of training, so they're experts about local planting. To find a master gardener near you, navigate to the American Horticultural Society website at *www.ahs.org*, then click on the "Master Gardeners" link.

VOLUMES OF VEGGIES

Maximize your garden savings. Instead of planting the same vegetables every year, determine which vegetables can help you keep more of your dollars, and plant those. To find out which vegetables will be your biggest money savers, choose the ones with these characteristics:

- You cook or eat them often.

- They are expensive at local supermarkets and farmer's markets.

- They are not available at local farmer's markets.

- They can be easily stored for a month or two.

Good choices include tomatoes, beans, broccoli, spinach, peppers, lettuce, peas, arugula, beets, onions, potatoes, and garlic.

Prevent plant problems with perfect partners. Companion plants can be surprisingly helpful in your garden, particularly when it comes to repelling pests. When planting your garden, arrange good companions together. On the other hand, some "enemy" companions may prevent nearby plants from thriving. Read more about plant friends and foes in this handy chart.

Plant this	Near this	But not near this	Here's why
marigolds	tomatoes		Marigolds reduce aphids on tomatoes.
French marigolds	tomatoes		French marigolds fend off nematodes.
cucumbers		potatoes	This combo results in poor plant health.
nasturtiums	squash		Nasturtiums help repel squash bugs.
mint	cabbage		Mint helps repel cabbage moths.
dill		carrots	Dill may slow carrot growth.
onions	lettuce		Onion scent helps keep slugs and snails away.
parsley	carrots		Parsley's fragrance can keep carrot flies from finding the carrots nearby.
tomatoes	asparagus		Tomatoes repel asparagus beetles.
summer savory	beans		Summer savory helps repel bean beetles.

Get your garden veggies earlier. You can have early vegetables every year by attracting bees. All you have to do is plant the flowering herb borage. Plant it in pots around your garden, and you will soon see bees buzzing among your vegetable rows. These busy pollinators may be a key ingredient for that early vegetable crop. For results that could stretch throughout the season, plant other flowering bee attractors, too. Cosmos, sunflower, zinnia, rosemary, and bee balm can be good choices if they grow well in your area. Contact your local cooperative extension agent for more details.

Foil common garden saboteurs

Like sleeper agents in a spy novel, some good plants may suddenly cause trouble if they encounter the right "trigger" plant, so avoid these chancy combinations:

- Apple trees near potatoes. Planting these close to one another can lead to potato blight.
- Sweet peppers near hot peppers. Cross-pollination can turn sweet peppers into blazing hot sweet peppers.
- Any member of the cabbage family near tomatoes. Something about cabbages, broccoli, cauliflower, turnips, and their cousins hampers the growth and fruit production of tomato plants.
- Jerusalem artichokes or sunflowers near any vegetable. These may limit the growth of neighboring plants.

Find hidden space for vegetables. If you are growing vegetables for the first time, or if you don't have room for a full vegetable garden, try adding vegetables like artichokes and tomatoes to your flower beds. Just be sure to take a precaution or two.

- Label your vegetable plants so no one will mistake them for unwanted plants.

- Be careful to place each plant where it can get enough light.

- Make sure each plant will avoid exposure to the wrong fertilizers, or to herbicides and pesticides that are not safe for edibles.

If you are unable to take these precautions, create a small, raised bed for vegetables, or plant vegetables in movable containers.

Double your space, halve your weeding time. These are two key benefits of interplanting, a different way of planting crops together. The trick is to find two different vegetables that can be planted close together without interfering with each other's growth. For example, consider these rapid growers that beat the weeds, and the slow growers you can pair them with. Speedy growers like radishes, lettuce, onions, spinach, and beets can shade the ground and prevent weeds while they grow. If you plant them among slower growers like broccoli, carrots, cabbages, and corn, they help keep the soil weed-free until the slow growers appear. Interplanting may also help fight pests and plant disease.

Reap the healthy rewards of gardening

An online survey found that gardeners are more likely to eat vegetables than people who don't garden. But that's not all. Figures from the National Gardening Association suggest a 180-pound person burns 80 calories in just 15 minutes of raking or planting seedlings, 90 calories during 15 minutes of mowing or weeding, and 100 calories during 15 minutes of digging.

Fit even more in your garden. Interplanting fast and slow growers is just one way to sneak more vegetables into your garden. Experiment with other kinds of interplanting, and you may discover you have even more planting space than you thought. For example, you can combine shallow-rooted plants like radishes, broccoli, or spinach, with deeper-growers such as carrots, parsnips, winter squash, or tomatoes. Or interplant heavy feeders like cabbage, squash, cucumber, or celery with lighter feeders such as carrots or garlic. Better yet, interplant those heavy feeders with beans or peas, which enrich the soil by adding nitrogen to it.

5 secrets to healthy plants. Here are five simple things to do to maintain the healthiest plants during growing season.

These help prevent disease, pests, and other plant problems, and they are practically guaranteed to give you great results.

- Make sure your plants have enough nutrients throughout the growing season, but be careful not to overload them.

- Mulch to prevent weeds and help keep the soil moist.

- Make certain each plant consistently gets the right amount of water, especially when rains are rare.

- Know when and how often to harvest each vegetable, and follow that schedule closely to foil diseases and pests.

- Clean up your garden regularly and at the end of the season. Remove dead or diseased plants and annuals that no longer produce.

Great reason to delay planting. Do you love warm-season veggies? Plant them too early, and they will actually grow more slowly. Discover the magic temperature that gives you the green light for greener plants. Plants like tomatoes, peppers, corn, melons, cucumbers, and squash don't grow at a normal rate until the soil temperature reaches 70 degrees. Even worse, planting too early can keep your plants in slow-growth mode for several months after the soil heats up. Don't take any chances. Push a soil thermometer 4 inches into the soil to determine if it's time to plant. If you can't wait until the soil warms, start some vegetables from seed indoors, and transplant the seedlings when the soil is warm enough.

Uncover plants that thrive with less care. Want more veggies, more blooms, and fewer dead plants? Just use Thomas Jefferson's simple selection method that made Monticello a gardening wonder. Jefferson didn't plant just one variety of a plant. He planted 15 or 20 varieties to see how they fared. Poor performers were removed and never planted again. Jefferson kept only the one or two varieties that thrived best. Although you probably can't plant 15 varieties of a particular vegetable, you can try Jefferson's technique by planting several varieties of each vegetable. Keep only the ones that produce the best quality and most vegetables with the least help from you. This is also a good technique to try with flowers, too.

The latest on homegrown broccoli and selenium deficiency

Broccoli is rich in selenium, vital for systems that protect against cancer, heart disease, depression, and asthma. So should you grow some in your garden?

That depends on where you live because the level of selenium in broccoli is determined by the soil it grew in. The amount of selenium available from soil varies from one county to the next, and some states have both selenium-rich and selenium-poor counties. What's more, phosphate fertilizers, acid soils, and many other factors can prevent plants from absorbing selenium.

Keep in mind, broccoli contains many vital nutrients and natural compounds that help prevent cancer and other diseases. Just don't depend on broccoli as your sole source of selenium. Instead, eat a variety of selenium-rich foods including celery, chicken, beef, dairy products, and whole wheat.

Revitalize your vegetable garden. Your vegetable garden isn't producing as many vegetables as it once did, so give it a power boost. Take note of which plants in your garden are:

- heavy feeders, like tomatoes, corn, or pumpkins, that devour soil nutrients like a hungry teenager.

- light feeders, like carrots or peppers, that carefully take in soil nutrients like a dieting beauty queen.

- legumes, like beans or peas, that add nitrogen back into the soil.

If heavy feeders grow in the same place too long, the soil nutrients can become too depleted to feed plants well. To fix this, rotate your crops among three plots using these rules:

- Place heavy feeders in the plot where legumes grew the previous year.

- Plant legumes in the space where light feeders lived the previous year.

- Grow light feeders in the previous year's plot for heavy feeders.

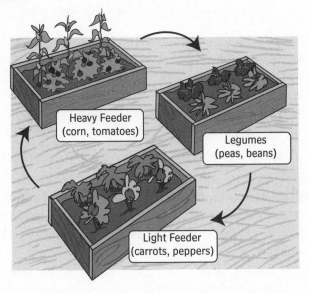

Slash pests and diseases the natural way. Many pests and diseases are specific to a particular vegetable or family of vegetables, so the troublemakers settle down where their target plant lives. That is why they come back so easily year after year. Crop rotation can help foil them, but you may need to change how you group your plants. For example, pests that like tomatoes may also love peppers, so you should not plant peppers where tomatoes have recently grown. To keep your pests from dining on extra courses, divide your plants into these groups and move each group to a new site each year.

- peas, beans, sweet corn, spinach, lettuce, pumpkins, and squashes including zucchini

- the cabbage family including broccoli, cabbage, cauliflower, turnips, rutabagas, and radishes

- tomatoes, potatoes, eggplants, peppers, onions, and carrots

Recognize rotation limits

Crop rotation in your backyard garden is less practical and effective than crop rotation in a farmer's field. Limited space may prevent you from placing the plants far enough apart to completely foil pests and diseases. You may also run into stumbling blocks like these:

- You have limited sunlight in parts of your yard.
- You want to collect seed.
- You cannot fit each grouping of plants into the same amount of space.

This doesn't mean crop rotation can't help you. Even a kitchen garden can benefit. But you are not likely to develop serious problems if you can't rotate your crops or you must settle for a scaled-down version of crop rotation.

Make pea trellises for pennies. Save your prunings from bushes and trees, particularly the ones about a yard tall that have plenty of forked twigs and branches. Look for branches with at least 5 continuous inches of straight, unforked branch at one end.

- If you have enough of these for all your pea plants, press the unforked end deep into the ground near each plant, and allow the pea to climb this trellis. If your pea plants are close enough to one another, you can even place one of these trellises between two pea plants, so both can climb it.

- If most of your branches have unforked ends shorter than 5 inches, it's time to improvise. Place posts in the ground at each end of your pea row, string wire between the posts, and tie one branch above each pea plant so the twiggy ends nearly touch the ground.

Add space to a chock-full garden

Even if every inch of your garden space is planted, you can still add one more crop if you have a garden arch. Grow vining vegetables like pole beans, cucumbers, peas, or summer squash up the arch. You can even grow pumpkins or melons if you attach onion bag slings to the arch to hold each fruit. Just make sure no one walks under the arch once the melons or pumpkins appear. Even the ones protected with slings can still fall.

Slash your grocery bill. Why pay for veggies and herbs when you can grow many of them yourself. Here's how you can build raised beds, even in small spaces, that practically guarantee success with tomatoes, peppers, squash, and more.

- Reinforce cardboard boxes with jute twine or duct tape, or use milk crates lined with corrugated cardboard. If you prefer boxes, choose boxes 2 feet deep for tomatoes, squash, and other deep-rooters. Be sure to discard them at the end of each season.

- Group up to nine boxes or crates together to form a rough square or rectangle. Leave no space between the boxes, but make sure you can reach the center box easily from the edge. If you can't, make two groups of crates or boxes with a single aisle between them.

- Fill each box with prepared soil, and plant a different vegetable crop in each one.

Harvest more from the same space. Stop planting your small vegetables in rows, and you may get up to four times as many vegetables without adding any more planting space. The secret is to plant carrots, lettuce, and other small veggies in beds or wide blocks. Plan the width and length of each block so you can easily reach the plants at the center without stepping into the block. As long as you leave walking space between the blocks, this technique can work well in regular garden plots or raised beds.

Spend less time weeding and watering. You may recognize the six-sided hexagon from the black shapes on soccer balls or the shapes in a honeycomb. But you can also use hexagons to reduce the workload in your garden. Instead of sowing seeds in rows, plant seeds in an interlocking hexagon pattern within beds. When you plant this way, the foliage of the vegetables fully shades the soil. As a result, weeds cannot sprout, and the soil retains more moisture — meaning less weeding and watering for you. To start sowing in hexagons, check the recommended spacing for the vegetable, and make sure every seed you sow is the recommended distance away from the seeds surrounding it.

Sow one seed at the center of each hexagon, and one at each corner as shown in the picture. Use this method with beans, beets, cauliflower, carrots, garlic, lettuce, onions, peas, peppers, and tomatoes.

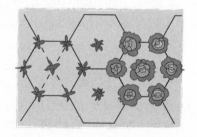

Reap more fresh vegetables every month. For the most productive garden, no part of your plot should sit unplanted for long during the growing season. Use these methods of succession planting to make that possible.

- Plant warm season crops where cool season crops were growing. Start seedlings inside, so plants can be ready the moment the ground is available and warm enough. Be ready to replace those warm season vegetables with cool season crops later in the year.

- Plant a small patch of a quick-maturing vegetable every two weeks for a continuous harvest throughout that vegetable's growing season. If possible, start seedlings inside, condition the soil, and reuse an area whose plants are spent. This also prevents gluts where far too many vegetables ripen all at once.

- Plant early-, mid-, and late-season varieties of a particular vegetable for a long, continuous harvest.

Grow lettuce on your back fence. Hang an inexpensive plastic rain gutter or two from a back wall or fence, fill with soil, and plant your lettuce. This not only gives you extra garden space, it may also foil ground level pests like rabbits. You can even hang the gutter garden at a height that will not strain your back or knees, or at a height that is wheelchair-accessible. Just be sure to resist the temptation to use rusty old gutters or any gutter painted with lead paint.

> ## *The scoop on dwarf varieties*
>
> Dwarf or miniature versions of your favorite vegetable plants can help you fit more plants in tight spaces, and many of them fruit earlier than standard varieties. But be aware that most of them don't produce as many vegetables per plant as standard varieties.

Harvest vegetables without a yard. Want a vegetable garden but don't have the yard for it? Reap a bushel of tomatoes, bell peppers, and lettuce by growing your vegetables in containers and planters. But take care to pick the right containers or your plants may not thrive long enough to deliver a harvest. For example, you must have containers large enough to house the plants after they reach full size. That means you need a one- or two-gallon container for peppers or chard, and at least a five-gallon pot for tomatoes or cucumbers. But you can get by with 6- to 10-inch containers for lettuce, radishes, and onions. For your best shot at garden-fresh vegetables, plant in containers that:

- have good drainage.

- have not previously held anything toxic to humans or plants.

- can hold soil without spilling it.

Easy vegetables and herbs to grow in small spaces. You can be your own grocer, and harvest your own delicious foods even in a small yard or patio. In fact, you can grow vegetables in planters, pots, and hanging baskets, even if you only have a sunny window, sun room, or concrete balcony. Just be sure to place your plants where they will get enough sunlight, and keep them watered. To help everything fit into your small space:

- select varieties that keep their growth compact.

- choose bush varieties of vining vegetables like tomatoes.

- train sprawling or large plants on trellises.

Also, stick with the best veggies and herbs to grow in pots and planters. The vegetables include carrots, lettuce, peppers, onions, tomatoes, chard, eggplant, cucumber, pole beans, summer squash including zucchini, and dwarf varieties of sweet corn. Good herbs to grow in small spaces include basil, rosemary, sage, mint, and parsley.

Grow anything anywhere without tilling. These may be the simplest instructions you will ever find for making raised garden beds.

- Grab a measuring tape, and go shopping for bales. Don't settle for hay bales, which often carry weed seeds. Instead, choose straw bales bound by wires or plastic twine. Measure the length of the bale, and buy enough bales to frame the size of bed you want.

- Choose a spot that gets full sun, and arrange the straw bales so they form a square or rectangle with empty space in the center. Don't remove the wires or twine wrapped around the bales.

- Link the wires or twine of adjacent bales together with cable ties.

- Fill the empty center of the rectangle with good-quality soil at least 20 inches deep.

Pick the best vegetables for raised beds. Raised beds are usually small, so stick with space-saving vegetables that can grow well when planted close to one another. Good choices include beets, carrots, lettuce, onions, peppers, radishes, spinach, and turnips.

Stretch a short growing season. Stop envying gardeners who have long, hot summers. Extend your growing season by up to three weeks and have earlier vegetables with these simple steps.

- Switch to raised beds. They naturally warm up earlier than beds in the ground.

- Build your raised beds from stone, brick, or concrete blocks. They warm the soil even earlier in the season and keep it warmer on cold nights.

- Site the bed so it faces south and paint the south wall black or wrap it in black plastic. This warms the soil even more, so you can plant earlier and end the growing season later.

Prevent contamination in raised bed vegetables

Don't use old pressure-treated wood to construct the walls of your raised bed. Older wood has been pressure-treated with chlorinated copper arsenate (CCA), a compound that leaches arsenic into the soil. Unfortunately, your vegetable plants take in this arsenic. While arsenic from these vegetables may not kill you quickly, it is hazardous to your health. So make your raised bed walls from one of these instead.

- Untreated wood. It's less expensive than pressure-treated wood and may last around five years.
- Pressure-treated wood made after 2004. It doesn't contain CCA, but you can line the interior of the raised bed walls — but not the bottom — with plastic sheeting if you prefer to play it safe.
- Long-lasting, termite-resistant plastic and wood composite boards.
- Cinder blocks, stone, brick, or another wood-free option.

Discover free plant ties in your house. Ties for staking tomatoes and clips for holding beans can be cheaper than you expect. Try these ideas.

- When worn-out Christmas lights are no longer worth taking out of the box, snip the strands into good lengths for plant ties.

- If you can't remove that mustard stain from an old shirt, make soft plant ties by literally cutting the shirt to ribbons.

- Cut a dry cleaning bag into strips and you will have nearly invisible plant ties.

- Your plastic, spring-loaded hair clip has become heavily scratched or discolored, but its curved tines can still make a gentle clip for beans or other climbing vegetables.

Gather more asparagus without adding plants. Forget about planting asparagus a foot deep in the ground. Research shows you can get more spears if you plant only 5 or 6 inches deep.

Save money on bean trellises. Before you buy a new bean trellis, try one of these clever cost cutters instead:

- Plant beans near corn when the cornstalk is about 10 inches high. Let the beans climb the cornstalk.

- Use a spare tomato cage.

- Grow beans on a screen door frame strung with fishing line or wire. Make sure your screen door trellis is fastened down or propped up securely. For even cheaper trellis netting, collect the plastic ring connectors from six-packs of drinks, and tie them together with leftover twist ties.

Enrich your carrots while they grow

Placing white plastic mulch over the soil around your carrot plants may increase the amount of beta carotene they contain.

Harvest straight carrots at last. Carrots don't like to grow long and straight in clay soil, so improve their chances with toilet tissue rolls. If you start your carrots from seeds indoors, sow them into toilet rolls. When it's time to plant outside, make sure each toilet roll has no more than two seedlings and transplant the roll straight into the soil. The rolls should help your seedlings grow in the right direction, so you can harvest long, straight carrots.

Help carrots break through a soil crust. Sow radishes in the same row with your carrots to break the soil crust so your carrots can grow through it easily. Radish seeds germinate faster than carrots, so the radishes do the hard work of breaking up the soil crust as they sprout and grow. By the time your carrots germinate, the soil crust may no longer be a problem for them. Just be sure to harvest the radishes before they can crowd out your carrots.

The truth about manure and root vegetables

Manure is not always bad for root vegetables. While fresh manure may cause root vegetables to fork or split, you may nourish and enhance your root vegetables if you dig well-rotted manure into the soil six months before planting. By spring, the manure will be helping your soil retain nutrients and water, so your root veggies will be more likely to thrive.

Prevent tasteless corn and missing kernels. If last year's corn ears had a bunch of kernels missing, the problem may be poor pollination. Plant your corn in several short rows instead of one long one. Winds can spread enough corn pollen across this shorter distance for all the ears of corn to fill in. But be careful if you grow more than one variety of corn. If two varieties cross-pollinate, you may end up with an entire crop of starchy, tasteless corn. Either plant the two kinds of corn about 600 feet apart, or make sure the varieties ripen at different times.

> ### *Grow free fire starters*
>
> Your next crop of corn can feed you in summer and warm you in winter. Just save the cobs, let them dry out completely, and they become excellent fire starters.

Sweeten bitter cucumbers. Your freshly picked cucumbers are surprisingly bitter. Peel them and cut off the stem-end, and they should taste better. But if they are still too bitter, slice them, sprinkle with salt, and let sit for 45 minutes. Then drain and rinse. They may not look as pretty as they did before salting, but they should be crisp and sweet. To help prevent bitter cucumbers:

- harvest them before they become overripe.

- water them regularly and apply mulch during hot, dry weather.

- plant bitter-free varieties.

Start peas early and transplant with ease. Use a cold frame, a length of plastic rain gutter, and these instructions to reap an early pea crop. Try a similar technique for earlier leafy greens, parsley, and basil.

- Cut the gutter to size, and drill drainage holes along the bottom at regular intervals.

- Fill with soil, choose an early variety of pea, and sow a seed every couple of inches.

- Place the gutter in a cold frame.

- When the seedlings are about 3 inches tall, dig a furrow outside to match your gutter.

- Ask a friend to hold up the gutter while you slide its contents into the trench. Then just tamp the soil and water.

- Protect the peas with cloches as needed if occasional cold weather is still a problem.

Retire toxic planters

Avoid using old tires as planters. Many locales now have local ordinances that forbid reuse of old tires. Even worse, tires may leach chemicals into the soil. Find other secondhand items to use as planters instead. Wrap your new secondhand planters in black plastic, or paint them black if you need them to help warm the soil.

Get bigger peppers with this salt. Here's exactly what to do for peppers that will make you proud. When your plants begin to bloom, spray them with one tablespoon of Epsom salt mixed into one gallon of water. Epsom salt contains magnesium, so your spray gives plants the nutritional boost they need to produce larger peppers. Some people say this has helped their plants produce more peppers, too. Just don't forget to spray your peppers again 10 days after the first spraying. If you have any spray left over, treat your other vegetable plants, too. It may help them produce larger veggies, too.

Grow super spuds in straw. Try this age-old gardening secret for growing potatoes without digging, planting, or hilling.

- Place the potatoes on the soil, and cover them in at least 8 inches of clean, high-quality straw. Don't use hay.

- Water the straw, and tamp it down with a rake.

- Apply another 8 inches of straw roughly halfway through the potato-growing season, and water the straw to prevent flyaways.

- Harvest the potatoes after flowering, when the plant is dying back. But don't get your shovel. Just push the straw back, and grab your potatoes.

- After all your potatoes are harvested, throw your straw on the compost pile.

Raise potatoes in a garbage bag. You don't need a big yard to have a garden. Grow your own potatoes inside a 30-gallon trash bag. Here's how.

- Prepare your seed potatoes at least one week before you begin planting.

- Cut several drainage holes in the bottom of the bag. Fill the bag half full with soil, and roll the sides down to near soil level. Place the bag where it can receive at least four hours of sunlight daily.

- Plant the seed potatoes 5 inches apart. Bury them 2 inches deep with eyes pointing upward. Water after planting, and keep watering regularly.

- When the plants are about 7 inches tall, add enough extra soil so only a few leaves remain above soil level.

- Keep adding soil as the plants grow.

- When the leaves yellow and die back, stop watering and wait three weeks.

- Slit the bag to harvest your potatoes.

Harvest potatoes before your neighbors do. Use these instructions to make potatoes mature more quickly.

- Lay down soaker hoses along the rows where you plan to plant.

- Cover each row in black polyethylene plastic, and bury the edges.

- Select an early-season variety of potato, cut slits or X shapes in the plastic, and plant.

Check with your cooperative extension agent to see if you can also plant earlier and less deeply than usual with this method. But be careful. Don't use black plastic with mid-season or late-season potatoes in raised beds. The higher soil temperatures may keep those potatoes from reaching full size.

Repurpose a laundry basket as a planter. You need a new planter and a new laundry basket. So turn the old plastic basket into a planter with these steps:

- Repair any tears with duct tape. Line the basket with a large, plastic yard waste bag.

- Poke holes in the bottom of the basket and the bag.

- Place it in a drip saucer, and fill the planter with soil.

- Plant potatoes or another root vegetable in the planter.

If you don't have a drip saucer for a large, rectangular-shaped laundry basket, check thrift stores, yard sales, or flea markets for a plastic laundry basket of similar size or larger. Cut off the bottom to use as your drip saucer, and place bricks between the two basket bottoms to serve as feet.

Cut better seed potatoes. For best results, remember these tips when cutting seed potatoes for the first time.

- Cut 2-ounce pieces roughly the size of a golf ball. The pieces don't have to be round. In fact, their shapes will vary.

- Leave two eyes on each piece.

- If the eyes are tightly packed on part of the potato, carve carefully for three eyes or less per piece. Cut additional pieces from eyes on other parts of the potato.

- Use a knife that doesn't have a serrated edge for a smoother cut.

- Avoid using supermarket potatoes. They are often treated to prevent sprouting.

The facts about ornamental sweet potatoes

An ornamental sweet potato vine can produce tubers just like regular sweet potato plants in your garden. After all, they are both sweet potatoes, and both are labeled *Ipomoea batatas*. But the ornamental sweet potato vine has been bred to produce colorful foliage, while regular sweet potato plants have been bred to make yummy sweet potatoes. As a result, any sweet potatoes that turn up on your ornamental sweet potato vine are perfectly edible, yet taste perfectly horrible. But don't eat them. Even if you have never sprayed your ornamental vine with pesticide, it may have been sprayed with pesticide before you bought it.

Speed up harvest with a garden colander. Give an old laundry basket new life, even if it's broken in places. Use it as a collection basket when you harvest vegetables, but don't take it directly inside. Instead, hose down your vegetables in the basket. Most of the water simply drains away, so you can easily sort the vegetables before their final cleaning. If you don't have an old laundry basket handy, use a large, plastic nursery pot the same way. When you rinse, the water will drain through the holes in the bottom.

Prevent powdery mildew without chemicals. Defend your squash crop against powdery mildew with a milk spray. Simply mix one-half cup of milk with four-and-one-half cups of water. Use whole milk, skim milk, or even powdered milk. It's up to you. Studies suggest this spray can work well for several members of the squash family, including zucchini and pumpkins. Experts also recommend it for squash and cucumbers. Just remember, this remedy works best if you spray the plants heavily before powdery mildew symptoms show up.

Beat tobacco mosaic virus with a jug

When you finish a jug of milk, refill the nearly empty jug with water, and water your tomatoes, peppers, eggplants, and potatoes with the milky water. This unusual solution may kill tobacco mosaic virus on these plants.

Coax fruit from stubborn indoor tomatoes. Your tomato plants flower quite nicely inside, but they never produce fruit. This may happen because tomato plants can't set fruit unless the flowers are pollinated first. So take a tip from commercial greenhouses and pollinate with an electric toothbrush. Simply remove the brush attachment from the toothbrush, turn on the brush, and gently rest it briefly against each flower on your tomato plant.

Collect seeds from tomatoes the easy way. Pick a well-ripened tomato, and scoop the pulp into a bowl or clear plastic container. Fill with water, and let sit for two days.

Dead seeds naturally float to the top, so skim them off and throw away. After the good seeds sink to the bottom, pour off the pulp. Look to see how clean the seeds are. If they look clean, spread them out to dry on a clean mesh screen for several days. This handy little secret also works well for harvesting seeds from watermelons and pumpkins.

Grow prize tomatoes in limited space

Measure out a 6 x 3-foot rectangle in a flat, sunny area. Mark the four corners and the midpoint of each long side. At each marking, loosen soil and pound a 2" x 2" 8-foot-long wood post about a foot into the ground.

Angle each pair of posts so they cross 1 foot below their tops. Tie each pair firmly together with thick, sturdy twine to make three triangle shapes.

Connect the triangles with horizontal 2" x 2" 6-foot-long wood posts. Place three along each slanted side of the triangles at equal intervals. Tie in place with twine. Rest the last 6-foot-long wood post on top in the V-shaped slots of the triangles.

Trellis tomatoes for amazing results. Cramming tomato plants in cages limits the amount of sunlight that can reach the fruits and leaves. But if you spread your tomato plant across a trellis, your plants get more sunlight and better air circulation, and they may reward you with more and better tomatoes, too. Trellises leave fewer hiding places for pests, and they can make pruning and harvesting much easier. Your trellis doesn't have to be expensive. You can use chain-link or wire fence, a flat metal trellis less than a yard high, or try an A-frame trellis. The A-frame trellis is essentially just chicken wire stapled to two rectangular wooden frames. The frames lean against one another to form the letter A. This may sound simple, but the A-frame trellis may help you grow more tomatoes with fewer pests.

Help for tomatoes that never turn red. You have always wondered why your tomatoes turn yellow or orange, but never red. Oddly enough, the same hot weather that makes your area good for growing tomatoes may also be part of the problem. Tomatoes can't do the inner magic that turns them red when temperatures rise above 86 degrees. So pick your tomatoes while they are still pale, and bring them in to ripen. One Georgia gardener even brings her tomatoes in to ripen while they are still green. Her tomatoes turn bright red, but that's not the only benefit. "The birds never get the opportunity to peck them," she says.

Fend off blossom end rot. Keep a container under your sink or near your stove to collect eggshells. Rinse them, and let dry in the sun. Add crushed eggshell to the soil for your tomato seedlings, and sprinkle a generous round of crushed eggshell in the soil when you put those seedlings in the ground. Gardeners say this provides extra calcium that may help prevent blossom end rot.

Enjoy richer flavors and more nutrient power

Heirloom varieties of vegetables have been around for decades, but they aren't grown by commercial farmers. Yet research suggests heirloom varieties are tastier and far more nutritious than the same vegetables from your supermarket. A study of 43 garden crops found that today's crops have significantly less vitamin C, calcium, iron, vitamin B2, phosphorus, and protein than the produce people ate in 1950. Experts suspect that breeding vegetables for the high yields sought by commercial growers results in less-nutritious vegetables. Grow heirloom vegetables, and you may enjoy both farm-fresh flavor and a richer treasure trove of nutrients.

Stop tomatoes from cracking. Use these two easy tricks to prevent spoilage of your prize tomatoes.

- Be very consistent with watering. Cracking is more likely when the plant receives wildly varying amounts of water over time. Water regularly, and don't let the soil dry out too much or stay too soggy.

- Grow crack-resistant varieties.

Improve the flavor of tomatoes and peppers. Plant basil beside your tomatoes or peppers. That fresh basil may smell wonderful to you, but it can help repel flies, tomato hornworms, aphids, mosquitoes, and other pests. Basil can also encourage your plants to produce peppers and tomatoes with even better flavor.

Little-known benefit of organic tomatoes

Tomatoes are not created equal. If you grow your own tomatoes organically, they may be more nutritious. After comparing several years of organic tomato crops to standard crops, researchers discovered organic tomatoes offered almost twice as much quercetin and kaempferol. These two powerful antioxidants may help reduce your risk of heart disease. More research is needed to find out whether the extra antioxidants consistently mean bigger health benefits, so stay tuned. But in the meantime, keep growing and eating those organic tomatoes. To get results similar to the study, avoid commercial fertilizers, and work a green manure cover crop and organic matter into the soil during the off season.

Prevent pests and diseases in container crops. You can rotate garden-based tomato crops to help them escape pests and diseases lurking in a particular patch of soil. But pests and diseases can overwinter in your tomatoes' potting soil, too. That means you are just inviting fresh rounds of pests or disease if you plant next year's tomatoes in old soil. What's more, the soil's nutrients have already been depleted, and that could make your new tomato plants more vulnerable to blossom end rot and other problems. Instead of rotating the tomatoes away from the soil, move the soil away from the new tomato plants. Throw out the soil and old plants in your tomato containers, and don't add them to your compost pile. When you plant next year, use new potting soil, and choose containers that weren't used to grow tomatoes this year.

Avoid common transplanting mistake

After removing most leaves from the bottom of your tomato plant, don't plant the newly bared stem and roots vertically in the soil. The deeper these go into the soil, the less oxygen and warmth they get. This slows down new root development, and it can cause the plant to develop more slowly. When you lay the stem and roots sideways in a shallow trench and bury them, the stem and roots receive more oxygen and warmth, and new roots can develop more quickly.

Right way

Wrong way

Make your own upside-down planter. Use an old garden bucket or five-gallon bucket with a handle and lid to make this tomato planter.

- Turn the bucket upside down, and drill or cut a 2-inch hole in the center of the bottom.

- Turn the bucket right side up. Cut a slit in the center of a coffee filter. Place the filter inside the bucket so the slit fits over the hole at the bottom. This helps keep soil from leaking out.

- Fill the bucket almost full with potting soil. Put the lid on securely, and turn the bucket on its side.

- Ask a friend to hold the bucket steady. To plant your tomato seedling, carefully thread the roots through the hole and slitted filter. Make sure it's firmly rooted.

- Ask two friends to help you hang your upside-down planter from a sturdy hook that can take plenty of weight.

- Water thoroughly.

What you should know about upside-down planters

Plan for these issues before you make or buy an upside-down tomato planter.

- These planters can weigh 70 pounds after watering. Use hardware and wall supports that can easily handle this weight.
- They may need watering as often as several times a day in hot weather. Keep a step stool near your planter to help you reach and water more easily.
- Water may run out of the bottom of this planter, just like it does in some hanging baskets.
- This planter works best for Roma, cherry, and grape tomatoes.

Gardeners say these planters produce fewer tomatoes than plants in the ground, but they also require no digging, weeding, or tomato cages. What's more, they are less likely to attract pests or diseases.

Super-size your tomato plants. One simple planting trick may beef up your tomatoes. Before you set each plant in the ground, remove all the leaves except the two top leaves. Dig a short, shallow trench as long as the stem and roots below the two leaves. Rest the stem and roots lengthwise in the trench while holding the leaves upright above soil level. Cover the trench with soil, and gently tamp the soil around the base of the plant. Gardeners have reported larger plants and more tomatoes using this method.

Speedy feeding secret for more tomatoes. Weekly sprays of fish emulsion can help tomato plants thrive, but some people hate the smell. If you are one of them, try this "Texas pot method," invented by Dr. Sam Cotner of Texas A&M University, for higher tomato yields. This method delivers high-nitrogen fertilizer directly to the root zone of the plants.

- Soak your tomato plants in a half-strength solution of water-soluble fertilizer for one hour before you plant.

- Collect one-gallon pots with three to five drainage holes. Sink them into the ground next to each plant. Be sure the top edge is an inch above the soil. Each pot should sit between two plants.

- When the tomatoes begin to set fruit, drop one table-spoon of 21-0-0 fertilizer in each pot, and fill with water. Let drain, and then refill with water twice.

- Repeat every 10 days until the end of tomato season.

Ban reusable containers with dark pasts

Don't use five-gallon buckets or metal trash cans for vegetable storage if they have ever held pesticides or other chemicals.

Take three aspirin for a top-quality crop. Want tastier tomatoes, peppier peppers, and healthier houseplants? Give them an aspirin. Just follow these super-simple instructions to make a powerful spray for your vegetable garden. Dissolve one aspirin in a cup of water. Discard four tablespoons of the liquid, and add enough water to make a gallon. Don't forget to remove the extra tablespoons, or you'll damage your plants. Applying this spray once every three weeks may improve the number and quality of tomatoes, basil, peppers, and other vegetables. It may also help your plants fend off diseases and some insects. To learn how aspirin water can also help houseplants like orchids, see *Surprising secret to bigger plants, better blooms* in the *Goof-proof houseplants* chapter.

> ## News you can use for container gardens
>
> Resist the temptation to use light, soilless potting mixes if you grow your vegetables in pots. Soilless mixes may not provide the plant with sufficient support for its roots or enough of the trace elements needed for growth.

Enjoy carrots during autumn and winter. Just rig up a compact root cellar. Here's how.

- Clean a five-gallon bucket.

- Remove the bottom, bury the bucket nearly up to its rim, and fill with newly harvested carrots.

- Place the lid on the bucket, followed by a brick, and a straw bale.

- Temporarily remove the bale, brick, and lid when you need carrots.

If gophers are a problem, try this instead:

- Clean a 20-gallon metal trash can.

- Drill drainage holes in the bottom.

- Bury the can so it rests on a layer of rocks for drainage, and its rim is 3 inches above the soil.

- Fill the bottom with a layer of straw, and alternate layers of straw and carrots until you run out of space.

- Place the lid on top, and cover with soil and 2 feet of pesticide-free straw or leaves.

Protect your crops from lead poisoning

Get your soil tested for lead contamination if you live in an older house or urban environment. Lead can seep into crops, making them hazardous to your health. Take these steps if levels are between 150 and 400 mg/kg.

- Place your vegetable garden far from driveways, roadways, and older painted homes and structures.
- Plant leafy greens and other hard-to-wash vegetables in pots or in a raised bed 6 inches above ground level.
- Wash all vegetables with soapy water. Rinse thoroughly.
- Peel root vegetables, and throw out the outer and older leaves of leafy vegetables.
- Ask your cooperative extension agent how much organic matter and lime to add to soil that has lead. Follow those instructions.

These steps are a good start, but you should contact your cooperative extension agent for more information, especially if lead levels are higher than 1,000 mg/kg.

Help scarlet runners beat the heat. Give your scarlet runner beans some valuable insurance against hot, dry weather. Before you plant them, dig a trench, line it with newspaper, and add a layer of finished compost. Plant your beans in the trench. The paper-lined trench and compost layer help your soil stay cool and retain moisture. The longer you can keep cool moisture around your bean's roots, the better off your plant will be during hot, dry weather.

Stop veggies from going on strike. Timing is everything when you harvest beans, squash, cucumbers, tomatoes, and okra. Don't leave even one overripe vegetable on the plant because that can trigger a chemical that discourages blossoming — and vegetable production. Check plants every other day during the growing season to make sure you harvest everything on time. This may mean you pick a few vegetables before you need them, so have a plan for what to do with extras.

Secrets to warm-weather spinach and lettuce. Choose heat-tolerant varieties of spinach and lettuce if you want to grow these crops during warmer weather. But don't stop there. Store your spinach and lettuce seeds in the refrigerator, even if you bought them weeks ago. These crops like the cold, so time in the refrigerator helps them germinate more quickly during warm or hot weather.

Make your own row covers

Measure the length and width the row cover must enclose. Plan for hoop supports every 2-3 feet. For each hoop, buy two pieces of 1-foot-long rebar and a 3- or 4-foot length of 1-inch-wide, flexible PVC piping. Or cut the rebar and piping to the appropriate size.

Pound rebar 6 inches into the ground where each hoop end should rest. Let the rebar lean slightly inward toward the row.

Slide PVC piping over each pair of rebar pieces to form arched hoop supports over the row.

Cover the hoops with fabric that allows sunlight and rain to pass through. Bury the fabric on one side, and weight down the other side with a line of bricks.

Put your shade to work. Place your trellises and tall plants at the north end of your garden, and you have kept them from shading sun-loving vegetables. But if you are growing lettuce or other crops that appreciate afternoon shade during summer, you may want to try one of these approaches:

- Place trellises and tall plants north of sun-loving veggies, but south of any crops that could benefit from afternoon shade.

- Angle each trellis so it runs from east to west, and plant lettuce or other part-shade vegetables on the north side.

Prevent club root with a simple trick. If club root infested last year's cabbage, broccoli, or turnips, don't grow the crop in the same place this season. The disease could still be lurking in the soil. Instead, select a new location, install each plant in its own cardboard box of potting soil, and sink the boxes in the ground. Just remember, use boxes at least 12 inches deep for cabbage or turnips and boxes at least 20 inches deep for broccoli.

Skip the lure of novelty plants

People who want to try the latest thing available in plant catalogues pay the price. Fancy new varieties of flowers and vegetables are most expensive when they're first offered. Let another gardener pay more to be a guinea pig. Wait a few seasons, and you can get the same plants for less.

SUPERB HERBS

Create a living spice rack. Even if space is tight, you can still have an herb garden in your home or on your patio. Just create a stacked herb garden with three containers.

- Find a container you like, and collect small, medium, and large versions of it.

- Fill the largest container two-thirds full with soilless potting mix, smooth the potting mix, and center the medium container on top of it. Finish putting soil in the first container.

- Fill the second container two-thirds full and center the smallest container on top.

- Finish filling the second container and completely fill the third container with soil.

Now you can plant herbs such as sage, trailing rosemary, lavender, basil, oregano, and chives. This ingenious — and attractive — idea could be just the trick for other types of plants as well.

3 ways to make fresh herbs convenient. Dried herbs from your spice rack may seem convenient, but fresh kitchen herbs are so easy to grow — and you won't believe how much flavor fresh herbs add to your meals. To enjoy beautiful, healthy herbs that are almost as close as your pantry, follow these tips.

- Plant them in containers, and place them outdoors next to the kitchen door.

- If that spot is not sunny enough, plant the herbs in kitchen window boxes, and water often.

- During winter, plant as many herbs as you can in small containers, and keep them together on your kitchen windowsill to share moisture.

Grow sun lovers and shade lovers together in herb spiral

Mulch a 5- to 6-foot circle in a sunny spot. Lay out the spiraling wall within that circle with stakes. Use bricks, cinderblocks, stones, or bottles to construct the wall at least 2 feet high, filling in soil as you go.	Plant sun-loving herbs in the spiral's highest level and in the south-facing half of lower levels. Plant shade lovers in the north-facing half except at the top. Herbs in the lower level will be shaded by those on top.

Create a traditional herb garden. If you were lucky enough to have an old wagon wheel, you could prepare the soil, rest the wheel on top, and plant herbs between the spokes. But you can modernize this time-tested, attractive garden design by using bricks or pavers instead.

- Prepare the soil for planting.

- Using string and stakes, lay out a circle and divide it into six "pie pieces." If your circle is too large for you to reach its center while kneeling outside the edge, make your spokes wide enough to walk on.

- Outline your circle and pie pieces with bricks or pavers. Sink them into the ground so that their tops are at soil level.

- Select six kinds of herbs that are low-growing and compact, and plant one in each pie piece.

Beware destructive new basil disease

Basil downy mildew may be new to the United States, but it has already struck down plenty of basil crops. So check the undersides of your basil leaves regularly for its telltale dark gray spores. If you find the spores on potted basil, remove all the leaves with spores, or get rid of the entire plant.

If you find the spores under the leaves of garden plants, immediately apply a phosphorous acid salt fungicide or a biorational fungicide like Actinovate to the tops and undersides of the leaves. Spray both diseased plants and healthy ones because these fungicides may help control basil downy mildew — but they are much better at preventing it. If none of your plants have spores, experts suggest you spray them anyway if basil downy mildew is already suspected in your area.

Make herbs more fragrant. Cut back herbs like basil and oregano at midsummer to improve their fragrance and prevent them from bolting. Just be careful to remove no more than half the leaves. If you grow your herbs in containers, fertilize them, but at a low application rate. Large amounts of fertilizer weaken the fragrance and flavor of herbs, but consistently limiting fertilizer may help your herbs develop stronger tastes and scents. And be careful even after harvesting your herbs. Some experts say that rinsing herbs too heavily may remove the essential oils that give them their flavor and scent. So rinse lightly, and pat dry with paper towels.

Heart-healthy ways to perk up flavor

Use your lovely herb garden to season your food without using salt. You will discover a whole new world of flavors, while adding ingredients that may help protect you from heart attack and stroke. Start with this herb list for all kinds of food.

Basil: fish, soups, stews, sauces, Italian or Spanish dishes

Bay leaves: lean meats, stews, sauces, French or Caribbean recipes

Chives: lean meats, soups, sauces, Chinese dishes

Cilantro: Mexican or Chinese dishes

Dill: fish, chicken, soups, German recipes

Fennel: fish, Italian or German dishes

Garlic: fish, lean meats, chicken, vegetables, soups, sauces, Italian or Greek dishes

Marjoram: French and Caribbean dishes

Oregano: soups; Italian, Greek or Mexican dishes

Parsley: lean meats, vegetables, fish, soups, sauces, Italian or Caribbean dishes

Rosemary: fish, chicken, sauces, French or Greek recipes

Sage: lean meats, fish, stews, Mexican dishes

Thyme: lean meats, soups, sauces, Caribbean recipes

Preserve basil flavor with salt. Basil does not always freeze or dry well by itself, so use some of your fresh basil to make basil-flavored salt. Lay down a layer of coarse salt followed by a thin layer of herbs and another layer of salt. Let sit until the herbs are brown and completely dry. Discard the herbs, store in an airtight container, and use the basil-flavored salt in your favorite recipes.

Creative ways to freeze basil. Mix a half cup of chopped basil with a quarter cup of vegetable or olive oil. Scoop up this mixture one teaspoon at a time, and drop each spoonful on a baking sheet lined with wax paper. Place in the freezer. When it is frozen solid, gently remove each teaspoonful from the wax paper, and store them in plastic bags. For a less messy alternative, freeze your basil and oil in ice trays. If you adjust the amounts of oil and basil to match those in your favorite hot recipe, you can simply add a cube or two directly to the cooking pot.

Tasty way to harvest garlic at the right time. The best time to harvest garlic is when the bulbs are at their biggest and the cloves have not yet separated. This will usually happen when the lower leaves turn yellow or brown. To check, dig up a few test bulbs, and cut them in half to see if the cloves fill the skins. They won't go to waste, even if they are not quite ready. You can eat garlic as much as a month before it is ready to harvest, before the garlic head has finished forming. At this early stage, you may not even need to peel it, but it already has that marvelous garlic flavor. For a lighter garlic taste without removing the bulb, harvest the edible flower stalks before they bloom.

Smart way to store your garlic harvest. Leave several inches of stalk on each garlic bulb you harvest to help prevent rotting. Braid the stalks of several garlic bulbs together, tie off at the top with string, and hang the bulbs in a warm, dry place for three to four weeks to cure. After curing, store garlic in a cool, dry place. Do not store it in the refrigerator unless you expect to use it within three days.

Save your herbs from fungus. Try this if you suspect one of your herb plants is developing a fungal disease. Grate one clove of garlic into one-and-a-half cups of water. Add another half-cup of water, and then pour the mixture around the base of the plant. This may not kill every fungus you find, but it can be effective on root fungus and many other plant diseases.

Dangers in the herb garden

Some herbs can put your life or health in serious peril. Avoid these seven herbs no matter what the supposed benefits are:

- aconite
- belladonna
- chaparral
- sassafras
- comfrey
- hemlock
- ephedra

Corral rampant growers. Mints and horseradish are just two of the herbs that spread like wildfire. Their sneaky shoots travel underground so they can turn up where you least expect them. From now on, plant them in a bottomless container such as a terra cotta flue liner, 12-inch-wide PVC pipe, drain tile, stove pipe, concrete pipe, or even a bottomless and topless box made from stacked timbers or cinder blocks. Sink your container 18 to 24 inches into the ground, but leave a couple of inches above the soil to keep wayward shoots in check. To solve the problem with less digging, choose a clay pot, or punch drainage holes in a bucket or jumbo-sized metal can. Turn this into a sunken planter, and plant your rampant grower inside.

Help rosemary thrive indoors until spring. Even gardening experts have sometimes failed when trying to overwinter their rosemary plants indoors, so leave rosemary outdoors if you live south of USDA Zone 6. Otherwise, combine all these secrets to help keep your rosemary alive and healthy until spring.

- Prune away at least one-fourth of the growth, and use the trimmings in cooking.

- Place the plant in front of a south- or west-facing window, or use fluorescent lights to make up for dim lighting.

- Plant the rosemary in a large pot with loose, well-drained potting mix.

- Keep the plant moist. Water as soon as the soil dries out.

- Keep rosemary cool. Aim for temperatures in the mid-60s, perhaps in a bright, unheated room or garage.

Grow herbs in a rock wall. You may have the perfect space for herbs if your rock wall is held together by soil instead of mortar and is sun-drenched most of the time. After all, herbs like thyme love dry, sunny spots with excellent drainage. Thyme also comes in many varieties, including scented choices like lemon thyme. So pick a seedling of your favorite thyme to start your wall herb garden. Simply tuck it in the soil between stones, add soil to fill in any gaps, and water very gently so you do not dislodge the soil or the plant. Other good herbs for your rock wall garden include trailing rosemary, prostrate sage, prostrate oregano, chamomile, and chives.

Make teas from herbs you grow yourself. Gather one to three tablespoons of fresh leaves for every 8-ounce cup of tea you plan to brew. Heat water until it just begins to boil, pour over your tea leaves, and stir. Or use a tea ball for easier preparation. Let steep for five to 10 minutes before drinking. Good herb choices for garden-fresh teas include lemon balm, rosemary, peppermint, bee balm, or sage.

Best time to cut herbs for drying. You can harvest fresh herbs anytime, but harvest leaves for drying shortly before the plants flower. That is when they are at the peak of their flavor and fragrance. Harvest the leaves in the morning soon after the dew dries. If you need to cut entire stems of leaves, snip the stems of annual herbs close to ground level, but only cut off the top third of perennial herbs.

Dry herbs in a parked car. Park your car in the sun on a hot day, and you have a great "oven" for drying herbs. Tuck your fresh-picked herbs loosely inside brown paper bags on the seats of your car, or lay the herbs out on newspapers or cleaned window screens spread on the seats. Leave two windows cracked open about one inch for ventilation. Check once every hour, and remove the herbs when they become brittle or crumbly. And here is a bonus — even after the herbs are removed, your car will still smell heavenly.

Prevent a microwave fire

Don't use paper towels or paper plates that include recycled paper content when you dry herbs in the microwave. Recycled paper may contain tiny metal fibers that can spark or even burst into flames.

Quick way to dry herbs. Microwave drying removes more essential oils from herbs than other drying processes. Yet microwaving may be your best bet when conditions are too damp for other drying methods to work or when you need to dry basil without losing flavor.

- Place one layer of leaves on a paper towel or paper plate.

- Microwave the herbs on low for 30 seconds and check them. If they are not dry, microwave on low for 15 seconds and check the herbs again.

- Keep microwaving and checking until the leaves are dry but green.

- Watch the herbs closely, and stop the microwave immediately if they spark, turn brown, or burn. This means you are drying the herbs too much — or even cooking them.

Hang herbs to dry without nail holes. Pioneer women had plenty of rafters to use for hanging herbs to dry, but most people do not. Try these options to avoid putting nail holes in your walls and ceiling.

- Use a spring-loaded curtain rod or shower rod. The curtain rods come in many sizes and are often expandable.

- Hang multiple bundles from discarded refrigerator, oven, or outdoor grill racks.

- Suspend hardware cloth or old window screens between two chairs or sawhorses.

Give herb flavors a longer shelf life. Your garden herbs will keep their flavor longer if you store them by freezing. Most people recommend drying herbs to store them, but fresh herbs stored by freezing taste better than dried herbs — for up to several months. However, you must freeze them as quickly as possible after harvest, so pick them at their peak flavor, wash, shake, and let dry. Then immediately spread them on a cookie sheet or drop into freezer bags, and place in the freezer. After freezing, store your cookie-sheet herbs in freezer bags, and label those bags. Some herbs may keep better or become easier to use if you chop the herb, blend with water or oil, and pour the mixture into an ice cube tray to freeze.

Prevent foul flavors in freezer foods. Be careful how you package herbs when you freeze them. Store strongly flavored herbs like chives or rosemary in closed jars before you put them in the freezer — even if they are already in bags or frozen into ice cubes. If herbs like these are not in jars, their scents may seep into nearby foods, making those foods taste odd or even inedible.

Easy reminders to use your herbs

You carefully picked your herbs at the peak of freshness, stored them in the refrigerator, and promptly forgot about them. Make sure the next batch of herbs does not suffer the same fate.

Pour an inch of water in a vase or glass. After harvesting the herbs, make a diagonal cut to trim the stems, and drop them in the vase. Cover with a plastic bag, and put the vase at the front of the refrigerator shelf. These herbs will keep for a week if you change the water every day.

If that still doesn't remind you, separate out a small bunch of herbs each week, and keep them in a water-filled vase on your kitchen counter or windowsill.

CONTAINER PLANTS

VERSATILE
HOME & GARDEN
ACCENTS

POTTING LIKE A PRO

5 sure signs it's time to repot. Some fast-growing plants need repotting more than once a year, while others will be happy with a new container every three years. Check for these telltale signs that it's time.

- The plant wilts soon after watering.

- A hard, salty crust forms on the soil surface.

- The plant is top-heavy and prone to toppling over.

- Leaves and stems don't seem to be growing or are growing very slowly.

- Roots are growing out of the pot's drainage holes or circling around the root ball inside.

Your plant will love having room to grow. Repot it in spring, once it wakes up from its winter sleep.

Cut plant back to keep from repotting. Repotting isn't the only answer for an overgrown plant. You can scale it back, instead, to keep it from getting bigger. Pop the plant out of its pot and trim off the outer roots. Put the root ball back in the pot, along with fresh soil. Prune away some of the foliage to accommodate the smaller root ball.

Perfect size pot prevents wilt and rot. Pots that are too small dry out fast. Those that are too large hold more water than the plant needs, which can lead to rot. When you get ready to repot, choose a container 2 inches wider and deeper than the current one. The plant will have room to grow and just the right amount of moisture.

Fast bleach bath prevents diseases. Go ahead — spend a quarter on that plant pot at the garage sale. Just be sure to sterilize it when you get home. Whether clay or plastic, soak it for at least 10 minutes in a bath of one part bleach to nine parts water. Follow up by washing it with soap and water. Sterilize pots every time you reuse them to avoid spreading diseases among your precious plants.

Easy-to-make mold helps you repot your plant at just the right height

Put soil in the bottom of the new pot, then set the old, smaller pot inside it.	If the rim of the old pot is not even with the new one, add more dirt. Fill the space between the two pots, too.	Carefully lift out the old pot and remove the plant. You now have a perfectly sized hole to replant.

Wet roots before repotting. Give plants a drink before removing them from their old pot. Wet roots are less likely to break off or tear when you slide the plant out of its pot.

Keep soil in and pests out. Cover the drainage hole in the bottom of plant pots with a clean coffee filter. Extra water will still drain out, but the soil won't go with it. It will also prevent pests from entering the plant through the drainage hole. Don't drink coffee? An unscented dryer sheet will do the same thing.

Gravel no good for drainage

Stop putting gravel in the bottom of potted plants. It can do more harm than good. Far from improving drainage, gravel and pottery shards can leave roots more waterlogged. Gravel actually slows water down as it moves through the pot, so the soil above stays wetter, longer. Skip the rocks. Simply use good quality potting mix and a planter with drainage holes.

Avoid narrow-necked planters. Elegant vase-shaped containers, with their narrow necks and wide bodies, look beautiful. Unfortunately, if you ever need to repot, you may not be able to remove the plant without breaking open the planter — or losing some roots.

Keep peanuts in their place. A layer of packing peanuts at the bottom of a big planter can make it lighter. They tend to scatter everywhere when you try to repot, however. Next time, drop them into a mesh bag, like an old onion bag, or use an old pair of pantyhose. Tie it closed and place at the bottom of the planter. The peanuts won't get loose when you're ready to repot.

Pick the top mix for growing success. Soilless mixes contain no top soil, making them very lightweight. Instead, they're a mixture of peat moss, shredded bark, perlite, sand, and, in some cases, compost. Not all mixes are made equal, though. Try these DIY tests in the store.

- Lift the bag. A good potting mix should feel light, not heavy.

- Squeeze the bag. If the soil inside feels springy, that's good. If it squishes together and stays that way, then it's too heavy.

Doctor the mix for better results. You can offset the downsides of soilless mixes by tweaking them at home. Combine one part garden loam or sandy soil with two parts potting mix. Be sure to sterilize the soil first to kill weed seeds, bugs, and diseases. Then pot up your plants as usual.

Don't pot with everyday dirt

It's tempting to save money by filling pots with dirt from your garden, rather than store-bought potting mix. But unless your yard consists of sandy, loamy soil, don't do it. The best soil for containers is not your "garden variety." Backyard dirt usually doesn't drain as well as potting mix, and that can starve plant roots of oxygen. And it's often loaded with weed seeds, unless you sterilize it first.

DIY recipe for simple soilless mix. It's easy to make your own no-soil potting mix.

- Combine half sphagnum peat moss and half perlite or vermiculite. Mix together thoroughly.

- Blend a slow-release fertilizer with ground limestone in a separate container. Check the fertilizer label to see how much to add. Use one tablespoon of limestone for every gallon of soilless mix. Add to peat moss mix.

- Sift the entire mixture through half-inch wire mesh. Or, if you plan to use it as seed starter, sift through one-quarter-inch wire mesh.

Store your batch in a watertight container, and moisten before using.

Get down and dirty with homemade potting soil. Sometimes a soil-based potting mix is the way to go — and you won't spend a fortune making it. Combine equal parts:

- coarse (builder's) sand, perlite, or vermiculite.

- moistened sphagnum peat moss.

- loamy garden soil, either from your own garden or pre-sterilized from the garden center.

You want loose soil that drains well. Test the texture with your hand. If it feels too sandy or gritty, add more peat moss. Too sticky, like clay, then add both sand and peat moss. Start with small amounts, mix, and test again until it feels just right.

Soil vs. soilless — best pick for plants. Soilless mixes work well for small houseplants but not the larger ones. They pack very few nutrients, and because they're so lightweight, houseplants can get top-heavy and tip over as they grow. Try using a potting mix that contains some actual soil for large or top-heavy potted plants, particularly those that are difficult to repot. A soil medium can help them thrive longer in the same container.

Free alternative to costly peat moss. Save even more money by skipping the peat moss in potting mix recipes. Make your own peat moss substitute out of leaf mold. Rake up fallen leaves and stuff them in a black plastic bag. Poke some holes in it for air to circulate. Leave it for a year, and you'll have a finished bag of leaf mold. Use in place of peat moss in all your potting recipes.

The lazy way to sterilize soil. Most potting soils you buy at the store are already sterilized. They've been heated to kill off diseases, insects, and weed seeds. If you opt to make your own potting mix, you'll need to sterilize it yourself. Let the sun do all the work.

- Find a sunny spot, preferably on concrete or asphalt, and lay out a black plastic garbage bag.

- Fill black plastic pots with your potting soil or soilless mix, and set them on the bag.

- Soak them with a water hose, cover the whole area with a clear plastic tarp, and weigh down the edges with rocks.

Two weeks in the hot summer sun, and your new soil will be ready to pot.

Breathe fresh life into old potting soil

Put nutrients back into tired soil. First, leach the built-up salts out of the soil. Fill a large pot with drainage holes with old potting mix and pour water through it. Let drain and repeat. Spread the soil out on a tarp to dry in the sun. Next, mix it half and half with weed-free compost sifted through a half-inch screen. Add a little powdered lime and a slow-release fertilizer. Moisten the mix and store for two weeks to cure.

Grill kills weed seeds and disease. Can't wait two weeks? Sterilize your homemade mix on the grill, instead. Fire it up and fill an old roasting pan with about 4 inches of moist soil or soilless mix. Cover the pan with aluminum foil. Poke a candy thermometer through the foil and into the soil. Set the pan on the grill, close the lid, and wait until the thermometer reads 180 degrees. Keep the temperature steady at 180 for 30 minutes, then turn off the grill and let the soil cool.

Boil up safer soil. Use your tea kettle to sterilize potting soil. Fill a large, clean, plastic pot half-full of potting mix. Pour two kettles of boiling water through the soil, letting the water drain out the bottom. Once it cools, it's ready to use.

Secret to season-long blooms. Want blooms that last all season long? Work granules of slow-release fertilizer into the soil before you put the plant in. Fill the pot with soil, and sprinkle the fertilizer on top. Massage it into the top 6 inches or so of soil evenly and thoroughly. Then put in your plants. If they look like they need an extra boost mid-season, apply a little liquid fertilizer.

2 quick ways to moisten soil. Wet your dirt before potting any plants in it. Otherwise, the water will simply drain down the sides of the pot, rather than reaching the root ball.

- If the soil is in a bag, simply pour water into the bag itself. Squish the mix around, and let it sit for an hour or two until it absorbs the water.

- If you're working out of a tub, add water to the soil slowly, and stir it in until the mix is moist.

Potting soil should be damp but not wet when you pot it up. Try this test to tell if it's ready. Gently squeeze a ball of soil in your hand, then open your palm. Press the ball lightly. If it breaks apart, it's ready. If it stays rolled up, it's too wet.

Wash salts out of soil. The simple act of watering your plants can cause soluble salts to build up in the soil. Eventually, those salts can lead plants to drop leaves and develop root rot. Leach the soil every four to six months to rinse out excess salt.

- Set the plant inside a sink or outdoors on the ground.

- Pour twice as much water through the soil as the pot will hold, and let drain out the bottom.

- Remove the top one-quarter inch of soil if it has a hard crust on top.

Leach plants before repotting or fertilizing, so you don't wash away all the nutrients you just added. Keep salts from building up in the future by overwatering the plant each time you give it a drink. Let the excess collect in a drip plate, and dump it out. Don't let the water sit, or the soil may reabsorb those salts.

Build a simple self-watering planter. You'll be able to pay less attention to your plants and keep them happier. Set an unglazed terra-cotta pot in the center of a larger planter. Fill the planter with potting mix, and situate your plants around the smaller clay pot. Add gravel to the bottom of the clay pot, and fill it with water. The water will naturally saturate the clay and slowly seep through to the surrounding soil, keeping it moist longer.

Double up pots for longer bouts between watering. This vacation secret can help plants thrive while you're away. Double-pot them before leaving. Place the pot holding the plant inside a larger container. Stuff Spanish moss, sphagnum moss, peat moss, or perlite between the two pots. When you water the plant, dampen the filler, too. This extra bit of insulation helps keep the soil cooler and the air around the plant more humid — both of which cut evaporation.

Battle wilt in hanging baskets. Hanging plants dry out notoriously fast, especially in wire baskets with coco liners. Try this to cut back on watering and keep them from wilting on even the hottest days.

- Lay a sheet of plastic tarp or a heavy duty garbage bag inside the coco liner. Trim the plastic to size.

- Poke holes in the plastic with scissors for drainage.

- Cut the absorbent center out of a disposable diaper. Cut the center into 1-inch squares, and wet them thoroughly.

- Mix these squares evenly into the potting soil. Fill the basket with the mixture, and plant as usual.

The plastic will stop water from evaporating through the coco liner as quickly. The diaper pieces, on the other hand, will absorb water and keep it available for plant roots throughout the day.

Create a tiny oasis for tropical plants. Some plants like it wet. They crave humid conditions. Give them what they want. Create a mini tropical garden. Fill a high-sided pan with a layer of pebbles. Then pour enough water in the pan to partially cover the pebbles. Set the plant pots in the pan, making sure the bottoms aren't sitting in water. The air around the plants will get humid as the water evaporates.

Secret to helping strawberry jars thrive. Strawberry jars aren't easy to keep watered, unless you know this seasoned gardener's secret.

- Cut a piece of PVC pipe just shorter than the pot itself.

- Drill holes up and down the pipe, on all sides.

- Cover the drainage hole in the planter's bottom with a coffee filter or old window screen.

- Stand the pipe in the middle of the strawberry jar and

- Fill the pipe with sand or fine gravel. Place a piece of screen across the top.

Water through the top of the pipe, and give a quick drink to each of the plant pockets. The drainage holes you drilled earlier will let water seep throughout the soil, all the way to the bottom.

Seal pots to stop evaporation

Cut down on watering by sealing your terra-cotta pots. Scrub the inside clean and let dry. Then, with a foam paintbrush, paint the interior with an oil-based, exterior-grade, polyurethane sealant. A polyurethane spray will work, too. Apply two to three coats, letting the pot dry between each.

Saturate pots before replanting. Soak terra-cotta pots in water right before putting plants in them. They will absorb water from the soak, instead of stealing water from the soil of your freshly repotted plant.

Turn everyday objects into playful planters. Leave the old plastic pots behind and get creative with your planters.

- Don't throw away your busted watering can. Fill it with dirt and trailing flowers, like petunias.

- Pull out the wheelbarrow with a flat tire. Dust off the cobwebs and park it in the yard. Fill with soil and colorful flowers and vines.

- Remove the metal drum from an old washer, and take out the agitator. Line the inside with plastic, leaving the last row of drainage holes uncovered. Paint the outside brown, and hot glue twigs vertically all the way around the tub.

Make cheap and easy lightweight planters. Buy more planters without spending a bundle. Transform Styrofoam ice coolers into indoor or outdoor planters. They're lightweight, easy to move, and a lot cheaper than clay pots. Paint the outside with latex paint, poke holes in the bottom for drainage, and fill with potting mix. If the coolers are too deep for the plants you plan to grow, simply cut away the top until you get them the right height.

Quick way to clean woven baskets. Vacuum woven baskets with a soft brush attachment, or dust with a paintbrush. Simply spray a cheap paintbrush with a dust-attracting spray. Work the bristles into all the nooks and crannies for a deep clean.

Build your own birdbath/planter combo. You can create a stunning planter that does double-duty as a birdbath.

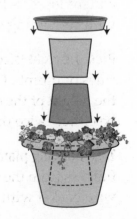

- Begin with a tall pot or urn. Drill a few drainage holes in the bottom if it doesn't already have some.

- Place a cheap pot upside down inside the larger one, and set a nicer pot right side up on top of it.

- Top this tower with a clay saucer.

- Fill the large pot with dirt and low-growing, brightly colored annuals.

- Fill the saucer with water for the birds, and enjoy the view.

You can attach the stacked pots and saucer to each other using Velcro if you're worried about them toppling.

Foolproof formula for container combos. Don't get hung up picking plant combinations for your pots. Just remember these rules.

- Keep it odd. Stick with an odd number of plant varieties, like three or five.

- Keep it simple. Make sure you have one trailing plant, one upright grower, and one mid-height plant in each of your containers.

Leave plants in their plastic pots while you try different arrangements. It's much easier than moving them around in the dirt. Slip them out once you've settled on a look.

Get gorgeous displays, no repotting necessary. Cut back on the amount of repotting you do, and instantly amp up the "wow" factor. Leave plants in their plastic pots when you combine them in baskets or planters. Arrange them the way you like, pushing the pots close together. Then tuck moss over and around to hide them from view. When the season changes or a plant loses its blooms, simply take out that pot and replace with something else. No dirt under your nails and no hassle.

Pick the right-sized plants. Container garden design has a few rules of thumb. Height is one of the most important. Measure the height of the container itself. The plants you put in should be either twice that height, or only half.

Take hanging plants from dull to dramatic. Get magazine-quality fullness from the most humble hanging planter. Line a hanging wire basket with moss or a coco liner. Cut holes in the sides of the liner every few inches. Fill halfway with soil, then start working small plants into the holes you cut. Finish filling the pot with soil, and place plants in the top to polish it off.

Pick a theme when grouping pots. Potted plants look great in groups, if the pots somehow match. Pick a theme to hold them all together — use different sized pots painted in similar colors, made of the same materials, or of similar shape or style. Or go wild by grouping dramatically different pots all holding the same type of plant.

Top off potted plants with a touch of whimsy. Soil toppers add more than beauty — they help stop mold from growing, soil from drying out, and nutrients from washing away. The prettiest are often free. Cover the top of the soil with old marbles, broken ceramic, small seashells, leftover tiles from a bathroom redo, or small river pebbles. Even nut shells are fair game.

Banish bugs with buried garlic

Bugs and germs hate garlic more than some people do. Give this gardening folk remedy a try. Poke holes in the soil around the rim of potted plants, about three holes in a 14-inch pot. Bury an unpeeled garlic clove in each hole, about 1-inch deep, to ward away pests and disease.

GOOF-PROOF HOUSEPLANTS

How to pick the healthiest houseplants. Dying houseplants may not be your fault. They could have been doomed from the start at the store. Learn to bring home healthy plants with the best shot at surviving and thriving. Shop for plants that look full, even bushy, and have plenty of leaves. Also, make sure they have buds just beginning to open, instead of in full bloom. Avoid plants with:

- tightly closed green buds, which usually don't open indoors.

- yellowed leaves, or leaves with brown tips.

- leaves that have been polished to a high gloss with leaf shine.

- dry soil shrinking away from the walls of the container.

- dark spots on leaves, or holes in leaves.

- webs or cottony material at the base of leaves.

- pots that feel too lightweight, since this can signal drought stress.

Discover the perfect bedroom plants. Every plant "breathes." Some simply do it at night, cleaning the air while you sleep. Leaves and stems contain tiny "pores" that allow plants to absorb carbon dioxide and release oxygen. Most plants open their pores during the day, but certain bromeliads and orchids, and many agaves and cactuses, do so at night.

Grow your own air freshener. Trash those store-bought air fresheners in favor of natural fragrances. One study discovered that scented air fresheners and laundry products released more than 100 chemicals into the air, 10 of which are toxic or hazardous. Freesia, cyclamen, garden petunias, fairy primrose, and white calla lilies are just a few houseplants with sweet-smelling blooms.

9 best natural air cleaners. Houseplants not only convert carbon dioxide to oxygen. Some super-flora can actually remove dangerous chemicals like benzene and formaldehyde from the air. These compounds are a staple in cleaners, plastic, cigarette smoke, car exhaust, paint, glue, and insecticide. In other words, your home is likely full of them. University of Georgia researchers tested 28 common houseplants. These nine were tops at removing pollutants.

- *Hemigraphis alternata* (purple waffle plant)
- *Hedera helix* (English ivy)
- *Hoya carnosa* (variegated wax plant)
- *Asparagus densiflorus* (Asparagus fern)
- *Tradescantia pallida* (purple heart plant)
- *Fittonia argyroneura* (silver nerve plant)
- *Polyscias fruticosa* (Ming aralia)
- *Sansevieria trifasciata* (Snake plant)
- *Guzmania* species (certain bromeliads)

Having just one type of plant won't do much good, however. Invest in a combination to really clean the air in your home.

> ## *Beware of polluting plants*
>
> Not every plant helps clean the air. Some may actually release harmful compounds. In a study at the University of Georgia, peace lily, weeping fig, and areca palm all released volatile organic compounds (VOCs) into the air. The plants themselves weren't the only source. Plastic pots, pesticides sprayed on them by growers, and microorganisms in the soil all gave off VOCs. You may be able to cut back on these toxins by potting plants in natural containers, like clay, and resisting the urge to treat them with chemical pesticides.

Easy way to tell it's watering time. A one-touch test can tell you if your houseplants need water — and no, your fingers won't get dirty. Simply tap on the side of clay pots. When the soil is dry, the pot will sound hollow. When it's damp, the pot will sound solid. For plastic pots, perform the lift test. A light pot means it's time for watering. A hefty one can be left a while longer.

When to skip misting. Some plants need misting. Others don't. If your plants seem to enjoy a little dampness, mist in the morning. This gives the water time to dry before the cooler night air sets in. Wet foliage at night invites disease.

- Skip the misting for most palms, cactuses, and other desert plants. Getting them wet outside of their normal watering encourages rot.

- Don't bother misting to raise the humidity. The spray won't bump it up enough to do much good. The fine water droplets evaporate too fast.

- Never mist a plant that you think has fungal leaf spot. The water will help spread the infection.

First aid for dried-out plants. Letting the soil dry out completely can spell certain death for your plants, unless you act fast. Set the pot, plant and all, in a sink or bucket. Add enough water to bring it one-third of the way up the pot's side. Let soak for a couple of hours, until the soil inside is damp again. Use a fork to gently break up any hard soil on top, so water can once again penetrate.

Leaves reveal light needs. Is your plant getting too much light or not enough? The secret is in the leaves. Use this handy table to decode your plant's SOS signals.

Too much light	Too little light
brown, burned-looking areas appear on leaves	leaves get spindly and seem to reach for the light
leaves dry out and fall off	lower leaves turn yellow and drop
leaves become pale	new leaves are small or don't form at all
foliage wilts in the middle of the day	leaves on variegated plants turn solid green

Perfect plants for low-light windows. North-facing windows get the least light, but don't despair of growing plants there. While African violets may never take to it, plenty of non-bloomers will. Cast iron plants, Chinese evergreens, corn plant, and lance and Malaysian dracaenas are just a few that will happily live in this low-light area.

Free ways to supplement the sun. Forget expensive grow lights. Boost the natural light your plants need with these free and cheap tricks.

- Clean the windows. Grime can significantly cut the amount of light that reaches your plants.

- Open curtains and raise blinds. Remove screens if they aren't needed.

- Prune shrubs and trees outside that block windows.

- Paint the walls and furniture in light colors, and use light-colored rugs and curtains to reflect more sunlight into the room.

- Hang mirrors on sunny walls to reflect more light toward the plant.

No-guess way to test light strength

The plant's label says it likes "medium" light. How do you know if that's what you have at home? Try this trick. Put a white piece of paper on the table where you plan to set the plant. Hold your hand one foot above the paper. If you see a:

- sharp, dark, well defined shadow, you have high or bright light.
- softer but still clearly defined shadow, you have medium light.
- a dim, barely visible shadow, you have low light.

Bring more light to sun-starved plants. The right artificial light can make up for lack of sun.

- Fluorescent bulbs generally work best for foliage plants. Cool, white lights are good for growing foliage, while daylight bulbs provide lighting similar to what plants would get outside.

- For flowering plants, consider a combination of 40-watt fluorescent and incandescent bulbs. Bloomers need infrared light, in addition to regular light. Fluorescent bulbs don't provide infrared, but incadescents do.

Place plants no farther than 4 feet away from a 100-watt fluorescent bulb. Closer is better. In fact, foliage plants can sit within 1 foot of the light. Flowering plants can go even closer, within 6 to 12 inches. Keep in mind, incandescent bulbs give off more heat. You may need to place plants farther away from these to avoid burning their leaves.

Swap around plants under tube lights. Fluorescent tube light bulbs put out more light in the center than they do on the ends. If you use these to supplement your plants' natural light, be sure to rotate the plants regularly. Move those at the bulb's edges in toward the center. Or place plants that prefer low light at the ends and high-light lovers in the middle.

The trick to year-round blooms. Turn a seldom-used pantry or utility closet into a secret growing room. Set up your fluorescent and incandescent "grow lights" in the room. This is where you'll keep plants between blooming periods. When one flowers, bring it out and display. Once it stops, return it to the grow room, and bring out the next one in bloom. You'll always have fresh flowers to enjoy as well as an out-of-sight place to stash dull plants in the off-season. Grow rooms like these are perfect for starting seedlings, too.

Feed with the right fertilizer

One size doesn't fit all when it comes to fertilizing houseplants. Flowering plants that put out lots of leaves but few blooms are a sure sign of nitrogen overload. Feed these with a fertilizer high in phosphorus to boost blooms. Give leafy green plants one high in nitrogen, to help them grow healthy foliage.

Surprising secret to bigger plants, better blooms. Want healthier houseplants? Give them aspirin. Dissolved in water, it will jump-start a stunted plant with just a sprinkle, plus make some plants bloom. Scientific research has shown that the active ingredient in aspirin can:

- prompt some orchids and lilies to bloom.

- counteract the growth-stunting effects of stress, plumping up foliage and fruit.

- help make plants more resistant to viruses, bacteria, and fungal infections.

Simply dissolve one and a half aspirins in two gallons of water, and spray directly on plants. Don't make the solution any stronger, though, or you could actually slow plant growth.

Kitchen gadget keeps plants healthy. Grab an apple corer to fertilize your potted plants. It's the perfect tool for making holes in the soil. Pour a few granules of slow-release fertilizer into the hole, where the roots will be able to reach it easily.

When it's OK to overwater. Never fertilize a dry plant. They need water in order to move the fertilizer up into their roots. Without water, fertilizer can come into direct contact with roots, burning them and potentially killing the plant. Water the plant thoroughly both before and after adding fertilizer.

4 ways to winter-proof plants. Even indoor plants like to "hibernate" a bit in winter. Switch to this easy care schedule to keep them lush and healthy.

- Don't bother fertilizing houseplants unless they are in bloom or actively growing. They generally don't get enough light or warmth in winter to do either.

- Cut back on watering. With less growth, plants need less water. Let the soil dry out between drinks.

- Group plants together to boost humidity and protect them from the dry, indoor heat.

- Consider setting plants in a pan filled with pebbles and a little water to generate more humidity.

Pinch back plants for better growth. Consider it a haircut for your houseplants. Prune out the unattractive or skimpy parts of the plant, and you'll generally be rewarded with healthier growth. One pruning cut can produce two new branches, creating lusher foliage. You can also prompt branching by pinching back new growth. Simply squeeze the soft tips between your thumb and forefinger.

Foolproof houseplants anyone can grow. These babies love to be neglected. For most, overwatering is about the only thing that will kill them. Pot them up and let them go.

- Cactus — pot in well-drained soil, and place in a sunny window.

- Bromeliad — pot in loose, well-drained soil, and water when soil begins to dry out.

- Rubber plant — use regular potting soil in a pot with drainage hole, and repot when it begins to look like it needs daily watering.

- Snake plant — give it bright but indirect light, and water occasionally.

- Chinese evergreen — grow in regular potting mix with extra humus added, and keep soil moist.

- Cast iron plant — give it low light, and let top two-thirds of soil dry out before watering.

Drop the temp for long-lasting flowers. No one likes to sleep in a hot, sticky room. Neither do plants. Lower your thermostat when you go to bed, and you'll mimic what happens in nature — a 10-degree drop after dark. The lower temperature helps plants recover from the heat of the day. The shift should also make blooms last longer and make their colors more intense.

Prep plants for the move outdoors. Going from the dim indoors to the bright outdoors can overwhelm, and even kill, most houseplants. Spending the spring and summer outside may do them good, but ease their way or you'll end up with scorched leaves.

- Wait until nighttime temperatures stop dipping below 50 degrees.

- Begin by setting potted plants outside in the shade, where they will get little if any direct light.

- Keep their trips outdoors short at first. Leave them there a little longer each day over the course of two weeks.

Reverse the process when it's time to bring plants back in for the winter.

Easy way to keep leaves clean. You don't have to wipe every leaf of your dusty houseplant. For some plants, simply setting them under the shower or outside during a good rain will do the trick. For the rest, this quick wash and rinse trick will leave them clean and shiny in no time.

- Fill a bucket with lukewarm water and a few drops of unscented liquid hand soap, like Ivory.

- Cover the soil surface of your potted plant with cloth.

- Hold the plant upside down, dunk the leaves in the water, and gently swirl it around.

- Rinse away the soapy residue with clean water.

Give hairy leaves a good cleaning. Soft, fuzzy leaves are a magnet for dust and dirt. Yet violet leaves hate being touched or getting wet. Instead of rinsing them off, try a dry cleaning. Brush each leaf clean with a small, soft, dry paint brush. It may take a little longer, but your plant will thank you.

Minimize harm when handling violets

Science has proven what gardeners have long known — African violets do not like having their leaves touched. Research shows they especially hate it if you've recently rubbed lotion on your hands. So respect their needs and keep your hands to yourself. If you must touch, wear gloves. Plants fared better from gloved hands than bare.

Trigger blooms with right amount of light. African violets need plenty of shut-eye or they won't bloom. They need eight hours of darkness each day, just like people, to be their best. Follow these guidelines to boost their blooms.

- Give them eight to 12 hours of bright, but indirect, light each day. To do that, place them about 3 feet from a west- or southeast-facing window.

- Read the plant's leaves. Too little light results in skinny, deep green leaves that seem to reach for the light. Too much turns leaves pale green or greenish-yellow.

- Make up for low-light conditions by giving them light for longer periods of time, up to 16 hours. The stronger the light, the less time they will need to spend in it.

Water violets safely with a wick. Trying to water the soil without wetting their leaves is next to impossible. The next time you repot a violet, soak an old shoestring in water. Slide it up through the drainage hole into the pot. Fill the container with soil and pot your plant as usual. Set the other end of the shoestring in a small container of water nearby. The woven string will wick water into the soil, delivering water directly to the roots.

Warm bath banishes mites. Mites love to munch on violets, begonias, gerbera daisies, and other delicate houseplants.

As if their webs aren't enough of an eyesore, their toxic saliva curls leaves and kills buds. Fight back by giving your plants a warm-water bath.

- Heat a pot of water over the stove until the temperature reaches exactly 111 degrees.

- Gently immerse the plants, pots and all, into the water.

- Stir the water slowly, and keep it at 111 degrees for 15 minutes. Then lift the plants out.

The heat should kill the mites without harming the plants. Gas stoves, not electric, work best because they heat more evenly. Use an accurate thermometer, preferably digital, to test the water. Let the water get too warm, or leave the plants in for too long, and the heat may kill them, too.

Turn on the fan for healthier orchids. Set up a small fan in the same area as your orchids. A fan improves air circulation, which thwarts bacterial rot and fungal diseases. It also strengthens the orchid's flower spikes and cools the plant off in warm weather. Moving air can dry out plants faster, though. You may need to water more often, but that's a small price to pay for stronger plants.

Kitchen spice fights fungal leaf spot. Reach for the cinnamon when you see fungal leaf spot on orchids. This spice acts as a natural fungus fighter. Sprinkle a little on the tip of your finger, and gently rub it over the damaged spot. A little cinnamon goes a long way, however. Using too much can burn the leaf.

Keep poinsettias growing year after year. Don't toss them out after Christmas. Keep them blooming through March. Set them away from direct sunlight and cold drafts, and leave the thermostat set between 65 and 75 degrees. These Mexican natives don't like winter weather. With the right care, you can keep them growing and blooming for years to come.

- Once the blooms finish fading, prune the plant back to 8 inches above the soil.

- Store it in the coolest part of the house for its winter rest.

- Water enough to keep the soil barely moist.

- Bring it back out in early spring, and place where it will get indirect sunlight.

- Move it outdoors to a deck or patio after the nights warm up.

Protect poinsettias from the cold

Ask for a wrapper the next time you buy a poinsettia in winter. These tropical flowers don't care for the cold, yet they're sold widely during the winter season. Have the sales clerk put a protective wrapper around the plant to guard against cold on the trip home. Chilly temperatures can make the leaves drop. Remove the wrapper once you get home, though. It will trap the ethylene gas the plant naturally releases. Ethylene buildup can lead to leaf drop and curling.

Train Christmas cactus to bloom on cue. Trick your Christmas cactus into blooming during the holiday season. These plants need plenty of darkness to trigger their blooms — about 12 hours a night for six to eight weeks. Start covering the plant with a black plastic garbage bag each evening, beginning in late October or early November. If you normally get up at 8 a.m., cover the plant at 8 p.m. Then remove the bag each morning. Tie it closed around the bottom of the pot, if needed, to keep out the slightest sliver of light. While you're at it, move the plant to a cooler location, between 55 and 70 degrees. Once you see buds begin to color, you can stop covering the plant and start enjoying the blooms.

Prompt a reluctant bromeliad to bloom. Put it in a clear, plastic bag with an unwaxed apple. Apples naturally release ethylene gas as they ripen. This triggers bromeliads to set blooms. Leave the two together for four days, then take them out of the bag. You should see flowers in as little as six weeks, although some species can take several months.

Turn unusual plants into eye-catching art. Tillandsia, or air plants, can grow almost anywhere, except in soil. Get creative with where you mount them.

- Sit one inside a conch shell.

- Mount several along a piece of driftwood.

- Glue a variety of air plants to a piece of lattice, and hang it on the wall like living artwork.

Soak the driftwood in fresh water for a few weeks to dilute the ocean salt trapped in it. Otherwise, the air plants may not thrive. If you put them in something that catches water, like a seashell, be sure to dump out the excess after watering them. Air plants can't stand wet feet.

Recycle glass light shades into interesting planters for exotic-looking air plants

Slip a sturdy piece of rope, something natural-looking like hemp, through the hole in the shade's top. Pull it through and knot the end.	Glue an air plant to the knot with waterproof glue, such as E6000.	Choose plants that are wide enough to plug the mouth of the light shade. If you only have small plants, tie a second knot in the rope, a few inches up, for the shade to hang from.

The secret to watering air plants. Air plants need watering, just like normal plants. They live in the air, but they don't feed off of it. Water at least twice a week by soaking the entire plant — leaves and all — in a bucket or sink filled with water. You can tell when it's thirsty by touching its leaves. Thirsty tillandsia leaves will feel soft, while happily watered leaves will feel stiff.

Have a care when mounting in air

You can mount an air plant to an object with almost anything — including floral wire, waterproof glue, and even Velcro. Don't try mounting them with copper wire, super glue, or a hot glue gun, though. These could damage the plant.

Easy, self-watering secret for houseplants. It doesn't get much easier than terrariums. They're self-watering, so they can go for long periods of time without additional water. Some can survive for years without it. And creating one is easy. You can leave plants in separate pots or plant them together in soil. Pots let you easily replace struggling specimens, but if you prefer planting them together, here's the way to do it.

- Put down a layer of small pea gravel first.

- Add 2 to 3 inches of soil.

- Tuck in your plants.

- Top the soil off with moss and rocks.

- Replace the glass cover and let them grow.

Creative containers make great terrariums. Turn old light fixtures, vases, and kitchen items into terrariums. All you need is something with a clear glass cover to let in light. Consider these creative containers.

- cake plate with glass lid
- glass apothecary jar
- old-fashioned rose bowl
- upside-down clear vase
- outdoor lantern or porch light
- bell jar
- pocket watch dome
- fish bowl
- indoor wall sconce

Set colorful saucers atop open-ended glass containers to transform them into closed terrariums. Saucers and shallow bowls also make great bottoms for holding gravel, soil, and plants under glass covers.

Strategies to beat ficus leaf drop. Buy your ficus young to give it the best chance at survival. These trees don't like changes in location, light, or humidity. Young plants, however, will ride out the move from greenhouse to your house better than older specimens. And since they cost less, you'll have less money on the line if they die. Bring it home in late spring or early summer to minimize shock.

5 foolproof tips for growing aloe vera. You can grow aloe vera, even if your thumb is less than green. It's one of the easiest plants to grow and among the hardest to kill.

- Set it in the sunniest window in the house.

- Put it in a shallow pot, not a deep one, to accommodate it's shallow, spreading roots.

- Pot it up in a potting soil labeled for cactus use.

- Feed it with a diluted fertilizer for flowering plants in spring, along the lines of a 10-40-10.

- Soak the soil when watering in summer, but let it dry out between drinks.

HALE & HEARTY PLANT PICKS FOR OUTDOOR LIVING

Easy recipe for mossy pots. Give your garden an old-world feel with moss-covered pots. Terra cotta, concrete, and stone planters will develop a mossy surface naturally, but that can take years. Here's how to speed up the process.

- Harvest some moss from your yard, chop it up, and let dry for a day or two.

- Combine the dried, chopped moss with two cups of yogurt or buttermilk.

- Paint the mix all over the outside and rim of your pot with an old paintbrush.

- Wrap the pot in a plastic bag to give the moss plenty of moisture.

- Leave in a cool, shady location for about two weeks, or until you see mold and moss starting to grow.

Take the pot out of the bag once the moss gets growing, but put a plant in the pot when you do. Watering the plant will give moss the moisture it needs to thrive.

Add interest to old birdbaths. Turn that birdbath you keep forgetting to fill into a pretty planter.

- First, make sure its base can support the added weight of soil.

- Since most basins are shallow, you'll need to mound the soil instead of leveling it off for planting.

- Pick plants with fairly shallow roots.

- If your area tends to get plenty of rain, then choose flowers that don't mind occasional wet feet, since bird-baths don't have drainage holes.

Well-placed rock keeps containers upright. Put a brick or heavy rock in the bottom of tall, decorative planters to keep them from blowing over. You'll need to pot the plant in a separate plastic container, then set it atop the rock. It's not a good idea to put rocks in the bottom of the soil itself. They keep the soil from draining properly.

Lighten up large pots

Fill your big planters part way with leftover Styrofoam or empty plastic containers, like water bottles. Most flowers only need 12 to 18 inches of soil. Don't try this trick with potted trees or shrubs, though. Unlike annuals and shallow-rooted perennials, they need as much soil — and growing room — as you can give them.

Pain-free way to move heavy planters. Don't try to move heavy potted plants by lifting them. Slide a dolly under the planter, then tie the container to the dolly with sturdy straps from the local hardware store. Don't have a dolly? No problem. Slip a piece of heavy-duty tarp under the planter, and pull the tarp, pot and all, to its new location.

Easy way to empty standing water. Over watering big containers can be a big problem. You can't let water sit in the drainage saucer. But the plants are too heavy to move and drain. Don't panic. Just reach for the turkey baster. Use it to suck standing water out of the saucer.

Low-cost alternative to clay. Love terra-cotta pots but not the price tag? Consider clay chimney flue liners, instead. Visit a local masonry yard. You'll find flue liners in all sizes, perfect for arranging beautiful outdoor displays.

Stop thieves from stealing pots. This trick is so simple you'll wonder why you didn't think of it sooner.

- Padlock a length of chain to something fixed and sturdy, like a mailbox or porch post.

- Run the chain under your container. Pull links up through the drainage hole of the pot.

- Insert a long nail sideways through the top link, so it won't slip out through the hole. Pull the chain back through so the nail rests on the bottom.

Pot up your plants as usual. This nail-and-chain combo will anchor each container, so no one can carry them off.

Bring woodsy beauty to plain pots. Find a use for all those overgrown vines in your yard. After you cut back grapevines or English ivy, wind them around plain plastic pots, buckets, or tubs. Use these dressed-up containers for outdoor plants. The vines will hide the plastic under a rustic charm.

Protect your deck with pretty feet. Planters that sit directly on a wood deck can foster wood rot and mildew stains. Solve this problem by putting pot feet on your planters. Don't waste money buying them at the store, though. Use items you already have or can get on the cheap.

- Glue large marbles to the underside of containers with waterproof glue.

- Cut wine bottle corks in half and glue to the underside of pots.

- Set smaller pots on kitchen trivets.

- Remove the burners from a defunct gas stove, and use as potted-plant trivets.

- Set containers on water-smoothed river rocks painted to resemble animal feet.

Make a small deck look larger. Arrange container plants to make your patio, porch, or deck larger than it really is. Place them in diagonal corners, and arrange each group in an L-shape. This will lead the eye across the sitting area and seem to stretch the space.

Clever trick to cover walls. Hide ugly walls or simply dress up a small deck with espaliered container plants. You can prune any slow-growing tree or shrub into an espaliered shape as long as it's hardy enough to survive outside in your climate. Just be sure to pick a pot big enough to give roots plenty of room to grow. Large containers also hold more soil, which insulates roots against the cold. Figure on a pot that holds at least 8 cubic feet of soil.

Train your own lollipop-topped topiary. You can train almost any tall plant into a lollipop-shaped standard. This style features a tall plant with a bare stem and round, bushy top.

- Start with a plant in a 6-inch pot. If it has more than one stem, pick the straightest, strongest one and prune off the rest.

- Prune away all of the side shoots on the main stem, up to where you want the foliage to start.

- Slide a stake that's as tall as you want the plant to be into the soil beside it.

- Tie the stem to the stake loosely with strips of fabric.

- Pinch off new leaf buds once the plant reaches the same height as the stake. This encourages the top to fill out.

- Trim the bushy foliage at the top into a round, lollipop shape.

- Prune off suckers as soon as you see them growing on the main stem.

Hang plants in shiny hubcaps. Turn old hubcaps into eye-catching outdoor planters. Drill holes around the rim for hanging, and a few more in the bottom for drainage. Run a piece of sturdy wire or chain through the rim holes, and hang from a hook on your porch. Then pot it up the way you would any other hanging basket. You can even spray paint the hubcap to match your home's exterior.

Quick care tips for metal containers. Keep your metal planters shining with some occasional love. Clean them with window cleaner and a soft cloth. If you have hard water, spills down the side can leave mineral deposits that mar the surface. Simply buff these out with another soft cloth. Wax the metal every once in a while with car wax to help prolong its shine.

Bring flair to everyday baskets. Skip the sphagnum moss and coco liner in hanging plants. Line wire planters with large sturdy leaves, instead. Prune the leaves off a large caladium or other variegated foliage plant. Lay them along the inside of the basket, with the colorful side facing outward. Layer the leaves on top of each other, along the basket's bottom and sides, until the lining feels sturdy enough to contain the soil.

Garage-sale find makes perfect hanging planter. Turn an old wire egg basket into a clever hanging planter. Line the inside with sphagnum moss, and fill with potting soil. Choose a trailing, flowering vine to creep over the edges and soften the wire. Keep in mind, planters made from wire and moss tend to dry out fast. Take steps to drought-proof your new creation with the tips in *Battle wilt in hanging baskets* in the chapter *Potting like a pro.*

Save money, repot container combos. You spent hours creating beautiful plant combinations in hanging basket and outdoor urns. It seems a shame to toss those plants at the start of winter. So don't. They may do well indoors in their current containers, but taking them apart is easy. Keep a supply of small, plastic pots on hand. Fill with potting mix, gently separate the roots of each plant, and pot them up in individual containers. Next spring, rearrange in their outdoor planters. You'll save money by reusing the plants year after year.

Tuber planting tricks for fuller caladium

The way you plant a caladium tuber determines whether you get a lush-looking plant with many small leaves or a taller plant with a few large leaves. Try these expert tricks for a fuller, more compact caladium.

- Plant the tuber upside down. You'll get more sprouts, and they won't grow as tall. They will take a little longer to grow, however.

- Cut a large tuber into four pieces. Let the cuts heal and dry for a few days. Then put the pieces back together and plant as usual.

- Pinch off the main bud, or eye, on the tuber. This forces the tuber to put its energy into making more but smaller buds.

Bring in plants, but not the pests. Dunk plants — pot and all — in a tub or large bucket of water before bringing them back inside at the end of the season. Place them in the tub, and fill it with water until it just covers the top of the soil. All the creepy crawlers will quickly drown. Replace the mulch or moss that topped the soil. You'll sleep better knowing no critters are hitching a ride inside.

Prep plants before bringing inside

Many container plants need to come indoors for winter. The transition can be tough, though. Make it easier on plants by moving them to a shady portion of the yard for a few weeks. This gets them ready for the darker indoors. Once inside, prune them a little, and place them in front of the sunniest window in the house. Water them less in winter but enough to keep them from totally drying out.

Overturn pots to prevent winter cracking. Large, heavy pots are a pain to move indoors in winter. So don't. Dump out the soil, then tip containers upside down and leave them outside. Emptying the soil will keep it from cracking the pot as it freezes and expands.

Simplest way to overwinter plants. Try storing plants in your garage during winter. They'll get shelter from the worst of the cold and wind, but feel enough chill to keep them dormant. Don't have a garage? Any room that stays between 32 and 50 degrees will work for most plants.

Prep plants for winter survival. Some plants are just too heavy to move inside for winter. Never fear. You may be able to keep them alive outside with a few simple preparations.

- Group container plants closely together against the protected side of a house or shed.

- Pile leaves around and on top of the containers for added insulation.

- Drape a tarp over them to trap heat on especially cold nights. Use a stake to prop up the tarp, so it doesn't touch the leaves or stems.

For more ideas on protecting outdoor plants from the cold, see the chapter *Zone defense: make climate & conditions work for you.*

Keep clematis alive in winter. Not all plants need to come inside for winter. Some hardy climbers, like clematis, can survive outdoors as long as you plant them in big pots. Soil helps insulate roots against the cold. The bigger the pot, the more soil it holds, and the warmer roots stay. For areas where the thermometer hits zero degrees in winter, plan on a container that holds at least 8 cubic feet of dirt. That means 2 feet tall, deep, and wide. Mulch the plant well for its winter rest.

Defeat the weather with solid pots

Some pots do better than others when left outside during winter. Clay, ceramic, and concrete all absorb moisture. That water expands when it freezes, then shrinks when it thaws. If that happens enough times, these containers can crack or even shatter.

Cheap, brittle plastics can freeze and crack, too. Fiberglass, resin, and high-quality plastics fare better in winter, but the weather will bleach them out over time. Your best bet is to buy wood and metal containers if you want your pots to survive the cold weather.

Bury perennials to beat the cold. Help potted perennials survive the winter outside by burying them — container and all — directly in the ground. Dig a hole a few inches deeper than the pot itself. Drop the container and plant in the hole, then fill in around it with mulch. Top dress the plant with more mulch to keep it warm. Come spring, simply dig it up, clean it off, and set it out.

WINDOWSILL WONDERS ANYONE CAN GROW

Secret to balanced window boxes. Buy window boxes that are either the same width as the window or slightly longer for a balanced look. If you also have shutters, then choose a box at least a total of 6 inches longer than the window is wide. Ideally, choose one long enough to extend to the middle of each shutter.

Stagger rows for lusher look. Resist putting plants in straight rows in window boxes. It's boring and won't fill out the container well. Plant in alternating rows, instead. Place a row of tall plants in the back. Then stagger midsize plants down the middle, between and slightly in front of the taller plants. Follow up with another staggered row of even shorter — preferably trailing — plants, nestled between and in front of the middle ones. This maximizes space and makes the planter look full and lush.

Smart planting adds privacy. Have your window box do double-duty as a privacy screen. Opt for tall plants with full foliage instead of the usual low-growing trailers. This trick isn't just for the bathroom window. Hang planters from deck and porch railings, and pot up the same way. You'll form a natural wall against nosy neighbors and get a beautiful, fragrant view to boot.

Quick-change tip for easy replanting. Make cleanup a cinch when the seasons change. Instead of planting directly in the window box leave plants in individual nursery pots, set inside the planter, and cover with moss. Then line the box with a plastic sleeve, and plant inside it.

Water less with this simple trick. Say goodbye to daily watering, and keep soil moist on the hottest days. Lay a baby diaper with the absorbent side up in the bottom of window boxes. You may need more than one diaper, depending on how long the box is. Then fill with soil and plant as usual. The diapers will absorb excess water and hold it for plants to use later.

Pick the right plants for light levels. Bear in mind how much sunlight each window receives when picking plants for your boxes. Windows that get between eight and 12 hours of direct light a day need plants that will tolerate full sun. For four to eight hours of light, pick partial-sun plants. For two to four hours of direct sun, choose shade-tolerant plants.

Save dirt from going down the drain. You probably know that putting a coffee filter in the bottom of a pot can stop the soil from washing out the drainage hole. But filters are too small for window boxes. So try newspaper instead. Line the box with two layers of black and white newsprint. The paper will eventually break down. Just change it out when you swap plants each season.

Don't forget to feed. Watering is all well and good, but remember to fertilize, too. Container plants rely solely on you for their nutrients, unlike plants in the ground. Give them a biweekly feeding in addition to their regular watering. They'll give you loads of blooms in return.

Easy DIY window boxes. Window planters aren't cheap. So make your own out of an old drywall mud pan. It has the same shape as a window box, although it may not be as long. Drill a few holes in the bottom for drainage, paint it a pleasing color, and plant as usual.

Amp up the "wow" factor. Set off flowers by painting the planters themselves. For wood, pick a durable exterior paint. For metal boxes, invest in a can of exterior spray paint. Decide in advance which flowers you plan to plant, then pick your paint colors to complement the flowers.

Dress up windows with salvaged shelves. Window boxes aren't the only way to display plants. Keep glass shelves from a bathroom makeover, or pick them up the next time you find them at a yard sale. Attach the shelves and their supports on the outside of windows. Then use them to hold small potted flowers. It's a unique way to liven up your home's exterior and perk up the view from indoors.

Free decor livens up winter windows. Make your Christmas tree keep on giving. Recycle the branches once the holidays are over into winter window-box decor. Prune off a few branches of healthy green needles, and lay the boughs in your planters. They will add a dash of color and festiveness to the barren winter landscape.

Be wary of metal

Skip solid metal window boxes in sunny locations. The metal transmits heat, which can burn plant roots in a window that gets lots of sun. Most metals also rust, and that in turn can stain your siding. Either choose one that won't rust, like aluminum, or keep the planter rust-free by cleaning and repainting it every few seasons.

TREES,
SHRUBS &
GROUND COVERS

PRETTY
PROBLEM SOLVERS

SURE-FIRE SUCCESS STRATEGIES FOR SHRUBS

How to pick healthy shrubs. Don't be shy about inspecting shrubs at the nursery before you buy them. After all, they're a major investment of money and time. Make sure the soil is damp, so you know the plant has been watered regularly. For container-grown shrubs, slide the plant out of its plastic tub. Check that the roots are white and fat rather than dried-out and shriveled. Look for injury to the main stem or trunk, too.

Solve landscape problems with the right shrub. The right hedge can make a better windbreak, privacy screen, and noise muffler than the tallest fence. They're more beautiful, too, and they don't need painting or sealing. To protect against the wind, choose a deciduous hedge. For privacy or to quiet noise from a busy street, turn to evergreens.

Think leaves when picking plants. Keep leaf size in mind when choosing hedges. Shrubs with small leaves look best up close.

If you will mostly see them from afar, pick plants with large leaves or a striking form.

Best plants to protect your home. Want thieves to steer clear of your property? Burglar-proof your home with beautiful but unwelcoming plants. Think thorns, dense branches, and razor-edged leaves. These plants, in particular, will make thieves think twice about breaking into your home.

- berberis, with some of the sharpest spines around

- acanthus, with its spiny flower heads

- pyracantha, perfect under windows

- climbing roses, ideal for training up drainpipes and walls that thieves might try to climb

- pampas grass, whose knifelike leaves make it perfect for dark corners where intruders might try to hide

Pick the ideal time to plant

Why wait until spring to buy your bushes? Pre-order shrubs through a nursery or mail-order company and specify a delivery date. Early fall works well for most evergreen and deciduous plants. Be sure you get them into the ground at least one month before temperatures drop below 40 degrees. If you live in a cold, windy area, plant evergreens in spring.

Gauge winter sun when choosing location. You may not think of winter sun as harsh, but it can burn evergreens just as easily as the winter wind can. When planting your shrubs, take into account where the sun will shine in winter, especially if you tend to get lots of snow. Here are a few more things to keep in mind.

- Snow reflects even more light onto tender plants.

- Deciduous trees that have dropped their leaves won't offer any shade for surrounding shrubs.

- Plants on the south side of a home generally get the most sun in winter.

Consider planting evergreen shrubs on the north side of your house, shed, or other structure, so long as they will get enough sunlight in summer.

Peak time of day to plant. Do your planting in the early evening, once the hottest part of the day has passed. It will be easier on you, and the young plant will have a night to get settled before enduring the scorching heat of the sun.

Quick check for hole depth. Get your planting hole the right depth without guessing. The hole for container-grown shrubs should be the same depth as the pot they came in. Dig your hole, set the root ball inside, and lay a yard stick across the top. The shrub's soil should be at the same height as the surrounding ground.

Build a cone for bare-root plants. Bare-root trees and shrubs need to be planted differently from container-grown or balled-and-burlapped plants.

- Dig the hole, but leave a mound of dirt in the center, shaped like a cone.

- Set the bare-root plant on the cone, and spread its roots out around it down the sides of the cone.

- Check the plant's height with a stick or ruler. The crown should sit about 2 inches above the surrounding ground.

- Add more dirt to the cone as needed to raise the plant higher.

- Fill the hole halfway with dirt, packing it down to eliminate air pockets.

- Fill the rest of the hole with water, let it soak in, then finish backfilling.

Protect new plants from harsh winds. Hedges make great windbreaks, but getting young shrubs established in a windy spot can pose a challenge. Give them a strong start. Stake a length of fabric mesh down both sides of a line of plants. Double the layers for even more protection. To guard individual plants, stake mesh in a circle around each one. Leave the netting in place until your shrubs get established, about three to five years after planting.

> ## *Space plants differently in sun and shade*
> Your hedge may end up spanning both sunny and shady areas. Plan for this by spacing plants in the shady areas closer together than those along the sunny stretch. Shaded shrubs won't fill in as much as sun-drenched ones. Plant them closer together, and no one will notice the difference.

Box up shrubs on cold nights. Baby shrubs can have a tough time surviving their first winter. Cover them on cold nights with cardboard boxes. Place the box over the plant with the flaps folded out. Then set rocks on the flaps to keep the box from blowing off. For even more insulation, mound straw or leaves over the plants, then cover with the box. Just remember to remove the box during the day.

Hedge your bets against shrub death. Buy a few extra plants when putting in a hedge. Plant the extras elsewhere in your garden until the new hedge gets established. You'll be able to replace any plants that don't make it with a same-size shrub from your extra stock.

Train the stems of young woody shrubs. Encourage young stems to grow farther apart if they rise from the ground too close together. Place a small block of wood at the base of the stems to force them apart. This will keep them from touching and give woody shrubs a graceful appearance. Remove the wood once stems are growing in the directions you want.

2 steps to better blooms. Take two simple steps, and you'll have the healthiest, most beautiful flowering shrubs in the neighborhood.

- Prune each shrub based on when it blooms. For instance, prune spring-flowering shrubs as soon as the blooms fade. Prune summer- and fall-flowering shrubs in early spring.

- Top-dress shrubs with 1 to 2 inches of compost every three years to naturally replenish nutrients in the soil. Southern gardeners may need to add compost more often.

Keep variegated leaves from going green. Keep your eyes open for signs that a variegated shrub is reverting to type. Prune out any solid green foliage as soon as you see it. Left to grow, it will out-compete the variegated leaves for light and could eventually take over the entire plant.

Nip suckers on grafted shrubs. Species grown by grafting onto a different rootstock, like many hollies, rhododendrons, camellias, and lilacs, can sprout suckers below the graft. The new growth will weaken the plant. Find the place where the sucker starts — probably below ground. Dig down a little, if necessary, and tear the sucker off. Don't bother cutting it off above ground. You'll just prompt the plant to sprout more suckers.

Simple trick for lush, full foliage. Force evergreen shrubs to bush out. Pinch off the buds on the ends of new branches as they appear. The plant will then put more energy into growing side buds on those same branches. The result will be a fuller-looking plant with lush, thick foliage. Just be careful not to mistake a flower bud for an end bud when you're pinching. For deciduous shrubs, cut new shoots to half their length during growing season. They'll react by sending out more side shoots.

Grow new shrub from old branch. Turn a landscaping disaster into a fortunate mistake. When you accidentally tear a branch off a beloved shrub, don't panic. Root it, instead. Shrub branches root best if they came off with a tiny piece of the main stem, known as a heel. Trim the heel, if necessary, and remove the lower leaves. Dip the end in rooting hormone and plant in a sterile sand-peat moss mix. Keep the plant moist by setting the pot in a plastic grocery bag.

Best shapes for handling heavy snow. Where you live may determine the shape of your hedge. Areas that get a lot of snow need shrubs that can shake it off. Give short shrubs and hedges a rounded top, like an upside-down bowl. For tall ones, try a popsicle shape, with a tall, narrow body and a rounded top. One rule holds true no matter where you live — always make the bottom wider than the top. Otherwise, the upper branches will shade the bottom ones and lead to leggy growth.

Final date for pruning hedges

Get all your pruning done well before winter. Find out when first frost usually falls in your area, and stop pruning at least six weeks before that. The tender new shoots that sprout after pruning need to harden off before winter hits.

3-stage plan for hard-pruning shrubs. A trim isn't enough when old shrubs get out of hand. You need to renovate them. Some shrubs can take tough love. For instance, you can cut a red-twig dogwood *(Cornus alba)* down to the ground all at once without harming it. Most need a staggered approach. Adopt this three-year pruning plan for overgrown deciduous shrubs.

- Prune one-third of the branches the first year, focusing on the oldest, sickest, and ugliest ones.

- Remove another third the second year, along with any new growth that looks weak.

- Take off the last third during the third year and trim up new growth to keep the bush balanced.

Cut branches all the way back to the ground or central trunk. And try to take off branches on all sides of the shrub, so it doesn't look lopsided.

Game plan for shaping overgrown evergreens. You can renovate broad-leaved, evergreen shrubs in much the same way. Do the work over the course of two or three years. Most evergreens can't handle losing all their leaves at once.

- Remove the oldest branches along with the sick ones the first year. Cut the remaining branches to half their size.

- Prune half the original branches during the second year, cutting them all the way back. Thin out new growth.

- Cut back the other half during the third year.

Give golden shrubs more light. Golden-leaved shrubs sometimes turn green if they don't get enough light. So instead of a showy specimen in your yard, you end up with just another green bush. Don't panic. Move it to a sunny spot, or prune away some of the foliage that keeps them in the shade, and the yellow color should return. Be sure to plant new golden-leaved shrubs where they will get enough light.

Beat iron deficiency with tea. Acid-loving shrubs grown in alkaline soil can end up low in iron. Watch for yellowing leaves on rhododendrons, azaleas, and blueberries. At the first sign, give them a sip of tea. Steep used tea bags and pour the cooled liquid around the base of these plants for an instant boost.

Smart way to prep for winter. Just because shrubs stop growing in cold weather doesn't mean you can stop watering. Winter puts a lot of stress on plants, and not just because of the cold.

- When the ground freezes, shrubs can't draw water up through their roots.

- The combination of icy winds and strong afternoon sun further dries out your plants.

Give them a fighting chance. Water both deciduous and evergreen shrubs thoroughly in the fall, before the ground freezes. Shrubs will absorb as much moisture as they can hold, giving watering as temperatures get closer to freezing.

The right time to winter-proof plants

Don't winterize plants too early. Wait until after the cold has come to stay. Deciduous shrubs and trees need to be fully dormant before you tuck them in for winter. Insulating actively growing plants can smother them and set the stage for fungal infections.

Foil wrap foils hungry animals. Prevent nibbling animals from girdling your shrubs. These hungry critters will eat almost anything in winter — including the bark on bushes and trees. Unfortunately, they can kill plants by eating a strip of bark all the way around the trunk. Clear weeds and ground cover from around the trunk, so the animals don't have a hiding place. Next, wrap the trunk with aluminum foil or layers of burlap cloth. Remember to remove the wrap come spring.

TRIED-AND-TRUE TREE TACTICS

Ingenious way to increase your home's value. Sure, flowers are pretty, but planting shrubs and trees really pumps up the value of your home. The U.S. Forest Service says that trees raise property values between 10 and 15 percent. And the Arbor Day Foundation says one mature tree can account for $10,000 in resale value for a typical home. In fact, prospective buyers in one study were willing to pay 15 percent more for a house with just two young red oaks. The simple message — plant more trees, and watch them and your home value grow.

Flowering trees for next to nothing. Every year cities around the nation give away free flowering trees to plant in your yard, often as part of Arbor Day celebrations. Check with your local Parks and Recreation department or nearby botanical garden to see if they're participating. Even if they aren't, you can still take advantage of a great deal. Join the Arbor Day Foundation for $10 and get 10 trees free. Choose from flowering trees, Eastern red cedars, oaks, redbuds, or other trees suited to your hardiness zone.

Best flowering trees to shade your patio. These five trees are perfect for planting near your patio. Their gorgeous flowers and foliage are stunning year-round, and they won't grow too large.

- flowering dogwood *(Cornus florida)*

- sourwood *(Oxydendrum arboreum)*

- autumn-flowering Higan cherry *(Prunus subhirtella 'Autumnalis')*

- Eastern redbud *(Cercis canadensis)*

- Snowdrift crabapple *(Malus 'Snowdrift')*

What you should know about fast growers. It's tempting to plant fast-growing trees, like Leyland cypress or Bradford pears, to fill in a barren landscape. Yet, there are a few things to consider before you make a decision. For instance, they may grow quickly, but they tend to have more problems than other trees. Fast growers usually:

- have weaker, more brittle wood that splits easily during storms.

- live much shorter lives, because they mature more quickly.

- need more growing space, and outgrow their space fairly quickly.

The quick shade or privacy these trees give may come at a higher cost in money and maintenance.

Pick different species to guard against disease. Avoid planting a line of all one type of tree or shrub. If disease strikes, it could wipe out your entire privacy hedge or windbreak. The same goes for trees in beds and borders. Vary the species as a buffer against insects and disease.

Bring more birds to your feeder. Give birds plenty of safe cover, and they will flock to your feeder. Plant trees around the feeder that do double duty as hiding place and food source, like serviceberries, redbuds, dogwoods, and flowering crabapples. Use trees that birds naturally love, and you'll draw more feathered friends to your buffet.

Trees you should plant in spring. You should plant most trees in fall, after they go dormant. This gives the roots time to get established before summer heat sets in. These trees, however, have roots that grow so slowly they need a spring start.

- red maple, birch, and hawthorn

- flowering dogwood and magnolia

- poplar, tulip poplar, and tulip tree

- many oaks, including red, white, bur, willow, and English

- willows, black gum, and goldenraintree

- silver linden and Japanese zelkova

The right time to plant containerized trees

Containerized and balled-and-burlapped trees can go in the ground at almost any time, as long as you can work the soil. That's because they come packed in their own dirt.

When to plant fruit trees. Put balled-and-burlapped and container-grown fruit trees in the ground in early fall, unless you live in USDA Plant Hardiness Zone 5 or colder. Then, spring is best.

Save money and labor with smaller saplings. You think you're getting a head start on landscaping by planting more mature trees. Think again. You'll save money and have healthier trees by planting young specimens.

- Older trees are more likely to suffer from shock and even die after transplanting.

- Young trees adapt better to new locations and grow faster.

Plus, young, small trees are much easier to plant. And while older trees start out larger and more majestic, in three to five years a young sapling will have caught up in size.

Right and wrong way to carry saplings. Always lift and carry balled-and-burlapped trees from the bottom of the root ball, not by the trunk. Holding it by the trunk will put too much stress on the inside of the tree. Hold the plant with your hands underneath the root ball. Or, if it's too heavy for one person to carry, set it on a tarp. Have someone help you lift the tarp, tree and all.

Little-known planting danger. Don't plant your trees too deep. Plant balled-and-burlapped and containerized trees at the same depth as they were in the container. Look for a ring of dirt around the trunk to tell you the soil level. Dig a hole that's any deeper, and the roots may grow upward instead of down into the earth. By growing up, they run the risk of wrapping around the trunk, slowly strangling the tree to death.

Wrong way to amend your soil. It's one of the biggest mistakes you can make — amending the soil in the hole where you plan to plant a tree. Experts once recommended it. Now they know it's a bad idea. Amend only the hole, and the roots of woody plants like trees may not grow beyond it. Instead, they'll act like container plants, becoming root bound over time. If you need to enrich poor soil, don't just amend the hole. Amend the entire bed to encourage the roots to spread out.

The latest scoop on burlap. Think twice before leaving the root ball wrapped in burlap. Most "burlap" nowadays is either treated to make it rot resistant or is actually made of plastic. Either way, it won't dissolve and set the roots free to grow. Materials that keep the roots bound up like this can eventually kill the tree. Play it safe. Cut away the wrapping once you settle the sapling into its hole.

When it's OK to stake a tree

Not every sapling needs staking, but some trees do benefit, including those:

- in windy locations.
- with bent trunks.
- with a wide canopy that could whip around in the wind.
- with poorly developed roots.

Only stake these trees for the first year they are in the ground. Tie them with soft, flexible tree tape or straps that allow the trunk to sway in the breeze. The movement helps strengthen the root system, giving you a sturdier plant.

Hold off hard-pruning new trees. Experts used to suggest pruning away one-third of the branches on a newly planted tree. Not anymore. Newer research shows it doesn't help. In fact, heavy pruning like this can actually hurt the new arrival. Fewer branches mean fewer leaves, so the tree can't make as much food from sunlight. The new plant needs as much food as it can get to build a healthy root system in its new home. So when planting a sapling, only cut off broken, pest-infested, or crossing branches.

Wait to prune after planting. Hold off pruning low-hanging branches and end buds when you first plant a tree. The low branches help the trunk build strength, while the end buds pump out hormones that boost root growth and leafing. Wait until the sapling gets established before removing these parts.

#1 mulching no-no. Don't mulch right up against the trunk of trees. It creates a dark, moist environment perfect for boring bugs and the fungi behind heart rot. It can also cause tree roots to grow up and around the trunk, choking the tree to death. Instead, create a donut-hole shape of mulch around tree trunks, with the trunk in the center of the hole.

Shape branches to grow up or out. Train a deciduous tree into the shape you want. Start by finding the buds emerging on branches.

Inward-facing bud

- To prompt the tree to grow tall and narrow, prune branches above an inward-facing bud.

- To encourage a wide, spreading shape, prune branches above an outward-facing bud.

Simple trick trains limbs to weep. Use old nylon stockings to train weeping trees. Drop a rock into the foot of a stocking. Then tie the other end around the limb you want to droop, or weep. The rock's weight will help train the

Outward-facing bud

limb downward. The nylon is soft and stretchy enough not to harm the bark.

The latest news on dressing wounds. Skip the wound dressing and pruning paint for most trees. Research has shown that applying it to cuts only makes you feel better, not the tree. It won't cure an existing infection or stop decay. It may even slow the healing process and keep the wound from closing. The only time you should use wound dressing — when treating a pruning cut or other injury on an elm or oak. Applying pruning paint during the elm's growing season or to the oak in spring can help protect these species from Dutch elm disease and oak wilt.

Tell these pros to hit the road. Just say "no" to so-called tree professionals who tell you to top a tree or who climb one while wearing spikes. Neither practice is good for your plant.

Expert advice for pruning crape myrtles

Some people think these trees won't bloom without a hard-pruning every year. Not true. In fact, cutting them back severely actually invites pests and disease. You can prune them, but you don't have to. They will thrive without it. If you want to trim them, simply prune them for health like any other tree, removing dead limbs, crossing branches, and low-growing suckers.

Heed the warning signs of heart rot. This fungal infection routinely topples trees. It all starts when a tree gets injured, whether by a lawnmower, sloppy pruning, storm, or animal. That wound opens the door for fungi to enter. They weaken the tree by chowing down on the wood fiber inside. Any tree that has mushrooms, shelf fungi, or other fungi growing on it has heart rot. Keep an eye out for these other signs.

- a cavity on the trunk, usually near the ground
- lots of woodpecker holes
- carpenter ant infestation

You don't need to take down these trees right away. They can live for years more. But you should remove those that have both fungi and an open wound or crack, before they fall on people or property. If you aren't sure how sick your tree is, call your city's forester or a certified arborist. They can diagnose the damage and tell you how much danger it poses.

Easy way to remove an unsightly tree stump. Skip paying to have your stumps ground out. Remove them yourself with minimal work. Stumps will rot naturally, though it takes time. Here's how to speed up the process.

- Drill lots of narrow holes in the stump.
- Fill the holes with a high-nitrogen fertilizer.
- Keep the stump moist by watering often.

The nitrogen feeds fungi that decompose wood naturally. They will break down its structure so you can easily knock out the rotten stump.

Creative ways to hide stumps. Dress up stumps while you wait for them to decompose. Make them part of your landscape. Build a flower bed around one, or create a compost pile on top. Both will help the stump decay faster. You can even turn stumps into flower pots. Just hollow them out and fill with potting soil.

Stop sap from dripping on your car

Tired of tree sap on your car every spring? It's probably not tree sap at all, but "honeydew" from aphids and scale insects. These bugs feed on leaves and secrete a sticky, sap-like substance as they eat. Get out your garden hose and get ready. Instead of using it to spray your car, aim a strong stream of water directly at the leaves of the tree you park under. The blast will knock these pests out of the tree for good. Once down, they can't climb back up.

Scrub off sap with shortening. Get pine pitch off your hands with Crisco. Rub it gently on the sticky spots, then wash well with soap and water.

Guard trunk against deer rubbing. Deer do more than eat your flowers. They can kill trees, too, by rubbing their antlers against the trunk in late summer and fall. Protect yours by wrapping the trunk in a black plastic drain pipe, the kind attached to the bottom of a downspout. Cut it to the length needed, then cut a slit down the middle. Slip the pipe into place around the trunk. An added bonus — it'll deter rabbits, voles, and other hungry critters from stripping the bark in winter.

Paint protects from winter sunscald. During winter days, unprotected tree trunks heat up in the sunshine. Then, when temperatures drop at night, the cells inside the trunk can burst. These temperature fluctuations can seriously damage young trees, especially those with thin bark like maple, cherry, and apple. Bark on the southwest side of a tree is most at risk. Protect against sunscald with white paint. Mix one part white latex paint with one part water and paint on the trunks. The white paint will reflect winter sunlight without harming the tree.

Special care for picky hardwoods. Be careful when landscaping around old trees. Many native hardwoods don't like to be disturbed. Paper birches, for instance, may die if you suddenly clear out the ground cover or mow the tall grass beneath them. California live oaks are similarly fussy. Don't regrade the ground nearby or add any soil on top of their roots.

Why you should plant grass under Bartletts. Grow grass under Bartlett pears if they are prone to fireblight. Excess nitrogen increases their risk of catching this disease. Grass helps use up nitrogen, so twigs become less succulent and less likely to catch this bacterial infection.

Surprising way to boost growth. Some grasses, including tall fescue, secrete a chemical that stunts the growth of surrounding plants and trees. If your young trees seem to be growing slowly, try mulching the area around them. Spread mulch over the grass about 6 feet out from the trunk. Missouri researchers found that stunted walnut trees grew twice as fast once mulch killed the surrounding fescue.

GROUND COVERS
CARE-FREE YARD SOLUTION

Unify your landscape. Ground covers are not just for slopes and shady areas. They can bring a whole landscape together. Plant the same type in all of your beds to unify seemingly unrelated plants, trees, and parts of your yard. Or use it as a living mulch in one main bed. A good, healthy cover will keep down weeds, control erosion, provide much-needed food and habitat for wildlife, and soften the transition between the lawn and taller bed plants.

Cut mowing time dramatically. Turn hard-to-mow parts of your yard into lush, low-maintenance ground cover. Corners, tight spaces, steeply graded strips, and the areas under trees are ripe for conversion.

Great ground covers put the squeeze on weeds. Try a "sweet" solution for that problem spot in your yard — poor soil, too little sun, or too many weeds. Sweet woodruff is a hardy perennial ground cover that will love the location and choke out those weeds, to boot. It's not your only choice, however. Other dense-growing covers such as white dutch clover and sweet violet will also keep weeds at bay.

Fill bare spots with ease. These easy-to-grow ground covers thrive in shady areas where grass struggles to survive. They'll save you money and time, since they typically need less water and fertilizer than grass, and rarely require mowing.

- wintercreeper *(Euonymus fortunei)*
- creeping phlox *(Phlox stolonifera)*
- pearlwort *(Sagina subulata)*
- periwinkle *(Vinca minor)*
- Japanese spurge *(Pachysandra terminalis)*
- English ivy *(Hedera helix)*

Find the right cover for any situation. Keep the plants in a bed looking balanced by choosing low-growing ground covers for small beds and taller ones for large beds. For steep slopes, pick tall, vigorous ground covers with extensive root systems. These provide better erosion control. Be wary of ground covers advertised as fast-growing under all types of conditions. They may take over your landscape.

Expert tricks for planting on a slope. Creeping ground covers are great for erosion control. They cling to steep slopes where grass can't. Getting them established at such an angle can be a challenge. Try these tips for success.

- Clear out existing weeds and grass, then plant your ground cover plants.
- Pin each plant into the soil with metal landscape pins to keep them from washing loose in a heavy rain.
- Check plants one month later to see if the roots have taken hold. If so, remove the pins.

Pruning made simple. Give vigorous ground covers like ivy a quick pruning every few years. Simply mow over them with the blade set high, leaving the foliage 4 to 6 inches tall. Do this in early spring, after the last frost, to keep them going strong.

VIGOROUS VINES & CLIMBERS FOR QUICK COVER

Get more mileage out of a flowering landscape. Train flowering vines to grow through trees or shrubs that bloom in a different season. Train a late-blooming clematis up the main trunk of a spring-blooming rhododendron or even an evergreen cypress. Your trees or shrubs will appear to be flowering again come summer.

A dozen vines guaranteed to grow. Create an enchanting garden wall with climbers that anyone can plant. Keep in mind that vigorous vines can get out of hand. Curb their growth with regular prunings.

- climbing hydrangea
- clematis
- bittersweet
- kolomikta vine
- silver fleece flower
- hardy kiwi
- honeysuckle
- Boston ivy
- wintercreeper euonymus
- Virginia creeper (woodbine)
- trumpet vine
- wisteria

Even the best climbers benefit from having supports. But mounting a trellis or wires flat against a wall won't do much good. Hang all supports at least 2 inches from the wall. This leaves enough space for tendrils and man-made ties to wrap around the back for a better grip.

Free supply of plant ties. Save that old string mop, once its cleaning days are done. Cut the strings off one at a time to use as plant ties. They're soft but strong, with just the right amount of give. Use them to train your climbing vines up a trellis or other support.

Easy-to-make supports for wall climbers. Not all vines are built for climbing. Some lack tendrils that twine or suckers that stick. They need help going vertical, but setting supports in brick, stucco, and wood can be a lot of work. Simplify things with some silicone sealant and twist ties.

- Head to the hardware store for a tube of clear, 100-percent silicone caulk.

- Fish out the extra twist ties you've saved from packages of garbage bags.

- Dab a spot of caulk in each place you want your climbing vine to cling.

- Bend the twist tie in half, and stick the bottom into the caulk.

- Do this up the length of wall you want the climber to cover.

- Let the caulk dry, then begin tying your vines. Place a vine into each tie and twist it closed.

You can spray paint the ties green or black, so they blend in with the plant. When it's time to prune back the climber, simply untie the vines.

Old Velcro trains new vines. Keep your eyes open for Velcro straps. These often come wrapped around electrical cords and fresh produce. Now they have a new purpose — tying up vines, roses, and other climbers. Best of all, you can reuse them again and again.

Cut your cooling bills in summer. Shade trees take time to grow, so it could be years before they actually lower your cooling bills. Get relief in the meantime. Plant a fast-growing annual climber, like moonflower, morning glory, or scarlet runner bean, under south- and west-facing windows in spring. Give them a trellis or other structure to climb, and they'll block the intense summer rays that heat your home. Live in an apartment or condo? Plant them in window boxes, instead. Come autumn, cut them back or let them die back from the cold to let in warming winter light.

Help new climbers fill in faster. Perennial vines take time to fill out and fill in. Bulk them up by interplanting with annuals for almost-instant greenery. Mix in a few sweet pea, morning glory, or nasturtium climbers amongst your slower-growing woody perennials for the first few years.

Secret to curbing wild wisteria. Cutting back wisteria in winter will make the plant go wild again come spring. If you're battling a vigorous wisteria, that's exactly the opposite of what you want. Wait until summer. Pruning it then won't trigger the same rampant growth.

When to skip the fertilizer

Save your money. Don't bother fertilizing vigorous, fast-growing climbers like wisteria and trumpet vine. Feeding them once a year actually results in fewer blooms. They'll put the extra nutrients into growing stems rather than flowers.

Give climbing plants extra oomph. Fertilizer isn't just for leaves and roots. You can spray it on the wall, too, to give climbing vines a boost. Once you've planted your climbers, or after you've pruned them back, spray their wall support with a liquid foliar fertilizer. The plants will absorb it as they climb.

Safer alternative to English ivy. You know planting ivy is asking for trouble, but you just can't help yourself. Spare yourself at least some pain by planting Boston ivy instead of English ivy against your house and other structures. While the English version is an evergreen, its Boston cousin is not. Because it loses its leaves each winter, it won't trap ice and snow against your home.

Inspire clematis to thrive. A few stone pavers or a layer of mulch can help your clematis thrive. These vines like to have their heads in the sun but their roots kept cool. Satisfy both needs. Plant them where they will get at least six hours of sun each day, but cover the root area with one of these options.

- Lay wide, flat paving stones around the base of the vines.

- Put down 2 inches of mulch.

- Plant a ground cover with shallow, noninvasive roots to shade the ground.

Free forms for creative topiary. Put old holiday decorations to use in your yard. Once the lights go out on a wire form, whether a reindeer or cone-shaped Christmas tree, remove them and spray paint the form green so the wire won't show. Set it in your garden, and plant flowering vines around it. Train the vines along the form for a whimsical topiary.

Dress up mailbox with the ideal vine. Vines twining 'round your mailbox may look romantic, but the wrong ones can easily take over. Ensure your mailman can open the box by choosing dwarf varieties of your favorite climbers. Dwarf clematis and miniature roses are just the right size for a short support, like a mailbox post.

Stake sweet peas for better growth. Give sweet peas support early on in their life. Otherwise, they'll never really take off. Stake them once they reach about 4 inches long. Simple kabob skewers will do the job fine. If you decide to start them in a container, move them outside once nighttime temperatures stay above 40 degrees.

QUICK TIPS
FOR LUSCIOUS
LAWNS

LAWN CPR
SIMPLE FIXES TO
REVIVE & RESTORE

Single step guarantees great grass. The secret to a lush lawn with less work and less money? Get your soil tested before fertilizing, sodding, or seeding. A basic soil test will tell you exactly how much fertilizer to apply for the type of grass you want to grow. There's no guessing and no wasted time or money. Take a soil sample, and send it off to your cooperative extension office for analysis. You'll receive a detailed report in a few weeks with fertilizer recommendations and lawn-care advice. Learn how to get a good sample in the chapter *Secrets to building better soil*.

Feed your lawn evenly. Make sure you fertilize every inch of lawn without feeding it too much in one place. Fill your spreader and set it to spray at only half the rate recommended for your lawn. Apply half the fertilizer walking left to right. Do the whole yard, then apply the other half walking top to bottom.

Foolproof trick for hitting every spot. Never miss another spot while fertilizing with this ingenious trick. Mix a little flour with the fertilizer. Whether you broadcast it by hand or with a spreader, you'll always be able to see the ground you've already covered.

Glaring signs of nutrient shortage. You can spot a lawn that is low in nutrients even without a soil test. Just watch for these warning signs.

Nutrient deficiency	Symptoms
nitrogen	Sparse, yellow to yellow-green grass with stunted growth. Weeds — particularly clover — are taking over the turf.
iron	Grass grows well but is yellow to yellow-green.
phosphorus	Dull, blue-green grass. The blades progressively turn purple along the edges, then develop a reddish tinge.

When fertilizer won't fix yellow grass. Pests and diseases can also cause grass to turn yellow. The difference — you'll see more dead, brown blades with these culprits than you would from nitrogen deficiency. The damage will also be more localized and less widespread.

Telltale signs of too much fertilizer. It's easy to go overboard with fertilizer. These symptoms say you've overdone it.

* dark green streaks in the lawn that eventually turn brown

* irregular yellow spots bordered by dark green

Don't fret if you see these signs. Your lawn can still recover. Simply water the area thoroughly to dilute the fertilizer.

Keep leaves on the lawn for less fertilizing. Don't waste your time raking fall leaves. Leave them on the lawn, and chop them up with a mulching mower. Shredding them where they lay will help them decompose faster and return much-needed minerals to your turf. Do this routinely, and your grass will gradually need less fertilizer to thrive. Sometimes leaves lie too thickly on the ground even after mulching. You'll need to rake these areas to keep them from smothering the lawn.

No-guess guide for feeding your grass. Check this chart to find out how much nitrogen your lawn needs for the whole year. Notice the range for each grass. Where you fall in that range depends on where you live. For instance, if grass has a long growing season in your climate, then feed it at the higher end.

Grass type	Pounds per 1,000 sq ft
centipedegrass	1 to 3
bermudagrass	2 to 6
tall fescue	2 to 4
fine fescue	1 to 3
St. Augustinegrass	3 to 6
Kentucky bluegrass	3 to 6
zoysiagrass	2 to 4
buffalograss	0 to 2
bahiagrass	2 to 4

Guard against nitrogen burn. Never apply more than 1 pound of quick-release nitrogen fertilizer per 1,000 square feet of grass at a time. Put down more, and you are likely to burn the grass you're trying to grow. Instead of heaping it on all at once, feed the lawn in small doses, and do it often. Or choose a slow-release nitrogen fertilizer. You'll still need to avoid overfeeding, though. Don't apply more than 3 pounds of slow-release nitrogen per 1,000 square feet of turf at one time. Otherwise, you'll spend all year endlessly mowing.

Top turfs for the least amount of work. Get a low-maintenance grass, and say goodbye to expensive fertilizers, wasteful watering, and weekly mowing. These grasses thrive on neglect.

- Fine fescues grow great in places where the summer doesn't get too hot. They love dry, nutrient-poor soil and hate being fertilized. They don't need much water, either, although drought conditions are not ideal.

- Centipedegrass grows low, so it doesn't need much mowing. Fertilize only once a year, twice at most. It's a good grass for acidic, nutrient-poor soil.

- Buffalograss tops the list of tough turf. Once established, it needs very little water. You don't even have to mow it, although it looks better when you do. Don't plant it if you live in a hot, humid climate, though. It prefers dry, windy weather.

Simple schedule for fertilizing grass. Not all grass needs fertilizing at the same time of year. Some need it more often, and some need it less. Use this table to keep track of what to feed, when.

Feed	Around
bermuda, zoysia, St. Augustine grasses	Easter, Memorial Day, July 4, Labor Day
centipede, buffalograss	July 4, Labor Day
bluegrass, tall fescue	year round as they grow throughout the winter

The lawn you'll never mow again. Let your mower collect dust. Go low maintenance with a no-mow herbal lawn. Many low-growing plants are fragrant, not to mention flowering. Think violets, creeping thyme, mazus *(Mazus reptans)*, or pearlwort *(Sagina subulata)*. For front yards where you rarely walk, consider yarrow, oregano, white Dutch clover, and phlox.

Miracle medicine for tough turf problems. A single all-natural treatment can both aerate and dethatch your lawn while conditioning your soil. And you won't spend hours on these otherwise backbreaking tasks. Just apply a light top-dressing of crumbly, finished compost to the lawn.

- The microorganisms in compost help break down thatch.

- Organic matter in compost helps clay soil particles clump together. This aerates the soil, improves drainage, and makes the dirt easier to work.

- Compost acts as a natural fertilizer, putting nutrients back into the soil.

Because it improves both the nutrients and physical structure of the soil, compost is considered a top-notch soil conditioner. Make a spray-on treatment by steeping a sack full of finished compost in a large bucket of water. Cover for several days, then remove the "tea bag." Dilute the liquid until it looks like weak tea, and spray on your lawn at a rate of one quart per 1,000 square feet.

Spiked shoes no good for grass

You've probably been told to aerate your lawn by wearing spiked golf shoes. Maybe you've even tried it. If not, don't bother. This trick won't work. Golf spikes aren't nearly long enough to penetrate the thatch on your lawn, much less the soil.

Simple trick to drought-proof lawn. Top-dress your lawn twice a year with a light layer of compost. Put down half an inch in the spring and fall to improve drainage and prevent drought damage. Compost helps dirt hold more water, soaking it up like a sponge. This makes your grass more likely to survive dry stretches.

Fall leaves defeat spring dandelions. Mulching your lawn with maple leaves could help rid it of dandelions. Researchers discovered that turf mulched with maple leaves had fewer dandelions the following spring. Sugar maple leaves worked best. Count yourself lucky if you have one of these trees in your landscape. Rather than raking up these leaves in fall, simply mow them with a mulching blade, and leave on the lawn.

Rake without aches. Make a few simple changes in your raking routine to spare your back and joints.

- Stick with a standard-sized, 24-inch rake. The larger the rake, the harder you have to push down to pull leaves across grass.

- Leave space between your hands when gripping the handle. This gives you more leverage.

- Thread a length of rope through the grommets on a tarp. Rake leaves onto the tarp, then pull it to the curb.

ID bugs to beat infestation. Find out what's eating your lawn by chasing bugs to the surface. Try this test on part of the lawn where you suspect an infestation.

- Cut the top and bottom out of an old soup or coffee can.

- Push the can a couple of inches into the soil.

- Fill it with water several inches above ground level.

- Keep the water level up for the next four to five minutes.

Bugs will start floating to the surface, desperate to escape drowning. Simply collect them in a container for identification.

Flush pests with soap and water. Squirt one or two tablespoons of unscented liquid hand soap into one gallon of water. Pour it across 2 square feet of pest-infested lawn, and see what crawls to the surface. Chinch bugs, cutworms, and sod webworms are just a few critters that can be flushed out this way. In fact, soaking the lawn with this solution can help control chinch bugs in a small area.

Get to root of soil problems. The reason your grass won't grow may have nothing to do with nutrients, pests, or diseases. The soil itself could be to blame. Sink a sharp shovel in the dirt. Dig straight down several inches and look at the soil layers. If you're lucky, you'll see nothing but dark, loamy soil. Most of the time, however, you'll see 2 or 3 inches of loam atop a bed of sand, gravel, or clay.

- Sand or gravel means your lawn dries out fast and struggles to survive during droughts.

- A bed of clay means just the opposite, that your soil holds too much water, making plants prone to root-rot.

Build up the good soil on top gradually, adding a light layer of compost each year.

Secret to finding a no-grass zone

Grass doesn't do well in shady locations. Look for moss. If it thrives in a certain spot, then skip the grass and plant a shade-loving ground cover there instead.

DIY fix for bare areas. Lawns are like carpet, and you can repair them the same way. Cut a patch of grass from a hidden part of the yard to repair a very visible bald spot.

- Sink a sharp, square-bladed shovel all the way around a section of grass. Make sure the cuts go a few inches deep.

- Slide the shovel blade under the soil and lift out the grass, roots and all.

- Move the square immediately to its new home, and water regularly until the roots take hold.

Stop soil from washing away. Need a grass to control erosion? Bahiagrass is your best bet. It's not the prettiest turf, but its roots can dig down 8 feet deep in search of water. That gives it a great foothold.

Guard grass from snow and ice. Stake out your yard in winter to ensure healthy growth come spring. Mark the boundaries of the lawn with tall stakes to alert passing snowplows where the grass begins. You'll benefit, too, by having a visual reminder not to park on the frozen lawn. Plus, the person who shovels your drive will know not to pile the snow onto staked-out lawn areas. Use stakes that will stand taller than the snowdrifts around them, and spray paint the tops a bright color for visibility.

Homemade repellant for blood-sucking bugs. Keep ticks and chiggers from latching on to your skin. Just dust yourself with a combination of baby powder and powdered sulfur, also known as flowers of sulfur. Mix the two ingredients half and half in an empty baby powder bottle. Then dust the openings of your shoes, socks, and pants before heading out to work in the yard or walk through the woods. You can also dust the skin on your arms, legs, and waist. Sulfur can irritate the skin, though, so try it on a small area first.

Easy-to-make tick trap. Ticks like to hang out on the ends of tall grass and shrub branches, waiting for you to walk by. Trick them with an easy-to-make tick trap, and quickly clear your yard of these bugs. Staple one edge of a large piece of white flannel to a wooden stick. Drag it along the grass and the edge of wooded or overgrown areas to attract them. For vertical plants like shrubs, wrap the flannel around a broom, and brush it against the branches. Simply pick the ticks off the flannel and kill them.

Show ticks they aren't welcome. Mulch along the edge of woods, stone walls, and lawn with a layer of cedar chips. This wood naturally repels ticks. Tall grass attracts ticks, so mow the lawn regularly, and clear out overgrown areas. Keep shrubby plants pruned back along the wood's edge and along any trails on your property, so passersby don't brush against them.

SEEDING

THE FIRST STEP TO
A BEAUTIFUL LAWN

Best time to reseed. Reseed your lawn in fall for greener grass and to crowd out weeds. The ground is still warm, the air is cooler, and there are fewer weeds to compete against for food and water. As trees drop their leaves, more sunlight reaches the ground. Seedlings are also less likely to be struck by disease in the fall.

Pick the right mix for fewer weeds. Buy the right seed from the start, and you'll have fewer weeds in the long run. Seed mixes often contain ryegrass, because it grows fast for an almost instant lawn. Unfortunately, it isn't hardy, and it crowds out the slower-growing but longer-lived grasses in the mix. Once the ryegrass dies, the weeds will take over. Pick a seed mix that contains mostly slower-growing, sturdy grass like red fescue or bluegrass and only a small percentage of rye.

Top 3 signs of good grass seed. Make sure you aren't wasting your money on the next bag of grass seed. Look for these numbers on the label.

- The noxious weed percentage tells you how many weed seeds are mixed in with the grass seeds. Don't settle for any amount other than zero.

- The germination rate on a bag of good-quality seed should be at least 80 percent. That means for every 100 seeds you plant, 80 of them will sprout.

- The test date tells you how old a bag of seed is. The germination rate goes down as the seed gets older. Buy the bag with the most recent test date. Never buy one more than nine months old.

Foolproof way to spread seed. Load up your spreader, and set it to spray at half the recommended seeding rate. Walk the spreader from left to right, covering the whole yard. Then walk it top to bottom. You'll spread in two directions, ensuring even coverage and no bare spots.

When less is more

It's tempting to put down more seed than the bag recommends. After all, more seed means a thicker turf, right? Wrong. Too much seed actually gives you thin, spindly grass. The seeds end up too close together, competing for nutrients and water. As a result, most of the sprouts will die. Overseeding also attracts disease. Putting down too much fescue, for instance, can lead to pythium blight. Play it safe and stick with the suggested amount.

Simple trick for planting fescue. Fescue requires even more clever spreading. Figure out how many pounds of seed you need for your yard. Set your spreader to spray at one-third of that rate. Seed your yard by walking left to right and top to bottom. Then finish up with a third, diagonal pass over the whole yard.

Sow with sand for even coverage. Grass seeds come in different sizes, depending on the species. It's easy to overseed when using a spreader to sow a small-seed species. The tiny seeds fall out too quickly. Mix them with sand in the hopper to slow them down for better coverage.

Keep beds free from grass. Ready to reseed your lawn? Cover the shrubs, flowers beds, and patios with old sheets or plastic tarps before you begin. This will keep stray grass from sprouting where it isn't wanted.

Give grass good soil contact. Seeds need to touch the soil to have any shot at surviving. Here's how to press them into the dirt without smashing them.

- Drag the back side of a lawn rake over small, seeded areas.

- Rent a weighted roller for large areas. However, don't fill it with water. Leave it empty and roll over the lawn.

- Aerate before seeding. Then drag an old piece of carpet over the lawn to break up the cores of dirt and move seed down into the soil.

#1 danger for new seeds. Seeds can sit on dry dirt for a long time. But once they get wet, you have to keep watering them until they sprout leaves and roots. If they dry out after they've begun to germinate, they will die — and they won't come back. Use the fine mist setting on your garden hose nozzle. Once they germinate, you can switch to a sprinkler.

Secrets to reseeding small areas. Don't settle for bare spots in the lawn. Reseed small patches and help them thrive with a few quick tips.

- First, mow the surrounding grass short, as low as half an inch.

- Loosen the dirt so seedlings can sink their roots into it, and rake up any twigs or rocks.

- Sprinkle grass seed across the bald area.

- Top the seeds with a quarter-inch layer of peat moss to keep them from drying out.

- Water the patch three or four times a day for about two weeks or until the seedlings get a foothold.

- Mow once the new grass reaches 3 to 4 inches tall.

Save money on sod. A new lawn doesn't have to cost a fortune, although sodding the whole yard can. Get the grass you want at a fraction of the price by strip sodding, instead. Simply buy sod from your local supplier and cut the squares into smaller pieces. Lay the pieces six to 10 inches apart on bare soil. The grass will fill in the gaps as it spreads. The closer you plant them together, the faster they'll fill in. Keep in mind, this only works with spreading grasses. That includes zoysiagrass, St. Augustinegrass, and bermudagrass to name a few.

Don't fall for these claims

Don't get duped by advertisements for grass seed or plugs that seem too good to be true.

- Mail-order companies that promise hundreds of plugs for next to nothing. They jack up the price by tacking on hefty shipping charges. Do the math, and you'd be better off buying sod from your local nursery and cutting it into plugs yourself. Locally bought grass is also more likely to survive transplanting.

- Hybrid grass-seed mixes that claim to grow anywhere, in any climate, all year round. No grass is this good. Do your own research. Ask your local extension office or nursery to recommend grass mixes for your area.

Sprig your lawn for big savings. Here is another way to plant a lawn without a lot of money. All you need are cuttings of a spreading-type grass, like bermuda, zoysia, or centipede. You can buy a bushel of sprigs from a nursery or cut some from the grass already growing in your yard. Cut runners about 12 inches long. Then make a furrow in the ground with a spade or hoe. Stick half the runner into the furrow, and leave the other half on the surface. Heel it in, pressing the soil back over the buried runner. Water it twice a day to keep it from drying out.

Top-dress edges to prevent drying. Protect sod seams from drying out and dying. Sprinkle a light layer of soil along the top of the seams and corners. Do this as you lay each line of sod, and you won't have to walk on the new grass later.

First aid for unused sod. Don't fret if you fail to get all your sod installed on the first day. It will keep for up to two days if you baby it. Move it to a shady spot so it doesn't dry out. If you have room, unroll it. If not, leave it rolled or stacked, and mist the sod to keep it moist.

Poke holes to help roots. Check the texture of the dirt you plan to lay sod on. If it's much finer or coarser than the dirt that comes with the sod, then plan to aerate about a month after laying the new lawn. Otherwise, the new grass won't root properly and will die. Aerating helps mix the two layers and lets oxygen and water move more freely between them. Aerate your lawn once a year for a few years to mix the soils together and improve drainage and root growth.

WATERING
DEWS & DON'TS

Take the guesswork out of watering. Established lawns need about 1 inch of water a week. Instead of guessing how long you should run the sprinklers, put some empty soup cans to work in the yard.

- Spread the cans around the lawn.

- Run the sprinklers for 15 minutes.

- Measure the water in each can with a ruler.

- Add the amounts and divide by the number of cans to get an average.

- Divide 1 inch by the average amount of water in the cans.

- Multiply the result by 15.

Say the cans capture an average of 0.2 inches of water in 15 minutes. Divide one by 0.2 to get five. Then multiply five by 15 to get 75. The answer — run the sprinkler for 75 minutes to put 1 inch of water on the lawn.

Get roots to grow deep. Give grass the weekly 1 inch of water it needs all at once, rather than watering it a little each day. Giving grass big gulps instead of small sips encourages its roots to grow deeper, which helps it survive in tough times.

Low-tech check for dry soil. Want an easy way to tell when you've watered enough? Stick a screwdriver in it. You can buy fancy water sensors that test moisture below the soil's surface. Or you can test it yourself for free. After watering, push a long screwdriver into the dirt until you feel resistance. It will slide easily through wet soil but stop when it hits dry dirt. Pull out the tool and check the dirt line to see how far the water has penetrated your lawn. Soil should be damp 6 to 8 inches deep after watering.

Telltale sign of a thirsty lawn

It's easy to tell if your lawn needs watering. Just walk across it. If your footprints show up for more than a few seconds, then the grass needs a drink.

Protect your lawn from drought. Make your turf more drought-tolerant before the summer season hits. Water it less often but for longer. Daily, light waterings create shallow roots. Deeper, less frequent waterings encourage grass roots to grow deep in search of water. Start training your grass now. Water it when it starts to wilt, and give it enough water to wet the soil in the root zone. Don't water it again until grass wilts again. The turf will gradually go for longer stretches between waterings.

Expert tip for beating the heat. Weekly watering may not be enough to keep the lawn alive during hot, dry days. Take a tip from the pros. When dry summer days hit 100 degrees, golf course groundskeepers mist the greens lightly with water, enough to wet the blades but not reach the roots. Their goal — to cool down the turf itself. You can do the same. Mist grass lightly with a garden hose as needed during the hottest part of the day. Don't use a sprinkler, though. It puts out too much water. The same technique can also keep newly seeded lawns alive and help diseased turf recover in summer.

When it's all right to water at night. Watering the lawn in the evening may be convenient, but it's generally not good for the grass. Wet turf can become a breeding ground for disease, especially if you live in a hot, humid climate. It's a different story in a hot, dry climate. There, the benefits of watering at night, when less moisture evaporates, outweigh the risks. Wait until the temperature drops below 55 degrees in the evening before you turn on the sprinklers.

Save time and slash water bill. Use less water and spend less time fertilizing. Put down a slow-release fertilizer only once or twice a year. Feed more frequently, and you'll need to water more often. Plants must have water to absorb these nutrients. Otherwise, the fertilizer will burn roots and sicken or kill the grass. Cut back on heavy feeding to see an instant difference in your water bill.

Special schedule for tricky soils. Clay and sandy soils are the exception to the watering rule. If you have either type, don't water the lawn all at once.

- Clay can only absorb a little moisture at a time. The rest runs off. Let the sprinkler go until you see runoff. Turn it off and let the water soak in. Wait one hour, then continue watering.

- Sandy soil absorbs water fast, but it drains fast, too. Slow down drainage by giving grass half an inch of water at a time.

Secret to growing grass on a slope. Slopes need special care. Irrigate them the way you do the rest of the lawn, and you're sure to end up with dead, brown turf. Water runs off a slope before the soil can absorb all it needs. Break up a long bout of watering into several short sessions. Water until you spot runoff, then wait a few hours for it to soak in, and water again.

Tell beetles to take a hike. Combat beetles by changing how often you water your lawn.

- Japanese beetles like to lay their eggs in moist soil in late July. Let the ground go a little dry to discourage them.

- European chafer beetles lay their eggs in dry ground around the same time. Crank up the sprinkler to send them packing.

Keep the kinks out of hoses

A hose can't kink when it's full of water. Leave the water turned on while you coil that unruly garden hose. It will be kink-free and ready to store every time.

3 fast fixes for a leaky hose. Garden hoses are too expensive to toss and replace every time one springs a leak. Try these quick fixes for a pinhole leak. All will work in less than a minute.

- Place a small piece of rubber, like a tire patch or a bicycle inner tube, over the hole in the hose. Attach a hose clamp over the patch and tighten.

- Light a candle and drip a few drops of melted wax onto the hole. Wrap with electrical tape for added reinforcement.

- Insert a toothpick into the hole. Break it off as close to the hose as possible. Wrap the area with electrical tape. The toothpick will swell and fill the hole as the wood absorbs water.

MOWING MASTERY
KEEPING IT
GROOMED & GROWING

Get better results by mowing less. Want a beautiful lawn? Then stop cutting it so short. Scalping is the number one mowing mistake you can make. It will cost you more time and money in the long run.

- Longer grass needs less frequent mowing. Short grass grows fast to make up for the loss of so much leaf blade. Taller grass grows slower, saving you time and sweat.

- Routinely cut the grass too short, and the roots will never grow deep. Shallow roots leave your lawn vulnerable to drought and less able to fight off weeds, diseases, and insect infestations.

Go low to thwart mold. Make the last cut of the year a short one, if you tend to have snow on the ground all winter. Cut the grass 1.5 to 2 inches tall during your final mow. The grass will look greener in spring once the snow melts, and it will be less likely to harbor the fungi behind snow mold.

The right height for your turf. Every grass has an ideal height. Check this chart to find the perfect mower height to make yours healthy and more water-efficient.

Grass species	Ideal height (inches)
tall fescue	2.5 to 3.5
fine fescue	2.5 to 3
Kentucky bluegrass	2 to 3
perennial ryegrass	2 to 3
zoysia	1 to 2
common bermuda	1 to 2
centipede	1.5 to 2
St. Augustine	2.5 to 4

Free way to cut down on fertilizer. Leave grass clippings on the lawn, and you'll use 20 percent less fertilizer. Clippings return nitrogen and other nutrients to the soil. Do this, and experts say you won't need to fertilize at all when grass is growing fast, unless the lawn shows signs of nitrogen deficiency, such as turning yellow or slowing its growth. Even then, you can get by with half the amount of suggested fertilizer if you're leaving clippings on the lawn.

When it's best to bag clippings. Grass clippings return nutrients to the lawn, but sometimes they can do more harm than good. Bag them if:

- the grass is infected with a disease. Diseased clippings can keep an infection going strong.

- weeds are currently setting seed. No one wants more weeds.

- you've let the grass grow too tall. Excessive clippings can smother the lawn.

- the blades are still wet when you mow. Clumped-together clippings can smother the lawn, too.

Stop the spread of lawn diseases. Give your grass a better chance at beating a disease, and prevent its spread at the same time. Raise the height of your mower blades. Sick grass needs more leaf blade, so it can make more energy to fight off the illness. Mow the diseased area last, and hose off the underside of the mowing deck afterward to blast away infected clippings.

Right time to mow new lawns. Mow newly seeded lawns once the grass plants reach 3 inches tall. By then, they'll be firmly rooted enough to withstand the wheels of a mower. Set your blade at its highest height for the first few mows. As the lawn begins to fill in, you can gradually lower the blade to the level you want. Sodded lawns need slightly different care. Wait three weeks before walking on or mowing new sod, even if the leaf blades are more than 3 inches tall.

Find the cause of excess thatch

Grass clippings don't cause thatch. If your lawn has that problem, it's due to something else. Overfertilizing, overwatering, or cutting the blades too short are the usual culprits.

Spur grass to fill in faster. Get your newly planted grass to fill in faster by mowing it.

- Mow when the ground is relatively dry.

- Move slowly, especially when cornering, so the wheels don't tear out the tender turf.

- Cut the grass high, leaving it around 2.5 to 3 inches tall, to keep weeds at bay and the soil cool.

- Mow often. Giving new grass a haircut actually helps it mature faster.

Sprinkle seed as you mow. Keep a salt shaker full of grass seed in your pocket while mowing. After you mow over a bald spot, simply sprinkle some seeds onto the bare soil. Some types of grass seeds are too big to fit through salt shaker holes. Recycle an old parmesan cheese shaker for these.

Trim first to minimize work. Edge and string trim your yard first, before you mow. It goes against the norm, but your yard will look tidier. Trim along edges and in tight spots where the mower won't fit. Then mow over the clippings later where they lay. The mower will chop them so finely that you won't need to rake and remove them.

Mow in patterns to save your lawn

Change directions each time you mow the lawn. If you mowed left to right the last time, then mow top to bottom the next one. You can even add a diagonal pattern for more variety. By changing directions, you keep the mower wheels from wearing tracks in the turf and compacting the soil.

Low-cost way to a better cut. The best golf courses in the country use them, so why not you? If you have a small yard, consider a reel mower. They're perfect for naturally short grasses like bermuda and St. Augustine. They cost less than gas-powered mowers, are quiet so your neighbors can't complain, and leave behind finer grass clippings, so you don't have to bag. Plus, they make cleaner cuts than other mowers, which discourages disease.

Cooking spray keeps mower turning. Keep your reel mower in tiptop shape. Wipe down and dry off the blades and bedknife after each use. Lubricate them with a quick spray of silicone lubricant, WD-40, or nonstick cooking spray.

Simple strip cuts trimming time. Line raised sidewalks, retaining walls, and fences with a buried stone border. Dig a shallow strip along the edge. Then lay inexpensive brick pavers in it deep enough so only the top 1 inch sticks up from the ground. This forms a perfect mow strip. You can mow over the pavers without tearing up your blade, and spare yourself hours of string-trimming these otherwise tough-to-cut areas.

Protect grass from gas. Move your lawnmower onto pavement before refilling the gas tank. Gas spilled on grass will kill it within a few days, and there is not much you can do. Clear out the dead grass. The lawn will most likely fill in on its own. You can help it along by sprinkling a little grass seed or cutting a sod patch from a hidden spot in your yard.

BATTLE PLAN TO WIPE OUT GARDEN FOES

WIN THE WAR
ON WEEDS

Target weeds easily in crowded beds. All you need is an old paintbrush to tackle the weeds next to your prized plants, where you don't dare spray. Clean the paintbrush thoroughly, and let dry. Dip the brush in a weedkiller like glyphosate, tap off the excess, and carefully paint the liquid on the weed. The weed now faces a death sentence, but the innocent plants around it remain untouched and untroubled. Just make sure you don't use this brush for painting anymore. Instead, label it as your official "weed assassin," and store it with your herbicide.

Get a jumpstart on planting season. Create weed-free beds in as little as two weeks. For best results, do this during summer:

- Mow weeds down.

- Rototill and water the bed.

- Cover the bed in either clear, thin plastic or black pond liner.

- Bury the edges of the plastic.

The sun cooks and kills any weeds, weed seeds, grass, or other plants under the plastic. It also kills everything in the first few inches of soil. This leaves your new bed ready for planting when you take up the plastic. To prepare a spring planting bed during winter, cover it for at least 8-10 weeks. Plant after removing the plastic, but disturb the soil as little as possible.

Tailor the weapon to the weed. Take painting your weeds with weedkiller to the next level. Keep several sizes of children's paintbrushes on hand, and you can match the size of the paintbrush to the size of the weed you need to paint.

Don't mistake natural for nontoxic

Natural herbicides — like vinegar, salt or rubbing alcohol — are convenient, but they can be just as toxic as any other weedkiller. Salt, in particular, can destroy your yard by burning plant roots, ruining your soil, and keeping seeds from germinating.

If you choose to use these products, protect your lawn by covering nearby grass with newspaper before applying. And save your prized plants by placing a bottomless soda bottle over the weed and spraying into the mouth of the bottle.

Slash your pesky plant population. Try this amazing trick that keeps weeds from sprouting in the first place. Till your garden bed at night with help from headlights. Studies suggest night tilling may lead to a dramatic drop in weeds, and here is why. When daytime tilling turns over the soil, weed seeds in the soil are briefly exposed to sunlight. Many weed seeds are dormant until light touches them, but they only need a quick flash of sunlight to trigger sprouting. On the other hand, light from a few headlights has no effect, so feel free to use them.

But think twice before tilling at night if you have poor night vision, balance problems, or any condition that raises your danger of falls.

Kill every weed in your yard. All it takes is this four-step, easy-to-follow plan:

- In spring, spray with a pre-emergent weedkiller to limit weed growth.

- When summer comes, apply a different herbicide. Many herbicides are limited, meaning each herbicide only kills certain kinds of weeds. That is why switching herbicides helps get rid of weeds your spring herbicide could not eliminate. After the summer herbicide has done its work, pull any remaining weeds by hand.

- As autumn takes hold, apply a general herbicide.

- Give the newly treated weeds time to die off completely, and then pull up any weeds that are left.

Erase weeds with this medicine cabinet cure. Rubbing alcohol may be cheap, but it can still rub out weeds. Just mix one tablespoon of rubbing alcohol into one quart of water, pour into a spray bottle, and spray the weed. If the first spray does not kill the weed, try again with a stronger recipe. Mix one tablespoon of rubbing alcohol into one 8-ounce cup of water. Just remember to be careful if other plants are growing near the weed. See the box *Don't mistake natural for nontoxic* for details on shielding those plants.

Boost the potency of your weed killer. All you need is a secret ingredient from your kitchen — dishwashing liquid. This soapy liquid is a surfactant, meaning it helps the herbicide stick to the leaf. It can also break down the waxy coating protecting weed leaves, so the plant is more susceptible to herbicide. Adding this cheap kitchen liquid may keep you from doing extra spraying or buying additional weed busters, thus saving money on lawn maintenance. Experts recommend you add anywhere from one drop to one tablespoon of dishwashing liquid for each gallon of herbicide. But remember, dishwashing liquid may burn the grass around the weed, so use the smallest effective dose.

When dish soap is not OK

Read the label of any herbicide before you add dishwashing liquid to it. If the instructions say you should add a "nonionic" surfactant to the herbicide, don't add dishwashing liquid, which is ionic. Mixing dish soap into this type of herbicide may help your weeds survive.

Find relief from poison ivy. You will not believe which common household items you can use to treat this problem.

- Rubbing alcohol. If you have been in contact with poison ivy within the last half hour, immediately clean the area with rubbing alcohol, and rinse thoroughly. Do this soon enough, and you may prevent the poison ivy rash.

- Baking soda. Try a soak to ease the itching. Empty half a box of baking soda into your tub water. Some people say a baking soda compress may also soothe the itch.

- Oatmeal. Blend two cups of oatmeal into a powder using a blender or food processor. Stir this into your bath while filling the tub, step carefully into the now-slippery tub, and enjoy a 20-minute itch-fighting soak.

- Buttermilk. Dab on to itchy areas for relief, but only if you are not allergic to dairy products.

Discover the best time to kill weeds. Pull, hoe, or rake out your weeds early in the growing season while they are still small. Young weeds with shallow roots are easier to get out of the ground, plus you can remove them before they make seeds that turn into more weeds. If you would rather use herbicide on your weeds, do that early in the season, too. Herbicides work best when weeds are sprouting new growth.

Attack the weed at its roots. You tried to pull the weed, but the top broke off — leaving the plant free to regrow from its roots. Use this two-step process to make sure that never happens again. First, do your weeding after a good rain, or water your weeds deeply before pulling. Weeds are easier to remove from soaked ground. Second, try this technique.

- Grab an oversized kitchen fork for small weeds or those in tight spaces, or a hand trowel for large or medium weeds.

- Plunge the fork or trowel down into the soil near the weed's main root.

- Press the fork or trowel against the root to help lever or scoop the weed out. At the same time, pull upward from the base of the plant with your free hand. The entire weed should lift out of the ground.

Create a lightweight weed bucket. You could leave weeds on the ground, rather than drag a heavy bucket around, but that can help spread plant diseases. Instead, turn a milk jug into a light carrier that hangs from your belt. Cut out a large square hole on the side opposite the handle to make an L-shaped container. You can even cut away the mouth of the jug to make a larger opening. Thread your belt through the handle, and refasten the belt. Now you can just drop weeds into the jug at your hip. Or try carrying an empty plastic ice cream tub that has an attached handle — or any other plastic tubs with handles. These will be smaller, lighter, and more manageable than your garden bucket.

Give your back a break. Use this simple technique when weeding the garden, and you could prevent a bad back in the future. Instead of bending at the waist, squat down to weed. This makes your knees and thighs do the work instead of your back. But if your knees and back are already a problem, try one of these.

- Create raised beds at waist height, so you no longer need to bend. For even better results, attach a board or bench along the top edges of the bed, so you have something to sit on while you weed.

- Use a long-handled trowel, long-handled weeder, or a grabber to help you weed without bending.

Prevent weeds from a surprising source. A study of 10 retail brands of birdseed found that each one contained at least three kinds of weed seeds — and the seeds sprouted into weeds when tested. But that does not mean you should stop feeding the birds to save your yard. Just use one of these methods to bake your birdseed, and the weed seeds will never sprout.

- Conventional oven. Spread the seed out on a long, flat pan. Bake at 300 degrees for 30 minutes.

- Microwave oven. Microwave one gallon of seed in a paper bag for five minutes on high. To bake less seed, place 1 or 2 pounds of seed in a bowl, cover with a paper towel, and bake one minute for each pound of seed. Do not place microwaved birdseed back in storage.

Don't forget to let the seed cool before putting it in your bird feeder.

Stop watering unwanted plants. Sprinklers water weeds right along with your prized plants. So lay soaker hoses or drip irrigation very close to your plants, and cover with mulch. The plants will get plenty of water while nearby weeds suffer from drought. This even helps prevent many new weeds, because weed seeds need water to germinate. But take these steps to prevent new problems.

- Check your mulch to make sure it does not remain damp long after a rain. This happens when mulches are too finely textured or too thick to dry easily, creating the perfect place for weed seeds to germinate.

- Keep an eye out for powerful, deep-rooted weeds like nutsedge and bindweed. These can grow through most mulches — including landscape fabric — so they may pop up in well-watered, mulched areas. Get rid of these weeds the moment you find them.

Nutritious, tasty weed for your salad

You expect to spend the entire season pulling up purslane, so why not eat what you will harvest anyway? Purslane leaves, stems, and flowers are free, edible, and make a crisp, raw addition to salads. Even chefs have become fans of its juicy, lemony tang and peppery kick. What's more, this nutritious weed contains beta carotene and high levels of the omega-3 fatty acid alpha-linolenic acid. But before you eat purslane, take these rules to heart.

- Never eat purslane if pesticide or herbicide may have been applied to it, and avoid harvesting near your pet's toilet areas.
- Only harvest from your own yard.
- Send a picture or sample to your cooperative extension agent or another expert. Do not eat any purslane from your yard until an expert identifies it as purslane *(Portulaca oleracea)*.
- Start with small portions.
- Always wash purslane before eating.

Free weed wiper aims to kill. A weed wiper applicator lets you paint herbicide directly on the weed. This gives you the most bang for your herbicide buck, while protecting other plants. But instead of paying for a paint-on weed wiper, make your own from an old roll-on deodorant container.

- Use pliers and a pen to pop or tease the roll-on ball out of the container.

- Put on rubber gloves, and pour herbicide into the container.

- Put the roll-on ball firmly back in place.

- Roll herbicide on the weed leaves.

Either label the deodorant bottle and store it in a locked container, or clean out the bottle and throw it away.

Know which plots you cannot till. Do not use a tiller in soil infested by weeds that either naturally spread by runners or cuttings or can regrow from bits of root. This includes weeds like bindweed, Canadian thistle, quack grass, and unwanted Bermuda grass. Rototilling an area infested by these weeds spreads bits of the plant, encouraging each one to grow into a new weed. So, unless you want to multiply the number of weeds in that area, do not even hoe the soil.

Prevent trespassers by your garden fence. You put up a garden fence to keep pets and wildlife out, but make sure you do not invite weeds in as a result. Weeds that spring up along your garden fence can invade your garden by spreading either their seeds or underground runners. If you would rather not spend hours hand weeding, spraying herbicides, or using a string trimmer, try this instead. Lay pavers, bricks, or a thick layer of bark mulch underneath the fence or along both sides of its base.

Make winter weeds work for you. Give weeds like chickweed, clover, and medic a stay of execution if they pop up in your vegetable or flower garden during winter or late autumn. Chickweed *(Stellaria media)* makes a good cover crop and can help prevent the ground from becoming waterlogged. Winter clover *(Trifolium sp.)* and medic *(Medicago sp.)* can also be good cover crops because they return nitrogen to the soil. Just be sure to till or shovel these weeds back under the soil before they flower and go to seed — and make certain they are well buried. Otherwise, you will fight extra weeds all summer.

Gardener's secret: the glove of death

The glove of death is a weed-killing technique developed by land stewards of The Nature Conservancy. Some gardeners have adapted this for home use. They put on thick rubber, latex, or nitrile gloves — but never neoprene gloves — and then place heavy cotton gloves over them. The gardener dips the fingers of the cotton glove in herbicide and applies the herbicide directly to the weed. Gardeners say this helps them put herbicide exactly where they want it, without affecting other plants.

But be aware that this is not a recommended or labeled use of herbicide. In fact, The Nature Conservancy advises its volunteers to wear eye protection and protective clothing when applying pesticide. They also recommend washing gloves with detergent and warm water before removing them, and washing hands and arms afterward. Gloves used for pesticide application should not be used for anything else.

Save your plants from pesky pests

Grow this natural pest control every year. These delightful flowers actually deter harmful bugs from your tomatoes, roses, peas, and more. That is why French marigolds were probably in your grandmother's garden. Rediscover what they can do for you today.

- Plant these marigolds among roses or tomatoes — or plant roses or tomatoes where French marigolds grew last year. Scientists have discovered the roots of French marigolds produce compounds that can repel or kill nematodes that infest these plants.

- French marigolds may help protect potatoes from eel-worms. They may also repel whiteflies or aphids from a variety of plants.

For best results, plant French marigolds throughout your garden.

Erase aphids with a pantry favorite. Try this low-cost milk mixture that spells the end to an aphid infestation. Just prepare nonfat dry milk according to the package directions, pour in a spray bottle, and coat your plant leaves with it. This may also prevent viruses spread by aphids.

Repel insects and aphids from your plants

Just soak the leaves from wild garlic in boiling water, and use it as a spray against aphids and scale. If wild garlic is not available, try this instead.

- Chop or crush some garlic cloves, and place them in boiling water.
- Stir in a pinch of cayenne pepper, and let the mixture steep for a while.
- Let cool, stir in a few drops of liquid hand soap, and strain.
- Spray plants with this mixture to free them from aphids.

Protect your plants from aphids with tea. Just follow these instructions:

- Bruise two large handfuls of basil leaves and stems, and drop them in a one-gallon jar.

- Pour in one gallon of water, and let sit in the sun for four to eight hours.

- Strain through a mesh strainer, or use a section of pantyhose if you don't have one. Add several drops of liquid hand soap, and shake to mix.

- Spray this tea remedy on your plants to fight aphids, leafhoppers, grubs, squash bugs, mites, cabbage loopers, and cucumber beetles.

Eliminate two pests with peels. Peel your breakfast orange carefully. As long as it is unbroken, you can use an empty half orange rind to zap aphids or trap slugs in your garden.

- Aphids. Place the orange rind close to a spot where aphids are suspected, and the orange rind should kill them by itself. If needed, poke two holes in the rind, and pass string through the holes so you can hang the rind from a branch or stem. Or slit part of one side of the rind, and wedge it in place.

- Slugs. Place the half rind, round side up, next to a plant you need to protect or in a nearby shady spot. The slug will crawl under your rind trap to hide. Check the trap once a day, and dump the slugs into a bucket of warm sudsy water.

Invite lacewings to an aphid feast. Lacewings are bugs that love to eat aphids, but they need a place to sleep off those heavy meals. Make one of these homes to tempt them to stick around.

- Cane cabin. Tie a bundle of hollow bamboo canes and twigs together with twine. Secure it with more twine near each end of the bundle. Create a rustic look by tucking pine straw or twigs beneath the twine.

- Tubular townhouse. Cut the top and bottom off a two-liter soft drink bottle so only a plastic tube remains. Measure the length of the tube. Cut a piece of corrugated cardboard slightly shorter than that tube. Roll up the cardboard, and insert it into the tube.

Hang your new lacewing house outside. Make sure it is protected from rain and will not blow away in the wind.

Summon pest-eaters to your garden. Some people fight fire with fire. You can fight bugs with bugs. Although some "pest" bugs eat or damage garden plants, other bugs eat those plant-eating pests. Pest-eating bugs are called "beneficials," and you can invite them to dinner by growing plants that produce plenty of pollen and nectar. For example, attract ladybugs to your garden by planting flowers like zinnias, yarrow, aster, daisies, and sunflowers, or herbs such as parsley, dill, coriander, anise, or fennel. Grow these near your pest-plagued plants, and the ladybugs will reward you. They will eat the aphids, mites, scale, thrips, and other pests right off your plants.

Safeguard baby ladybugs

This "gift to gardeners" will eat voracious pests and leave your flowers untouched. You might not recognize ladybug larva, but they can eat up to 40 aphids a day for you. These long, alligator-like bugs are black or blue with bright yellow, orange, or red markings. Not only do they eat more aphids than their parents, but they also stick around when adult ladybugs have moved on.

What's more, each baby ladybug may eat up to 5,000 aphids during its childhood and adult life. So protect your ladybugs and their kids. Try to avoid using insecticides in your garden. And when you must use them, either use selective pesticides or use limited treatment to avoid killing your ladybug population.

2 substitutes for dangerous chemicals. Coffee and cigarettes for your plants? Not exactly, but caffeine and nicotine are two of nature's own plant-created pesticides. Discover how to use them.

- Coffee. Caffeine is deadly to snails and slugs. It can even kill plants if you use too much. So make a few cups of not-too-strong caffeinated coffee at sunset. After dark, grab a flashlight, and spray your plants with this coffee. Rinse the plants with your hose sprayer the next morning.

- Tobacco. Pour one gallon of boiling water over 2 to 3 ounces of chewing tobacco. Steep for 20 to 30 minutes, let cool, and strain. Spray this on plants to fight Japanese beetles, aphids, mites, and thrips. But take precautions. Nicotine is highly toxic to people, pets, birds, fish, and beneficial garden insects. Also, do not use this spray on tomatoes, other nightshade plants, or beans.

Protect your skin from nicotine sprays

Before using any pesticide that contains nicotine, wear gloves and other protective gear such as a face mask. Nicotine is easily absorbed through your skin and through mucous membranes in your nose and mouth.

Stop cutworms with 3 clever tricks. Pick your favorite or try all three.

- Draw the outline of a comma around the plant using a small amount of cornmeal. The worms will die when they eat it.

- Make a protective collar to fence out cutworms. Cut the bottom half off a 3-ounce or 5-ounce plastic cup, and use the top half as a collar. For smaller plants, cut a toilet tissue roll into two rings, or make a similar ring from stiff paper. Press the collar 1-inch deep into the soil.

- Sink a tenpenny finishing nail into the soil beside the stem of each tomato plant, leaving the head 2 inches above the ground. This prevents the cutworm from wrapping itself around the plant's stem, so it cannot ravish your tomatoes.

Enjoy a flea-free yard without harmful chemicals. Grow plenty of the plants fleas hate, and grow them throughout your yard. Try favorites like pennyroyal, fennel, rosemary, and basil. Chrysanthemums may also help because they are the source of pyrethrum, an insecticide used against fleas. For extra coverage where no flea-fighting plants grow, harvest some fennel or rosemary, or crush pennyroyal or dried basil leaves. Then spread these herbs around your yard. You can also scatter eucalyptus, cedar shavings, or ground red pepper.

Chemical-free ant repellent

You can stop ants both indoors and out without a drop of toxic chemicals.

- Indoors. Wipe down your countertops with a 50-50 mixture of white vinegar and water. Also, spritz white vinegar around window and door frames, splash it under appliances, or apply it anywhere else you have noticed ants. Vinegar erases the scented pheromone trails ants leave behind and leaves an odor ants simply despise. Just remember not to use this remedy on granite, marble, or painted surfaces.
- Outdoors. Pour vinegar on ant mounds, and ants will come boiling out of the mound, never to return. But be very careful to keep the vinegar from splashing or trickling onto nearby grass and plants.

Repel moths and ants naturally. Keep ants and moths at bay without using toxic pesticides or smelly mothballs. Start with these nine varieties of plants that keep away ants:

- pennyroyal
- southernwood
- onions
- chives
- sage
- catnip
- tansy
- bay leaves
- cucumbers

Some of these even do double duty. You can eat a cucumber and then scatter its peelings wherever you need to repel ants. Bay leaves and easy-to-grow pennyroyal may also be twice as nice. Not only do they send ants marching, but they also help repel moths. That is good news because some animal studies suggest mothballs may contribute to your risk of cancer. So sprinkle bay leaves in your drawers instead of mothballs, and enjoy fragrant moth-free clothes.

Banish mosquitoes without a bug zapper. You can repel mosquitoes without using gadgets or chemicals. Just use these seven tips to eliminate their breeding sites.

- Get rid of anything in the yard that can hold water, including buckets, plastic sheeting, and old tires. If you cannot remove an item, turn it upside down so it can no longer hold water.

- Water lawns, gardens, and individual plants carefully to avoid creating standing water that lasts overnight.

- Change the water in birdbaths and watering pools twice each week.

- Clean out rain gutters and downspouts regularly to prevent standing water.

- Keep your pool clean and well-chlorinated.

- Repair leaky faucets or air conditioners if they create long-lasting puddles.

- Fill or drain ditches, swampy areas, and dips in the soil that can hold water.

3 new ways to stop slugs cold. An unusual pet, extra guttering, or horsehair can help you keep slugs out. Here is how.

- Gardeners who keep chickens or pet ducks say these birds are enthusiastic slug hunters that help provide long-term pest control.

- Lay a border of aluminum guttering around the edge of your garden, and coat it with soap. Slugs cannot escape from this trap. Clean the gutters regularly, remove the slugs, drop them into a bucket of soapy water, and reapply soap to the gutters, as needed.

- Place horsehair around plants that need protection. For best results, cut or chop it into very short lengths.

Keep hungry pests away from vegetables. Forget pesticides. Cedar may be the one sneaky trick you need to make pests willingly give up feasting on your vegetables. Scatter cedar shavings or cedar mulch around plants you want to protect. You can even try cedar blocks or cedar leaves. Cedar not only repels vegetable pests outside but also moths and fleas indoors. Be sure to take advantage of cedar trimmings from your yard or a friend's yard before you spend money on cedar products.

Combat earwigs with "lamp" traps. Eliminate earwigs with a whimsical garden trap that resembles a lamp with its lampshade. Just stuff a flowerpot with straw, hay, or even crumpled paper, turn it upside down, and hang it on a dowel or bamboo cane near the plants you want to protect.  Earwigs will hide in the flowerpot during the day, so remember to empty the trap into a bucket of soapy water before sundown. Setting out a shallow bowl filled with vegetable oil will also trap earwigs.

Get rid of 10,000 garden pests this summer. A single adult toad can eat 10,000 insects by the end of one summer — not to mention large numbers of slugs, says the U.S. Department of Agriculture. Best of all, you never have to see or touch the toad. Just attract it to your yard by providing water and shelter. For shelter, make one of these easy toad homes, and place it in a shady spot.

- Turn an old flowerpot on its side and partially bury it.

- Arrange two parallel piles of bricks at least 3 inches apart. Make each pile at least 3 inches long and 3 inches high. Use bricks or flat stones to make a roof connecting them.

Place a low-rimmed old dish nearby, fill with water, and change the water regularly. Meanwhile, avoid using pesticides, or you may kill your bug-eating champion.

Purge pests with a fiery pepper spray. Bugs will run screaming from your garden rather than face this searing spray. That is also why you should wear gloves when you spray or mix it. Here is the bug-busting recipe.

- Place two cups of hot peppers in a blender. Or use two tablespoons of hot red pepper sauce.

- Add two cups of water and one clove of garlic.

- Add several drops of liquid hand soap. Do not substitute dishwashing liquid because it may damage plants.

- Blend for several minutes.

- Dilute with one gallon of water. You can let it steep overnight if you want.

- Strain and spray on plants every day for up to a week. Be aware that certain plants may be harmed by your fiery brew, so proceed with caution.

Evict squash bugs. Start saving your pizza boxes if squash bugs are troubling you. Snip two adjacent corners on each box, so you can fold a side down later. Place several open boxes around your squash plants early one morning while the temperature is still cool. Jiggle or tap each plant to make the squash bugs fall into the pizza boxes. Then pick up each box, fold down a side, and tilt the box toward that side to dump the squash bugs into a bucket of soapy water.

Keep cabbage root fly maggots out. These root-eating brassica pests may have killed last year's broccoli, but you can make sure that does not happen this year. As soon as you plant each seedling, cover it with a tight-fitting mat that surrounds the seedling. You can make the mat from Bubble Wrap, tar paper, foam rubber carpet pad, or cardboard.

- Cut a circle or square 9 inches wide.

- Snip a single slit from the outside edge of the circle or square inward to its center.

- Slide the mat around the base of the seedling so the seedling sits at the center of the mat, and the mat fits snugly around the seedling.

Reduce health risks from pesticides

Your danger of experiencing health problems from pesticides depends on how toxic the pesticides are and how much exposure you receive, says the National Pesticide Information Center. So if you must use pesticides, choose the least toxic option that will get the job done. Most toxic pesticides are required to display signal words on the label to let you know how dangerous they are. Look for the signal words on the front label, usually next to the statement KEEP OUT OF REACH OF CHILDREN.

- The most toxic pesticides are labeled DANGER.
- Moderately toxic pesticides display the word WARNING.
- Less toxic pesticides are labeled CAUTION.
- The least toxic pesticides are not required to display a signal word.

Medicine cabinet cure for infested houseplants. Scales look like oval bumps less than one-quarter inch wide on plant stems and the undersides of leaves, but mealybugs resemble tiny cotton balls. If these are moving, or you find odd deposits on leaves, your houseplant is infested. Here's what to do.

- Dip a cotton swab in rubbing alcohol. Touch each mealybug with it, or use it to crush scale bugs.

- Use insecticidal soap if your plant is too heavily infested.

- For a severe case of mealybugs, try a spray that is nine parts water to one part rubbing alcohol.

If you use insecticidal soap or alcohol spray, test it on a small part of the plant first to make sure it will not damage the plant. A spray of rubbing alcohol and water can kill some plants.

Send wireworms to their soapy doom. Small holes in your potatoes may mean you have wireworms or slugs. If your usual slug-stoppers do not work, try one of these traps for wireworms.

- Skewer an old whole potato or carrot on a stick or coat hanger. Bury it, but leave three inches of skewer above the soil with a brightly colored tag attached so you know where your trap is. When you dig up the vegetable, drop it in soapy water, or burn it immediately.

- Dig a shallow hole, drop some potato or carrot pieces in, and cover with a board. Weigh down this cover with a few rocks or bricks. When you check the traps, drop the potato pieces — and any loose wireworms — into the bucket of soapy water right away.

Also, consider growing buckwheat as a cover crop during the off-season. It may help you fend off future wireworms.

Make your own insecticidal soap spray. Mix one and a half tablespoons of unscented liquid hand soap into one gallon of warm water. Just be sure to test this spray on a small portion of the plant before spraying on the whole plant. Homemade insecticidal soap has a higher risk of injuring plants than commercial products.

Foil corn earworms with oil. Don't wait for corn earworms to rear their ugly heads. Use a child's medicine dropper to

315

apply several drops of canola or mineral oil into the tips of corn ears when the silk appears. To play it safe, you can also tighten the tip of the husk by placing a clothespin, twist tie, or rubber band where the silk enters the corn.

Beware this Japanese beetle cure

Planting geraniums among your roses sounds like the perfect way to prevent rose damage from Japanese beetles. After all, research has shown that Japanese beetles become paralyzed within 30 minutes of feeding on geranium petals. What's more, they stay paralyzed for up to 24 hours, which gives local predators plenty of time to finish them off.

Unfortunately, research also suggests geranium-laced rose gardens actually suffer more Japanese beetle damage than rose gardens without geraniums. So this is one time you don't want to go with the sensible solution.

Head off cicada damage in prized plants. Cicadas may not show up every year, but they can still damage some of your best landscaping plants. To lay their eggs, female cicadas split open branches in your small fruit trees, small yard trees, and shrubs, causing them to brown and wilt. In fact, some plants may lose most of their branches. Here's what to do when you hear cicadas are coming.

- Cover threatened bushes and trees with cheesecloth, tulle, or another netting with holes less than one-half inch wide.

- Tie the bottom of the netting with twine to close it off, and secure it around the trunk with clothespins.

- Skip large, mature trees or any plants that lack woody stems or branches. These plants can either avoid or recover from cicada damage.

- Unwrap your netted trees when local authorities give the all-clear, usually in July or August.

CREATIVE CRITTER CONTROL

Chase away cats with a fragrant barrier. Cats turn up their noses at the smell of citrus, so sprinkle orange peels, lemon peels, and lime peels around plants that need protection. This keeps unwelcome cats away naturally.

Guard against produce munchers. Save your pantyhose, cut the legs into sections, and slip a section over each vegetable. Tie a knot at each end so the vegetable is completely enclosed and protected. This pantyhose shield deters birds, snails, and other wildlife from picking at your garden. Each shield also dries quickly and stretches as your vegetable grows.

Keep dogs from doing their business in your yard. Try this simple formula to keep dogs and other critters out of your garden.

- Chop up several cloves of garlic, one onion, and three hot peppers. Toss it all in your blender.

- Add one teaspoon of Tabasco sauce, and puree the mixture.

- Pour into one quart of warm water, and let sit overnight.

- Put on gloves, and pour this wherever dogs have visited in your yard. As soon as they get close enough to smell this pungent potion, they will leave in a hurry.

The powerful ingredients in this spray may also make cats, rabbits, and bugs turn tail.

Shut out nibbling birds and snails. Surround your seedling beds with stakes, and spread cheesecloth over them. Use enough cheesecloth to leave several inches of extra fabric along the sides of the bed. Seal in your seedlings by weighing down the edges of the cheesecloth with an unbroken line of bricks. Leave no gaps between the bricks, or snails may sneak in.

Beware of this 'safe' pest repellent

Mothballs may seem safe and natural, but they are made of either naphthalene or paradichlorobenzene, two toxic chemicals. That is why mothball labels say you should only use mothballs in a tightly closed container. In fact, using mothballs for anything not specifically approved on the label is illegal and unhealthy — and that includes fighting pests in your garden or attic.

Placing mothballs outside may endanger pets and children and contaminate your soil and plants. Using mothballs indoors can be dangerous, too. If you smell mothballs, their vapors have reached unsafe levels. Intense or long-term exposure to these vapors may cause headaches, dizziness, nausea, and vomiting, and may damage your red blood cells, eyes, liver, nervous system, and kidneys.

Mothballs have also been identified as possible cancer-causing substances by the U.S. Department of Health and Human Services and the Environmental Protection Agency.

Creative way to chase birds away. Scare birds away from your fruit, vegetables, and other plants at zero cost. Just use an empty plastic two-liter or 16-ounce bottle.

- Draw three rectangles around the bottle, leaving equal space between them.

- Cut along the top, right, and bottom line of each square to make a flap, and bend each flap outward to catch the wind.

- Glue strips of aluminum foil on the bottle's upper section.

- Leave the cap on, poke a hole in the bottom of the bottle, and slide the bottle over a rod or bamboo cane.

- Place this contraption near plants you want to protect. Birds will not like the way the bottle flashes and spins noisily in the wind and will avoid your garden.

Easy potion persuades moles to leave. Make moles move out of your yard when you give them this nontoxic soak.

- Pour 6 ounces of unflavored castor oil and one cup of water in the blender.

- Add 3 ounces of unscented liquid hand soap, but do not use the antibacterial kind.

- Run the blender until the mixture is frothy.

- Put a cup into a 15-gallon hose-end sprayer, and apply to your yard and garden.

This coats the mole food in your yard with castor oil, lending a particularly vile flavor to every possible item on the mole's menu. The mole does not like castor oil any more than you do, so he will go elsewhere to hunt for food.

Music to move a mole. Moles are sensitive to sound waves, so try one of these tactics to get them to leave.

- Bury a line of glass bottles nearly up to their necks. When the wind blows across them, the resulting sound interferes with the mole's ability to hear and hunt.

- Find an old battery-powered radio that you will not mind putting underground for a while. Put in fresh batteries, set it to a station that plays hard rock, turn up the volume, and slip it into a plastic bag. Once the radio is underground, the sound vibrations naturally encourage the mole to find a new home.

Send pesky birds packing. Turn potential trash into garden treasure. Scare birds away from your prize plants with these ideas.

- Pull the tape out of an old videotape, or use an old, deflated Mylar balloon. Cut the videotape or balloon into 1-foot strips, and attach the strips to a line of string between two stakes. The strips flap, flutter, and flash in the breeze to frighten birds off.

- Save your next batch of plastic grocery bags. Fill each one up with air, tie it shut with a rubber band, then hang them all from stakes throughout your garden. The wind makes them move and rattle so crows and other birds stay away.

Build a mole shield into your raised bed. Lay down quarter-inch hardware cloth or wire mesh right before you lay the frame for your raised bed. This keeps moles, voles, and gophers away from your plant roots.

Combat gophers with pretty flowers. Try surrounding your garden or yard with a ring of daffodils or oleander. These plants have a reputation for keeping gophers away.

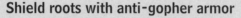

Shield roots with anti-gopher armor

You can build a cage to keep pesky gophers away from your plants. Check the recommended size for your planting hole, and construct your anti-gopher armor to match that size.

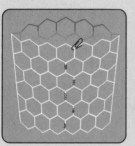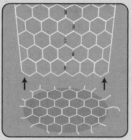

Cut a piece of half-inch hardware cloth or 1-inch chicken wire 1 foot long by 3 feet wide. Bring the foot-long sides together to form a cylinder. Connect the sides and reinforce with twisted paper clips, if needed.

Cut a round bottom for your cylinder from the wire mesh. Make it slightly wider than the cylinder's base. Attach this bottom to the cylinder's base by twisting protruding wire ends together.

Dig your planting hole. Place the anti-gopher armored cage inside, leaving 2 inches above the soil. Plant as usual.

Cheaper ways to fence out deer. An 8-foot-high chain-link fence keeps deer out but can cost up to $7 a foot. Consider cheaper alternatives like these.

- Some gardeners have kept deer out by hanging a line of plastic grocery bags on a rope or wire attached to posts. Keep in mind that this has only worked for small gardens.

- String chicken wire between 8-foot-high metal posts instead of installing an expensive chain-link fence.

- For small gardens or flower beds, a 5-foot-high fence may work well. Deer are far less likely to jump this "short" fence if they will land in a small space.

- Consider a one- or two-strand electric fence. It is easy to install and costs around 30 cents a foot, but do not install this kind of fence if children or pets visit your yard.

Give raccoons a fiery welcome

Fight back when raccoons dig up your newly planted flowers or herbs. Sprinkle black pepper around new plantings and in areas where you suspect raccoons visit. They will not like it one bit.

Combine deer defenses for better results. The best way to keep deer away from your plants is to combine several defenses. For example, you could try these three tactics all at once.

- Protect seedlings, young plants, or low growers by placing a dish rack over them. Place landscape pins over a tine on each side of the rack, and plunge the staples into the dirt, so the deer cannot simply shove the rack aside. This may keep rabbits out, too.

- "Fence in" beds or groups of plants. String one strand of fishing line 24 inches above the ground and another strand 48 inches above the ground. Gardeners say this really works.

- Place a motion-activated sprinkler where deer enter the yard or visit frequently. When the deer arrive, a sudden spray of water scares them off.

Give rabbits a prickly reception. During autumn, put on your garden gloves or grab a pair of tongs to collect "gum balls," the round bristly pods from the sweet gum tree *(Liquidambar styraciflua)*. If you do not have a sweet gum tree, ask if you can collect them from a neighbor's yard. Many people hate gum balls and will be glad to be rid of them. Store the gum balls in a dry place until you need them. To protect plants from hungry rabbits, surround each plant with a wide mulch of gum balls, and press them firmly into the ground. Rabbits do not like to walk on things that hurt their feet. So as long as you have made your mulch too wide for the bunny to reach across, he will leave your plant alone and seek food elsewhere. Gardeners report that gum balls keep snails away, too.

Make your plot repulsive to cats. Forget chasing cats out of your garden. This is much easier.

- Save several glass bottles with narrow necks, such as root beer bottles, or even wine or beer bottles.

- Fill each one three-fourths full with either bleach or a mix of equal parts ammonia and water. Do not use bleach and ammonia together, or you may inhale dangerous toxic fumes.

- Bury these bottles nearly up to their necks along the edges of your garden or in smaller areas you want to protect from cats. The vile smell keeps cats from coming too close.

- Remember to check the bottles regularly to see if they need refilling.

Smart fix for Fido's digging

Give your dog his own place to dig to stop him from digging in your garden. Make a sandbox frame using wood, an old child's wading pool, or simply dig a broad, shallow hole in the ground. Fill the sandbox with sand, bury a few toys and treats, and leave a few more toys and treats on top. If you catch your dog digging elsewhere, just escort him back to his sandbox.

Convince birds to bypass your fruit. Spray blueberries with sugar water when they begin to ripen, and the birds will learn to leave them alone. Cornell University researchers say this works because birds are only equipped to eat the simple sugars in fruits such as fructose and glucose. Regular table sugar gives them an upset stomach because they do not have the enzymes to digest it. To make the same table sugar spray the researchers used, heat two quarts of water until warm. Then dissolve five pounds of sugar in it to make a one-gallon spray. If you need two gallons of spray, dissolve 11 pounds of sugar in one gallon of water. Let the mixture sit until the sugar dissolves and the water looks clear. Spray this on blueberries, strawberries, or other ripening fruit. Just remember to reapply after each rain.

Say bye to bunnies. Sprinkle baby powder, black pepper, or garlic powder around your plants to make them taste bad to rabbits. Remember to apply a fresh round after every rain so the rabbits do not come back.

Simple way to banish bunnies

Plant plenty of onions, garlic, lavender, and catnip around your garden or yard to keep rabbits out. They also hate foxglove and monkshood, but these plants are poisonous and should not be used if children or pets visit your yard.

Protect seedlings from rabbit raids. Collect onion bags and large, wide tin cans to help keep bunnies from eating your seedlings. Here is how to use them.

- Remove the bottoms and tops from the tin cans.

- Cut the onion bags into circles a few inches wider than the rim of the can.

- Secure the onion bag circle over the top of the can with a rubber band, and reinforce it by taping the mesh's bottom rim to the can with duct tape or Gorilla tape.

This allows rain and sunlight into the can but not hungry rabbit mouths. Remove the can when the plant is almost tall enough to grow through the onion bag.

Block furry nibblers from digging. You just put your new plants in the ground yesterday, and chipmunks or squirrels are already digging them up. Make sure that does not happen again. From now on, surround every new planting with hardware cloth or a double ring of 3-inch-wide, flat river rock. When you lay down your barrier, be careful to cover virtually all the soil near the plant, so your furry nibblers have no place left to dig.

Stop your doe-eyed destroyers. Mix one egg white with one-and-a-quarter cups of water in a blender at low speed. Spray this on your plants, and they will taste like rotten eggs to browsing deer. Spray once a month and after it rains. If you spray broadleaf evergreens during winter, be sure to do it on a cloudy day. Spraying deer repellent on these plants on a sunny winter day can cause sunscald.

Eliminate clogs in your sprayer

If you use an egg-white spray to repel deer and it clogs your sprayer, try this. Either strain the spray before pouring it into the sprayer, or switch from regular egg whites to an equal amount of liquid egg whites such as Egg Beaters. Either one should end the clogs.

Create a cat-free zone. Grow plenty of coleus canina (*Plectranthus caninus*) among your flowers, and cats may start avoiding your garden. Gardeners report that this easy-to-grow annual truly can keep cats away, but you need plenty of these plants to do it. Start with a few plants, and root cuttings from them to produce the extra plants you need. This plant sends cats elsewhere because cats can smell its skunky stench better than humans can — and they do not like it one bit. Gardeners say they only smell the plant when it is watered or disturbed. But wear gloves when working with coleus canina because it can be sharp or spiny, and its smell can transfer to bare hands.

Shield young trees from trunk-chewer doom. Mice, voles, and rabbits can literally gnaw a tree to death by chewing its roots or trunk, a process called girdling. To prevent this, install a homemade tree tube. Wrap quarter-inch hardware cloth or metal window screening loosely around the base of the tree, sink the bottom edge 2 inches into the ground, and secure the top with twine. You can also make tree tubes from plastic corrugated drainpipe or field tile. Cut a piece at least 18 inches tall, slit one side, and spread it open just enough to slip around the base of the tree. Press the bottom of the drainpipe 2 inches into the ground. Whether you use wire mesh or corrugated drainpipe, make sure the tube extends high enough so that rabbits cannot chew the tree while standing upright on the snow.

Build a better mousetrap. Make a cheap, humane mousetrap from a spare garbage can or five-gallon bucket. Simply rest a board against the rim so the mouse can climb, and place a dollop of peanut butter in the bottom. The mouse will fall in the bucket while trying to reach the peanut butter. Release the mouse as far away from your home as possible. If this does not work, upgrade your trap.

- Drill holes just below the rim on opposite sides of the bucket.

- Drill holes in the lid and bottom of a 16-ounce soda bottle or large plastic pill bottle.

- Thread the bottle on a dowel or wire coat hanger.

- Thread the dowel or hanger through the bucket holes.

- Smear peanut butter around the middle section of the bottle.

When the mouse attempts to get the peanut butter on the bottle, the bottle will spin, dumping him in the bucket.

Grow plants deer hate. Gardeners often complain that deer eat their plants even though they are on the "deer hating" lists. But reports also suggest three plants nearly always remain untouched — lantana, oleander, and any variety of salvia. But those are not the only plants deer hate. Deer rarely eat powerfully scented herbs such as rosemary, catnip, dill, garlic, lavender, mint, oregano, and thyme; or flowers like bee balm, cleome, coreopsis, daffodils, heliotrope, lily-of-the-valley, and verbena. So consider growing these plants in place of the ones your deer have been devouring. Some people have reported that growing a border of strongly scented herbs around a deer favorite is enough to protect the plant.

How to stop a geese invasion. Last year, geese ate your grass, young plants, and even your seeds. Start taking action in January to make sure they do not frequent your yard again.

- Make a large flag from a black trash bag and a 4-foot stake. Place it where the geese can easily see it from anywhere in your yard. Move it to a new location once a week.

- Scare the geese regularly with loud noise from an air horn or leaf blower if that does not violate your local noise ordinances.

- Reduce the amount of fertilizer you give your grass so the lawn becomes less yummy to geese.

- Allow tall, thick plants to grow up around ponds or open spaces.

- Never let anyone feed the geese.

Outwit deer with ingenuity and bamboo. Your stash of bamboo stakes can prevent deer from eating your flowers or damaging young trees.

- Flowers. Before their flower buds appear, interplant perennials or annuals with green bamboo stakes. Position several bamboo stakes with each plant so their tops rest just beneath the top leaves. As the plants grow, move the stakes upward so they stay slightly below those top leaves. Constantly knocking into bamboo poles makes eating the plants difficult for the deer. By the time your flowers bloom, they may have already given up and moved on to other plants.

- Trees. To prevent damage to young trees by rubbing antlers, place four bamboo poles around the tree. Bend the poles inward and tie the tops together with sturdy twine, forming an arching pyramid-like shape over the tree. Hang bells or rattles from the twine for an additional distraction.

ADD PIZZAZZ WITH SPECIAL GARDEN FEATURES

FUN ATTRACTIONS
BIRDS, BUTTERFLIES & MORE

Invite beautiful cardinals into your yard. Cardinals don't migrate. If you play your cards right, you could have a family of cardinals in your yard for years. Here's how to start.

- Entice them into your yard during winter with a special seed mix of safflower and black oil sunflower seeds. Place this in a pole-mounted bird feeder about 5 feet above the ground. To help protect against climbing squirrels and cats, snip the base off a one-gallon milk jug, remove its cap, and thread it over your bird feeder pole. Attach it near the pole's top.

- Provide a water source, such as a birdbath, and change the water regularly.

- Offer a tempting nesting site. Cardinals like a mix of evergreens and deciduous trees, but they often nest in shrubs that border lawn space. Consider adding such nesting favorites as viburnum, dogwood, hawthorn, elderberry, or hackberry.

Reap a bumper crop of butterflies. The plants below are among the best herbs and flowers to attract butterflies. Make sure you select plants that feed butterflies throughout the season. For example, you could plant dill, nasturtium, and sedum for spring; cosmos, purple coneflower, and butterfly weed for summer; and asters and Joe-pye weed for fall. Also include plants butterfly larvae or caterpillars eat. Good choices are fennel, parsley, milkweed, oregano, marigold, or snapdragon. Once you have the right mix, fill in gaps with other butterfly favorites like borage, heliotrope, coreopsis, zinnias, chives, and butterfly bush.

Attract butterflies like a magnet

Try any of these seven plants for an instant "butterfly garden."

- bee balm
- black-eyed Susan
- daylily
- dianthus
- spider flower
- viburnum
- yarrow

---

3 ingredients for a bird-filled yard. To attract the most birds to your yard, you need some plants that produce berries, others that produce plenty of edible seeds, and a few that entice the insects eaten by some birds. Below you will find some of the best herbs, flowers, and other plants to attract birds in each of these categories. Include plants from all three of these groups.

- Plants for seed-lovers — fennel, sea lavender, English marigold, angelica, bachelor's button, cosmos, Mexican sunflower, nasturtium, purple coneflower, snapdragon, sunflower, and sweet alyssum.

- Plants for berry-lovers — beautyberry, blueberry, chokeberry, Cornelian cherry, Juneberry, Oregon grape holly, rose, Sargent crabapple, snowberry, and viburnum.

- Plants for insect-lovers — barberry, cotoneaster, dogwood, elderberry, or holly.

Keep squirrels out of your bird feeder. Squirrels can jump at least 10 feet. So hang your bird feeder on a horizontal wire, and make sure the feeder is at least 12 feet away from trees, bushes, poles, buildings, or any surface a squirrel could reach. To keep them from running along the wire, string "spinners" along the entire span of the wire. The squirrels fall off these spinners like lumberjacks in a logrolling contest. Good choices for spinners include foot-long lengths of gar-

den hose or PVC pipe, capless empty soda bottles with a hole poked in the bottom, and tennis ball canisters or wide pre-scription pill bottles with a hole added to the lid and bottom.

Convert a Frisbee into a birdbath. Just follow these steps:

- Find a hanging basket chain, the kind with a hook on top and several chains hanging down to support the basket. Pick up a few S-hooks that can fit the chains.

- Scrub the Frisbee clean with warm, soapy water. Disinfect it by soaking it in a solution of 10 parts water to one part bleach for 20 minutes. Rinse thoroughly, and wipe dry with a clean cloth.

- Drill holes for the hanging basket chains in the rim of your Frisbee. Position the holes to match the locations of the chains.

- Slip S-hooks in the Frisbee holes and thread the hanging basket chains through the S-hooks.

Lure butterflies with water and heat. Butterflies can't drink unless they have a dry place to perch. What's more, butterflies are cold-blooded, so they love sun-heated rocks where they can bask and warm themselves. You can provide both. Just place your birdbath in the sun, drop a few pale, flat stones in the water or around its edges — and watch the colorful fly-in begin. If you don't have a birdbath, bury a shallow lid or flat pan in a sun-drenched spot, fill with sand and dirt, and add water regularly. For best results, place this dish where it can get plenty of sunshine in the morning, and tuck a few light-colored rocks around its edge. Butterflies can't fly until their body temperatures reach 85 degrees, so these ground level rocks can help them warm up enough to fly.

Create a suet feeder for pennies. Grab a log from your firewood pile. Drill seven or eight holes 1 inch deep and 1 inch wide in the log. Place the holes on both sides of the log so every hole is several inches away from the other holes. Insert a small screw hook in the top end of the log, so you can hang it up. To fill the holes, melt suet in a pan on the stove, and mix in peanut butter, cornmeal, and some birdseed or raisins. Let the mixture cool until warm, pack it into the log's holes, and hang your new feeder outside.

> ### *Remove a birdbath hazard*
>
> Birds can get so wet from bathing that they become too heavy to fly more than a few feet. On open ground, this temporary handicap can make them easy targets for predators. Place your birdbath near a tree with overhanging branches, so the birds can easily reach a perch. This gives them a safe place to preen and shake off water.

Turn an old mailbox into a new birdhouse. Keep an eye out for old mailboxes at yard sales. Turning them into birdhouses is easy. Just find out what size hole your favorite variety of bird likes, and drill a hole that size in the back of your mailbox. Then simply attach it to a post and wait. When the birds leave for good, open the mailbox door, clean out your birdhouse, and prepare it for the next nesting pair.

Attract hummingbirds with herbs and nectar-rich flowers. Want hummingbirds to grace your garden? Attract the tiny beauties by planting herbs with heavenly scents, such as rosemary, sage, hyssop, mint, and anise hyssop. Or try gorgeous, colorful flowers like fuchsia, columbine, petunia, garden phlox, trumpet creeper, rose of Sharon, daylily, cardinal flower, hollyhock, cuphea, bee balm, and butterfly bush. But be careful. If you plant all your hummingbird attractors in one part of your yard, the hummingbirds will fight over that plot, and fewer hummingbirds will visit. To host as many hummers as possible, spread hummingbird-friendly herbs, flowers, and feeders throughout your yard.

Block ants from your hummingbird feeder. Make an ant-proof barrier for your hummingbird feeder.

- Tie a thick knot in the fishing line your feeder hangs from.

- Find an old spray can top, like the kind from spray paint or hairspray. Poke a hole in the center.

- Coat the inside surfaces of the spray can top with Tanglefoot.

- Turn the spray can top so the open side is facing down, and thread it on your hummingbird feeder line so it hangs from the knot.

Ants can't reach your hummingbird nectar without crossing the sticky underside, so you shouldn't see them in the nectar anymore. The barrier also will not collect dust or pose a threat to your hummingbirds. But regularly check the inside for other kinds of build-up. It may need cleaning and a fresh coat of Tanglefoot once in a while.

Transform a problem spot into a showplace. Don't fret if you have a sunny slope that constantly erodes or is too tough to mow. That annoying slope can become an eye-catching rock garden. Move a group of large stones or boulders from other spots on your property, or have them delivered from a stone yard. Place the larger stones along the bottom half of the slope and smaller stones around the top half. Bury each stone so one-third is below soil level. Slant the stones so the largest part of the top surface directs rain to the upward slope behind the stone — to direct water to your plants. Fill in the surrounding area with smaller stones and plants such as dianthus, thrift, creeping phlox, and hens and chicks.

Easy way to find rock garden seeds

Finding seeds for the alpine plants suited to rock gardens can be a challenge, and the seeds may be expensive. Fortunately, the North American Rock Garden Society (NARGS) may be able to help. If you apply for membership and pay the $30 annual fee, you can participate in their seed exchange. That means you collect five packets of seeds from your rock garden, send your seed donation to NARGS by the deadline, and receive 35 packets of free seed in January or February. For more details about membership and the seed exchange, visit *www.nargs.org* or write to: NARGS, P.O. Box 18604, Raleigh, NC 27619-8604.

Easily clean tight spaces in hummingbird feeders. The same pipe cleaners you used as a child can help clean tiny tubes and other tight spaces in your hummingbird feeder. Use three pipe cleaners to do a thorough job. Dip a pipe cleaner in water, put one drop of mild hand-dishwashing liquid on its end, and use it like a bottle brush. Rinse the area with water. If you can't do that, dampen a second pipe cleaner, and use the same bottle-brush technique to rinse where you just cleaned. Soak the other end of the pipe cleaner, and rinse again. Dry with a third pipe cleaner.

End the bird droppings on your deck rails. You love birds, but hate the droppings on your deck railing. To keep birds from landing, place stones or shards of brick every few inches along the railing, or string wire 3 inches above it. Before using harsh commercial products to clean off the droppings currently on the railing, try scrubbing with a stiff brush, water, and a small amount of mild dishwashing liquid.

Give mom-to-be birds a treat. Female birds give up a lot of calcium to lay eggs, so they must eat plenty of calcium before egg laying begins. You can help. Save your eggshells, which are rich in calcium. Rinse the shells thoroughly, boil them for five minutes, and bake them at 250 degrees until they are dry, but not brown. Let cool, crumble into seed-size pieces, and spread them on your platform feeder. Female birds will flock to your yard just to enjoy this treat.

Shield your bird feeder from squirrel raids. Follow this two-step process, and you may never fight squirrels again. First, move your pole-mounted bird feeder away from trees and any other jumping-off point squirrels could use. Then add this clever squirrel baffle.

- Remove the lid from a plastic five-gallon bucket. In the center of the bucket's bottom, drill a hole large enough for the bird feeder pole to pass through.

- Drill two nail-size holes on opposite sides of this large hole. Position each one 2 inches away from the large hole.

- Slide the bucket over the bird feeder pole, and thread a length of strong wire hanger through the small holes in the bucket's bottom.

- Hang the bucket from the feeder using the free ends of the wire hanger.

Disinfect your bird feeder to keep birds healthy. Clean and disinfect your bird feeder every time you refill it. After emptying the old seed, scrub and rinse the feeder. Prepare a solution of one part bleach to nine parts water. Soak your bird feeder in this solution for five minutes. If the feeder is too large for soaking, pour the bleach-and-water mixture in a spray bottle, and spray the feeder thoroughly and generously. Rinse carefully with clean water, and let it dry completely before you refill it.

Tempt birds with nest ingredients. Provide nesting materials, and you will make your yard even more attractive to birds. Save mesh vegetable bags, or use a wire mesh suet cage. Fill with cotton batting, 6-inch lengths of string or yarn, human hair trimmings, sheep's wool, or 1-inch strips of cloth the same length as a dollar bill. Attach the bag or cage to a fence post, tree trunk, or deck railing, and the birds will take what they need.

No weeds from nyjer seed

Nyjer seed from Africa and southeast Asia is sterilized with high heat before you buy it, so it won't sprout into weeds if birds spill it on the ground.

Let birds do the work of planting. Include whole sunflower seeds in the mix you put into your bird feeder, and place the feeder where you want flowers to grow. Hungry birds will drop seeds while they eat, and sunflower plants will follow naturally. You can even move your feeder around your yard from season to season to spread the crop.

Create an affordable pedestal birdbath. You can make an inexpensive birdbath if you have an old vegetable cage or bean tower. Here's how.

- Anchor your vegetable cage or bean tower in the ground.

- Measure the width of the top ring, and buy a plastic "imitation terra cotta" plant saucer to fit that opening.

- To help cover and decorate the tower or cage, plant a fast-growing flowering vine nearby, or substitute a potted English ivy plant.

- Thread green twine or fishing line among the rings of your tower or cage, so your ivy or vine can climb in to fill the empty spaces.

MAKE A SPLASH WITH WONDERFUL WATER

Test drive a water garden. Consider a water garden in a container if you've never tried water gardening before, or don't have space for one. You can create a water garden from a child's plastic wading pool, a large plastic tub, or a wooden half barrel. Just make sure it can hold your submerged plants, pots, and soil, plus at least four gallons of water. Also, read up on water gardening to help you learn about:

- managing potential mosquito problems.

- overwintering your garden.

- choosing plants for your climate and container.

Place your water garden in a spot that receives six hours of sunlight daily, fill with water, and add your plants. Just remember to fertilize with a water-soluble fertilizer, and use no more than half the amount recommended for the size of your container.

Spend less on floating pots. Make your own floating pot with three inexpensive ingredients and these instructions.

- Pay no more than a few dollars for a round, open-topped oil drain pan to serve as your pot.

- Select a children's swim noodle that can easily wrap around the rim of the pan.

- Set out some zip ties.

- Drill a few small holes in the bottom of the drain pan to allow water in.

- Drill one hole slightly below the pan's rim. Picture that as midnight on an imaginary clock resting on the rim. Drill three more holes at 3:00, 6:00, and 9:00, all slightly below the rim.

- Thread zip ties through the holes near the pan's rim.

- Wrap the swim noodle around the outside of the pan close to the rim, and cut to size.

- Pull each zip tie tight to secure the swim noodle to the pan.

Save money on fish

Contrary to what you may have heard, koi and other expensive fish are not a requirement for your water garden. One koi may cost $10 or more, and each koi needs more than 2 square yards of space. Goldfish or mosquito fish *(Gambusia)* are inexpensive, need less space, and are excellent choices for any water garden. What's more, these money-saving fish are readily available at many stores that sell water garden supplies.

Cut your water gardening costs. Slash several water gardening expenses with these tips.

- Instead of buying specialty potting mixes for water gardening, mix regular potting mix with unscented cat litter.

- Stop planting water lilies in expensive basket planters, and start planting them in old plastic dishpans or other containers. Just remember to top off the soil with a layer of gravel, so it doesn't float out into the pond water.

- Get water garden plants without breaking the bank. Ask a friend with a water garden to share or trade plants with you, or organize a plant exchange among several water gardeners.

Figure your pond's square yardage. You often need to know your water garden's square footage or yardage to follow instructions for maintaining your pond. Use these steps to calculate that number. For a square or rectangular water garden:

- Multiply the length times the width in feet to figure square feet.

- Divide this result by 9 to figure square yards.

A circular water garden is more complicated, so use these directions instead:

- Divide the width by two to get the radius.

- Multiply the radius times itself.

- Multiply that result by 3.14 to calculate square feet.

- Divide square feet by 9 for square yards.

For example, if your pond is 10 feet wide, divide 10 feet by 2 for a radius of 5. Multiply 5 by itself for a result of 25. Multiply 25 times 3.14 to equal 78.5 square feet. Divide 78.5 by 9 for a square yardage of 8.72.

Recipe for a successful water garden. Choose the right mix of plants, and you are less likely to be plagued with algae and other water garden problems. To start your pond off right, follow this recipe.

- One medium-size water lily for every square yard of pond surface, or enough water lilies, lotuses, and floating plants to cover 50 to 70 percent of the pond surface during summer. Shade from water lilies and floating plants help prevent algae growth.

- Two or three bunches of submerged or oxygenating plants for every square yard of pond surface. These plants help purify the water, and keep enough oxygen in the pond.

- Enough marginal and bog plants to cover one-third of the water garden's edge. These add a little extra algae-fighting shade.

Prevent fish problems right from the start

Adding too many fish to your pond can lead to disaster. To determine the right number, imagine several fish lined up end to end with each fish's tail touching the nose of the next fish. That line of fish can be no longer than the square footage of your pond multiplied by two.

For example, if you had a 12-square-foot pond, you would multiply 12 times 2 for a result of 24. That means your line of fish can be 24 inches long. In other words, you can have four 6-inch-long fish because 6 times 4 equals 24 — or you can have eight 3-inch-long fish because 8 times 3 also equals 24. Just keep in mind that koi are the exception to this rule because each koi needs 25 square feet of space.

Beware these algae-fighting mistakes. Don't rush to apply algaecide or replace the water when your pond turns an algae-ridden pea green. Do this instead.

- Keep the same pond water. Algae forms when sun exposure and nutrient levels are high. Change the water, and you give the algae fresh nutrients. Just leave the water alone, and nutrient levels will dwindle naturally. Also, include surface-covering plants like water lilies to reduce the algae's supply of sunlight.

- Think twice about algaecide. Algaecide can be dangerous to fish and plants, but healthy ponds with algae don't harm fish — except when algae are excessive. To determine whether you have too much algae, attach an aluminum pie plate to the bottom of a yardstick, and submerge the plate. If you can't see the plate when it's about 18 inches deep, ask your local cooperative extension agent how to safely and quickly reduce algae.

Twirl your pond algae away. Your beautiful clear water garden suddenly developed a mat of green, but you can get rid of it quickly. Push a rake, pitchfork, or long stick into the matted mess, and twirl it as if it were spaghetti on a fork. The long ropes of algae will wrap around your twirler, so you can easily dump it on your compost pile. When the algae are cleared away, clean the rake or pitchfork with bleach, and rinse it thoroughly.

Create a leaf netting dome. Keep decaying autumn leaves out of your water garden with this clever trick.

- Remove the cloth from an old patio umbrella.

- Place the umbrella so the center post is in the center of your pond, and the ends of the umbrella tines rest on dry land.

- Pin each tine to the ground with garden staples or landscape pins.

- Lash each pin to the garden staple with sturdy twine.

- Place leaf netting over the umbrella frame, and secure it with tent spikes or small stakes. Reinforce by tying the netting to the spikes or stakes with twine.

If you don't have an old patio umbrella, place a plastic beach ball or two in your pond to hold the netting above the water.

Keep pond walls from cracking. When your pond ices over, the water doesn't just freeze. It also expands. That puts pressure on your pond walls and can cause them to crack. Fortunately, you can prevent this easily if you live in an area where freezes don't last long. Before the first freeze, place one of these in your water garden.

- Planks or small logs.

- Tennis balls or other rubber balls.

- Empty but loosely capped milk jugs, bleach bottles, or economy size juice jugs. Fill with just enough gravel to keep the top third of the bottle above the water surface.

The ice puts pressure on these items, relieving the pressure on the walls of your water garden.

3 "harmless" mistakes that kill fish. Avoid these fatal errors when adding water or fish to your water garden.

- Buying fish right away. Your new pond needs at least four weeks to develop enough helpful bacteria to control ammonia levels in a fish-filled pond. Add only a few fish at first, and begin adding more after a month or so.

- Ignoring water chemistry. Call your water company, and ask what chemicals they use or allow in the water. For example, you may need to test for chlorine and chloramine in tap water, and apply chorine and chloramine removers to that water before fish can swim in it.

- Using rain barrel water. Don't add rain barrel water drained from your roof to a fish-filled water garden. Roof rainwater contains small amounts of contaminants that may harm fish.

Sink pond plant aphids. You may have heard that you should hose aphids off your water lilies and other water garden plants, but aphids are tricky. They often rush back on the plant leaves before they drown or can be eaten by fish. To get them off your plants for good, submerge the leaves for up to 24 hours using chicken wire or plastic mesh. Add weights to the wire or mesh, if needed.

Prevent a spring burst of pond algae. Start searching for a source of dried barley straw after Christmas. You apply the straw in late winter to help prevent algae outbreaks when the water warms. As barley straw decomposes, it produces a compound that prevents algae from growing. Plan to use 1 pound for every 100 square feet of water garden surface or roughly one-fourth pound for every square yard. To apply, place your straw in mesh produce bags. If your water garden is less than 6 feet deep, tie a stone to the bag so it stays near the bottom. For a deeper pond, consider tying the string to an empty plastic bottle to prevent it from sinking too deep. The straw lasts between two weeks and four months before it needs replacing, so keep extra straw on hand.

Quash water garden mosquitoes. Invite dragonflies to visit your water garden. They won't bite or sting you, and they love to gobble mosquitoes, diving beetles, gnats, and flies. Even better, they can devour enough bugs in one day to equal as much as 15 percent of their body weight. Because dragonflies can also fly at speeds up to 35 miles per hour, mosquitoes don't stand a chance. To invite dragonflies to your water garden, add water lilies to your pond, avoid using pesticides, and include a few rocks and sticks at the water's edge.

Plot a perfect hole for your pond liner. Dig the hole for your hard-shell pond liner more easily and efficiently. Outline it first with one of these clever tricks.

- Trace a simple silhouette. If your pond liner is a symmetrical shape like a circle, rectangle, square, or oval, simply turn the liner bottom side up, and trace around the rim with spray paint or a line of evenly spaced garden staples.

- Frame an irregular form. If the pond liner is not symmetrical, ask friends to hold the liner in place right side up while you use a tall stick, shovel, or stakes to mark the area directly below the rim. Move the pond liner out of the way, and either spray paint a thick line over the markings, or connect your garden staples or stakes with lines of spray paint before pulling them up.

Smart way to install a preformed pond liner

Don't make the mistake of digging a hole that exactly matches the depth of your preformed pond liner. The ground beneath the liner may contain sharp-edged rocks or other items that can tear or puncture the liner or bumps that tilt the liner so it will never be level. To work around these problems, dig a hole about 2 inches deeper than the liner, so you can fill the bottom with 2 inches of sifted soil. This sifted soil creates a smooth protective base layer for the pond liner to rest on. Not only does this protect the pond liner from sharp edges or bumps, it also helps you level the pond properly.

Prevent leaf litter on your water garden. Before you spend money on a pond skimmer, wrap netting around the prongs of your garden pitchfork. Temporarily secure the netting with clothespins or office binder clips to make a leaf scooper for your pond. But when autumn comes, try a new tactic. Place netting over your entire water garden to catch the leaves. That could save hours of leaf-skimming.

FENCES, TRELLISES & ARBORS
PRETTY & PRACTICAL ADD-ONS

Soften a lattice fence instantly. Your flowering vines will take weeks to cover your new lattice fence, but you have company coming and cannot wait. So rearrange what you already have. Select several of your hanging baskets that have beautiful flowers or stunning foliage, and hang them from the top of your lattice fence. Fill in gaps with tall house-plants or topiaries placed at the foot of the fence. Move a gazing ball, quaint birdhouse, or wind spinner from another part of your yard, or put up outdoor holiday decorations if a holiday is less than a month away.

Fix yard flaws for less. You could hide eyesores and solve privacy problems with a fence, but consider these cheaper options first.

- Hide the compost heap, garbage cans, tool shed, or a bare wall with a trellis. For best results, grow an evergreen vine on your trellis. Contact your local cooperative extension agent to learn which ones grow best in your area.

- Turn a chain link fence into a trellis. Train vining vegetables like beans on the links of the fence. Or fill in with a fast-growing annual vine like morning glory while waiting for a flowering perennial vine to gradually cover the fence.

- To sit on your deck or patio without being in full view of the neighbors, plant support posts in the ground nearby, and hang lattice panels from them. Grow fragrant vines on the lattice, and hook hanging baskets from the support posts.

Easy trellis for hard-to-climb fences. Twining vines cannot climb your flat wooden or vinyl fence, and you do not want to use hooks or nails. But if you can fit nylon string, fishing line, or twine between the fence's slats, you can make a fan trellis. To start, pound a notched two-foot stake into the ground near the fence. Pick a slat to start with, and follow these instructions for every two to three slats until you complete three lines.

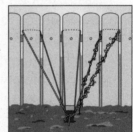

- Tie one end of your line around the stake inside the notch.

- Thread the line to the top of the fence and down between the two fence boards until you reach a cross board.

- Pass the line behind the slat and into the gap on the other side.

- Unwind the line down to your stake, and tie it off.

Beautify a plain wood privacy fence. For privacy and security, choose a tall wood fence with no gaps between the boards — but top it with flowers. Hang flat-backed, half-barrel planters along the top of the fence, and fill them with long-blooming annuals. This transforms your stockade-style fence into something straight out of an Alpine village. To further disguise the fence's harsh lines, fill in the gaps between the barrel planters with trees and bushes of different heights. Include small trees like dogwoods or flowering cherries, midsize shrubs like forsythia, and small bushes such as dwarf euonymus or dwarf fothergilla.

Turn old junk into a new trellis. Pick up an old metal headboard from a yard sale. To prepare it for use, remove the rust or let it be part of the headboard's charm. You can even prime and paint the headboard. To anchor your new trellis:

- Choose metal stakes or posts at least 2 feet high, but not taller than the headboard's outer posts. You can paint these stakes to match the headboard, but let them dry completely before using them.

- Pound a stake a foot deep into the ground where you want each headboard leg to sit.

- Sink the headboard legs into the ground in front of the posts.

- Attach the headboard to the posts with wire or a few zip ties near the top of each stake and several more a few inches above the ground.

Spruce up your front entry. Add an arbor to a plain, porchless front entry for almost-instant charm. Your arbor should be 3 to 4 feet wide to allow enough room for people to pass through. To save money on a large arbor, buy the plainest wood arbor you can find, and adapt it to match your house. For example, you can paint it to coordinate or contrast with your house color, your door, or your shutters. You can also add wood molding, metal accents, or finials that complement your home's style. The choices are up to you. To finish, top the new arbor with a lovely flowering vine like morning glory or moonflower. Your neighbors will be amazed at your picturesque new entryway.

Save plants from death by rain shadow

Don't place plants close to a fence if they need plenty of water. The ground within the first 2 feet of your fence is a rain shadow, meaning it receives less rain than the rest of your yard. This happens because rain falls diagonally when the wind blows. As a result, rain falls against one side of the fence, instead of reaching the ground on the other side.

So place your water hogs at least 2 feet away from the fence, or plan on giving them extra water when they need it. For even better results, reserve that strip near the fence for plants that like a dryer environment.

What not to grow on your arbor. Before you plant anything on an arbor over your front entry, porch, or patio, get answers to these questions about the plant.

- Does it have thorns? Roses and other thorny plants may need constant pruning to keep them from scratching your visitors.

- How big does it get, and how fast does it grow? Some vines can grow up to 40 feet or grow very rapidly. That also means plenty of pruning.

- Does it drop plenty of flowers, fruits, or leaves? You don't want splattered berries all over your porch or your guests.

- What does it look like during winter? You can pull down a dying annual vine until next year. But if you choose a perennial plant, make sure you are comfortable with its winter look or have an easy way to camouflage it.

Solve 2 twig arbor problems. Twig arbors have a rustic beauty, and you can make them from free branches and twigs gathered from your yard. But these arbors never last as long as you would like, and you may have trouble finding enough twigs to complete an arbor. To help your arbor last longer, strip the bark off your twigs and branches, and plunge the ends into a preservative before you set them in the ground. To make the same arbor with fewer twigs and branches, try one of these tactics.

- Instead of seating your arbor on the ground, nestle each end in a soil-filled container such as a half-whiskey barrel, washtub, or a plastic pot of similar size.

- Find a source of free saplings to use for the sides of the arbor so you only need enough twigs and branches for the top section.

Block sunlight or snow with a temporary fence. Try a roll of wire-bound reed fencing when you need an inexpensive temporary fence. This fencing features long, vertical reeds tightly bound together by woven wire. You can quickly put up a roll of this fencing to block sunlight or drifting snow. If you need fencing that can temporarily keep animal pests out of an area, a stronger or taller fence may be necessary. Contact your local cooperative extension agent for advice specific to your pest and local conditions.

Help a fence or arbor last longer. Seal your fence or arbor within two months if it is made from pressure-treated lumber. The pressure treatment only protects against damage caused by bugs, fungus, and rodents. It does not protect the wood from weathering, or from the warping and cracking that may occur during the months following pressure treatment. If the wood in your arbor or fence didn't have a sealer applied at the factory, seal it within two weeks with a sealer designed for pressure treated wood. But wait until two or three months have passed before you paint or stain it.

Avoid the fences burglars like

A tall, solid wood fence may be a poor choice for a security fence if you live in the city. That fence may hide you from nosy neighbors, but it also hides any potential burglars or other intruders that find a way inside it. A chain link fence is not much better because someone could cut it with wire cutters or easily climb over. A security fence should be:

- at least 6 feet high.
- made of a metal like wrought iron, tubular steel, aluminum, or welded wire so it can't be cut or breached.
- difficult to climb due to a lack of footholds and handholds, or because the top of the fence is spiky or veers outward.
- open enough so you can see what's inside.

Create your own custom-built trellis. Learn how to work with bamboo, and you can tailor a trellis to any size and shape you need. Use these tips to help you get started.

- Buy bamboo from garden stores, hardware stores, or online.

- Cut bamboo to size with a handsaw. Always cut upward-facing ends just above a node so they won't hold water and trigger rot.

- On a flat surface, lay out cut canes to match your trellis design. Use a ruler to space the canes the right distance apart.

- Temporarily hold intersecting canes in place with loops of painter's tape, so they don't shift when you lash other canes together.

- Lash canes together with zip ties, twist ties, or garden wire.

- If you use wire, wrap it around several times, twist the ends together with pliers, snip short, and curl the sharp ends inward toward the bamboo cane.

Make tough soil easier to dig. Rock-hard clay soils make digging a post hole painfully difficult. But you can soften your soil with a little help from your hose and a one-gallon milk jug.

- Dampen the spot where your first post hole will be.

- Dig a hole roughly 8 inches deep, but several inches wider than you need.

- Fill an empty one-gallon milk jug with your hose.

- Empty the entire jug into the hole. You may have to pause to prevent an overflow.

- Repeat this process for each post hole.

When little or no water is left in the first post hole, deepen the hole with your shovel or post hole digger. If your digger strikes rock-hard dry clay before your hole is deep enough, water the hole again, wait one or two hours, and finish digging.

Keep your dogs out of your garden. Your dogs own the back-yard, but you want to start a garden there. Here are a few nifty ways to protect your garden.

- Enclose a small garden patch using the panels and gate from a chain-link dog kennel. This is easy to install, and you can secure it with tent stakes or landscape pins.

- If you don't have large dogs, consider a cheaper option. Fence in a large garden or several individual beds with a roll of chicken wire. Drive long stakes into the ground to anchor and support your chicken wire fence. Tie an old baby gate to two stakes to use as your gate, and reinforce the fencing with landscape pins or tent stakes.

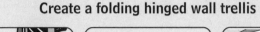

Create a folding hinged wall trellis

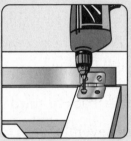  

Mount a strip of wood just below where you expect the bottom of your trellis to rest. Attach half of a metal hinge to the wood strip or block and the other half to the trellis.

Mount a second wood strip near where the top of the trellis will be. Attach screw eyes to it. Fasten hooks to corresponding locations on the back of the trellis so you can hook and unhook the trellis from the wall.

Train soft-stemmed vines like Virginia creeper to grow on your trellis. Vines with woody trunks will not fold down.

Keep your fence on your property. Before you fence along the edge of your yard, make sure you don't place that fence on your neighbor's property. Check the plat map you received when you bought your home, or contact your city or county assessor's office for a copy. Using that map, look for the metal stakes that mark the corners of your property. Most properties have these stakes, but not all. You may find them easily, or they may be buried underground. Renting a metal detector can help you locate underground stakes, and connecting the corners with string should show where your lot lines are. But if you are concerned about a dispute or possible legal action, hire a surveyor to legally certify where the lines are.

Turn ladders into an arbor. Pull your old wooden ladders or stepladders out of storage, and put them to work. You need three ladders or two stepladders to follow these instructions.

- Remove the backs if you use stepladders.

- Cut the ladders to equal size if they are not the same height.

- Attach posts to the legs of each ladder with screws.

- Position the two ladders so a stepladder back or third ladder can span the space between them.

- Sink each post deep in the ground so it's firmly seated.

- To complete the arbor, fasten the ladder-back or third ladder across the tops of the standing ladders with screws or twine.

- Grow grapevines or annual flowering vines up the arbor.

Wind protection for your plants. A solid fence only blocks the wind for a distance equal to the fence's height, so a 6-foot fence only provides 6 feet of protection. But studies suggest "open fences" may extend wind protection up to eight times as far — nearly 48 feet for a 6-foot fence. These open fences include lattice fences or slatted fences with 1-inch gaps separating the boards. The gaps disrupt the wind and slow it down, providing significant protection for your plants. The zone of best protection occurs at a distance between five and eight times the height of your fence. For a 6-foot fence, that zone would be between 30 feet away from the fence (6 times 5 equals 30) and 48 feet away (6 times 8 equals 48). Place your fence so the plants that need the most wind protection fall in that zone.

INS & OUTS OF GARDEN PATHS

Eliminate weeds safely with vinegar. Start watching for weeds between your pathway pavers in early spring. As soon as you see the first sprout, pour undiluted vinegar into a spray bottle, and spray it directly on the weeds between the pavers. But don't stop there. Spray between weed-free pavers as well, and you may not see weeds all season. Just remember two things when you use this spray.

- Spray weeds when they are small. Older, taller weeds may need more than one spray of vinegar to take them down.

- Vinegar can kill any plant it touches. Protect plants growing near your pathway with this. Trim off the bottom of a plastic 2-liter bottle, and place the bottle over the weed. Insert the sprayer nozzle into the mouth of the bottle, spray the weed with vinegar, and wait 30 seconds before lifting the bottle.

Save money on walkways. Enjoy brick pavers without the sticker shock of an all-brick walk. Install a poured concrete walk with decorative brick strips or edging, and pocket the savings. If your heart is set on a concrete paver walk, you can still save money if you already have leftover wall bricks. Just use those bricks to edge your walk instead of buying more concrete pavers. Line the bricks up lengthwise in two parallel trenches, and place the concrete pavers between these lines so the bricks can hold the pavers in place.

Garden path materials for cheap or free

Clever gardeners say you don't have to spend a lot on the ingredients for your path. Copy their methods and see how much you can save.

- Check construction sites in your area for piles of broken concrete. Ask permission to take a few small pieces from each site. Only choose those with at least one broad, flat surface. Turn these into a stepping stone path by digging deep enough to set them flush with the ground.
- Call commercial tree trimmers, and ask if they offer leftover wood chips for free. They may even deliver right to your driveway.
- Contact your city or county government public works department. Some cities regularly give away wood mulch to their residents.
- Restore an old pathway with a generous layer of playground mulch.

Low-cost alternative to poured concrete. "Fines" or "crusher fines" are a mix of stone dust and tiny gravel readily available from stone yards. Fines cost less than concrete, but it can bind together to create a durable trail. Before purchasing fines, ask about the cost of delivery and whether additives are needed to bind the fines together. Meanwhile, design your trail with almost no slope, and make sure it doesn't pass through spots where water puddles or runs. To lay the trail, follow these steps.

- Dig a square-bottomed ditch 4 to 6 inches deep and slightly wider than your planned path.

- Line the ditch with landscape fabric secured by land-scape pins.

- Fill the ditch with fines and tamp down.

- Rake the path smooth

- Mist the entire surface sparingly until barely damp.

The dust and gravel particles compact tightly together forming a solid surface.

Prevent falls with a slip-resistant surface. You didn't like skinning your knees and hands when you were a child, and you certainly wouldn't like it now. If you have concerns about falls or balance, don't choose gravel as your path surface, and remember that brick and slate paving are slippery when wet. Consider nonslip surfaces like these instead.

- Porous concrete. This drains water quickly, but you will pay more for it.

- Traditional concrete. It is less expensive, but you must lightly score it with a stiff-bristled broom before the concrete sets if you want to create a nonslip surface.

- Interlocking pavers. Available from home improvement centers, these offer good traction if they are correctly laid on a bed of sand or stone dust.

You can also get good traction using slabs from a coarse-grained stone such as bluestone.

Add design features for garden carts and wheelchairs. Set up your path to accommodate wheelbarrows and garden carts now, and it will also accommodate a wheelchair if you should ever need one. Include these cart- and wheelbarrow-friendly features.

- Make the path at least 3 feet wide with a 5-foot-wide space for turning around.

- If the path must pass over a slope, shift dirt from the higher side of the path to the lower side. You'll have a level path that doesn't tilt with the angle of the slope.

- Make sure the rise or descent of the path is never steeper than 1 foot for every 20 feet of length.

- Don't include stairs in your path plans.

Make a fines path safe for wheelchairs

A garden path made of crusher fines doesn't usually offer the kind of rock-hard, even surface that wheelchairs need. To make a wheelchair-ready path, mix a stabilizer or hardener like lime into the fines so your path will become even harder when it sets. Ask the stone yard or landscaping company if they offer options like this with their products. If they don't, ask what hardener they recommend and how to use it.

Choose bug-fighting patio lighting. You and your guests will never enjoy your garden pathways at night if you must pass through a patio full of flying bugs first. So choose yellow-tinted patio lighting bugs cannot see. Install a 150-watt high-pressure sodium bulb in an eave-mounted or tree-mounted fixture. Many bugs are attracted to lights that produce more ultraviolet and blue light, but this soft, pinkish-yellow light produces very little. Instead of swarming around this light, bugs go elsewhere. What's more, the high-pressure sodium bulb may save you money because it is very energy-efficient and long-lived. Supplement this light with candle-powered lanterns, light from a chiminea, or small table lamps with low-wattage yellow light bulbs.

Make a small yard look bigger. A garden path can help you create the illusion of extra space in your yard, but you must plan it wisely. Lay out your path diagonally so it crosses your yard once — or even twice — before reaching the back border. This focuses the eye on the long, diagonal lines in your yard instead of the shorter width and length. If you can create meandering curves that veer around or disappear

---

Creative ways to light up your garden

Down lighting. Place lights above eye level to light your patio or walkway. Light fixtures can be mounted from the patio, eaves, or even from trees.

Spread lighting. Use short, low-voltage lights that are partly or fully shielded so they direct the light downward. This helps light your path without adding glare that can trip you up.

Silhouetting. Add beauty to your walkway by placing a light below and behind a tree, bush, statue, or bed of flowers to emphasize its lovely shape or structure.

---

behind structures or plants, your yard may seem even more spacious. You and your visitors will no longer feel as if you can take in the entire yard at a glance. Instead, the meandering path and hidden areas suggest that your yard offers more to see than what initially meets the eye.

Age new bricks to match old ones. The bricks you bought to repair your walkway look too new to match your old bricks. If you can't exchange them for a closer match, try one of these techniques.

- Rub the bricks against one another to age them.

- Apply mud, sand, or a mix of mud and chimney soot to the brick, coating it thoroughly. Let dry in the sun or in a place sheltered from rain.

- Buy yogurt that promises "live and active cultures" on its label. Apply a heavy layer to the brick, and let it sit under shelter for two weeks.

Rinse the brick, and see how much older it looks.

Avoid laying crooked pathway pavers

Laying pavers on a bed of sand or gravel can be tricky. Lay just one row out of alignment, and the end of your path will be crooked, too. To prevent that, stretch a line of string over the pathway every few feet, and pin it in place. This string serves as a guide. If the pavers don't line up with a string, you can quickly realign the last few feet of pavers and correct the mistake before it turns into a major headache.

Rescue your walkway from freeze damage. Frost heave can push flagstones or cobblestones out of a garden path, so prepare the ground correctly before laying that path. Frost heave happens when the ground keeps alternating between thawing and freezing, usually during late autumn or early spring. Water caught in the soil freezes and expands, pushing the soil upward. That shoves your stones upward, too, sometimes rolling them aside. But if you leave extra room for the ice to expand, you may save your stones from frost heaving. So dig an 8-inch-deep trench as wide as your path. Fill it with crushed stone, tiny gravel, or coarse sand, and lay the cobblestone or flagstone path on top of it.

Prevent water from eroding your path. Water can damage your garden path or simply submerge it. Take these steps to prevent both problems.

- Before constructing your path, examine your property after each heavy rain. Make note of where water streams, pools, or takes a long time to drain away. Lay out your path to avoid these spots.

- Slope your path so rain naturally drains off. Make the center line slightly higher than the edges. Set the center one-quarter inch higher for every 2 feet of path width, so the path slopes downward from the middle to each side. That means the center of a 4-foot wide path should be one-half inch higher than the edges. If that won't work, make the path higher on one side than the other. Experts recommend one-quarter inch of height for each foot of path width.

Design comfort and safety into outdoor steps. Steps that are too high, too wide for your stride, or too short for shoes may raise the danger of tripping and falling. You can create steps with the right proportions by focusing on two measurements:

- height, sometimes called the rise.

- tread, which is the length of the part you step on measured from the step's leading edge to its join with the next step up.

Experts recommend a rise ranging from 4 to 6.5 inches. To find the right tread, use the formula Tread + (2 x Rise) = 26. For example, if you want a 4-inch rise, you would plug 4 into the equation and end up with 18 inches for your tread (18 + [2x4] = 26).

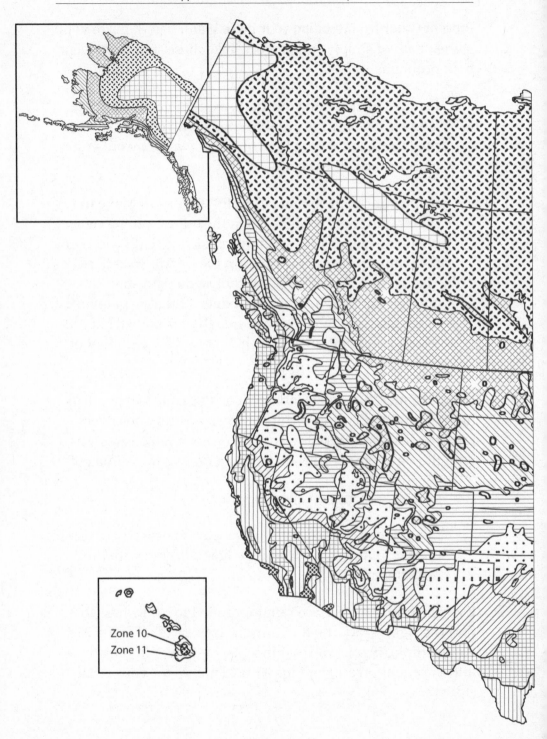

Zone 10
Zone 11

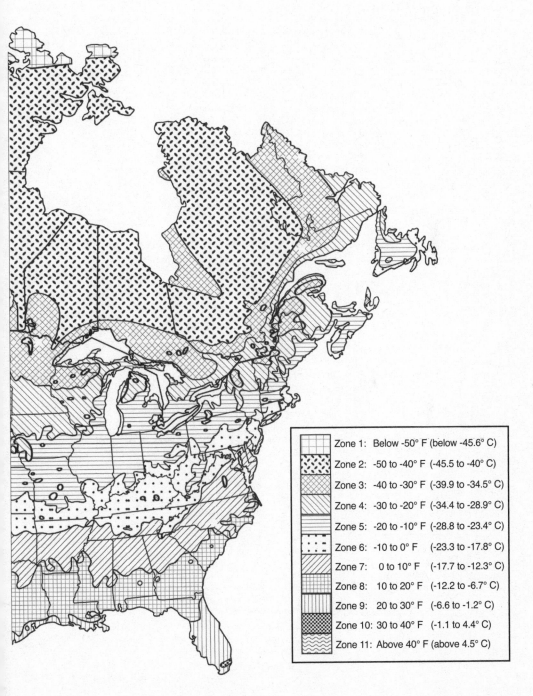

Zone 1: Below -50° F (below -45.6° C)

Zone 2: -50 to -40° F (-45.5 to -40° C)

Zone 3: -40 to -30° F (-39.9 to -34.5° C)

Zone 4: -30 to -20° F (-34.4 to -28.9° C)

Zone 5: -20 to -10° F (-28.8 to -23.4° C)

Zone 6: -10 to 0° F   (-23.3 to -17.8° C)

Zone 7:   0 to 10° F   (-17.7 to -12.3° C)

Zone 8: 10 to 20° F (-12.2 to -6.7° C)

Zone 9: 20 to 30° F (-6.6 to -1.2° C)

Zone 10: 30 to 40° F (-1.1 to 4.4° C)

Zone 11: Above 40° F (above 4.5° C)

INDEX

A

Acidic soil 39, 59
Aerating
  compost 53
  lawn 277-278, 286
African violets 100, 231-233
Air fresheners 224
Air plants. *See* Tillandsia
Alcohol, for plants 57
Alfalfa 36, 37
Algae 341-342, 344
Alkaline soil 26, 39, 59
Aloe vera 237
Alpines 9, 335
Aluminum foil. *See* Foil
America the Beautiful Fund
  126
American Horticultural
  Society (AHS) 124
American Iris Society (AIS) 139
American Rose Society 150
Ammonia 56
Animals, deterring from
  garden
  cats 317, 323, 325-326
  deer 321-322, 325, 327, 328
  dogs 27, 317, 323, 352
  gophers 321
  moles 319-320
  rabbits 322, 324
  raccoons 322
  squirrels 136, 325
Annuals
  planting with perennials
    124-125

  self-seeding 122-123
  transplanting 127
Ants 52, 310, 334
Aphids 305-307, 344
Apples
  pest control for 154-155
  picking 156
Apron 71
Arbors 348, 349-350, 354
Arch, for growing vegetables
  175
Arsenic 180
Ashes 58-59
Asparagus 181
Aspirin 194, 228
Autumn. *See* Fall
Azaleas 85, 147

B

Baking soda
  for gardening 150
  to relieve itching 299
Bamboo, for staking 112, 328
Banana 57
Bargains, gardening 6
Bark split 147
Basil 191, 201-203
Beans 181, 196
Beds. *See* Raised beds
Beer, and gardening 57
Bees 168
Beetles
  European chafer 290
  Japanese 149, 290, 316

Begonias 103, 127
Berries 161. *See also* specific
 berries
Bin, for composting 49, 50
Bird feeder
 cleaning 335, 336
 shielding from squirrels
  331-332, 336
Birdbath 220, 239, 332, 333, 337
Birds. *See also* specific birds
 attracting 146, 330-331
 feeding 333, 336
 nesting 337
 protecting fruit from 156,
  158, 159, 160, 324
 protecting seedlings from
  318
 scaring away 319, 320,
  327-328
 trees for 260
Birdseed 337
 baking 301
Black walnut tree 11, 64
Blackberries 159
Blanket, for plants 17
Bleach 152, 211, 323, 336
Blueberries 159
Borage 168
Borders 25, 30-32
Bottles
 for scaring birds 319
 for watering 115-116
 to protect plants 16-17
 to repel cats 323
 to repel mice 327
Boxwoods 111
Bricks, aging 359
Broccoli 172
Bromeliad 57, 230, 235
Bubble Wrap 19, 87, 314
Bucket 77-78, 129, 326, 336
Bugs. *See also* Pests

beneficial 307-308, 344
Bulbs
 dividing 102, 138-139
 fertilizing 138
 forcing 140
 marking 70-71, 135
 moldy 138
 planting 132-136
 sand and 133
 storing 138
Burs 71
Bushes. *See* Shrubs
Butterflies 330-331, 332
Buttermilk
 as fertilizer 57-58
 to relieve itching 299

C

Cactus 230
 Christmas 234
Caffeine 308
Cage, to deter gophers 321
Caladium 243
Calcium, for plants 57, 190
Canes, training 148, 159,
 163-164
Cardboard
 for planting 25
 to block weeds 32
 to protect apple trees 154
Cardinals 330
Carrots 181, 195
Cast iron plant 230
Castor oil 319
Cats 317, 323, 325-326
Chalk 80
Chicken wire 143
Chickweed 304
Chiggers, repelling 281
Chlorine 120
Christmas tree, recycling 248

Cicadas 316
Cinnamon, as fungicide 88, 233
Clay soil 41, 280, 289
Clematis 245, 272
Climate Zone Map 14
Cloche 17
Club root 198
Coffee
    filters 212, 219
    grounds 56, 128
    to repel snails and slugs 308
Cold frames 19
Coleus 325
Color, in gardens 12, 26-27, 31
Companion planting 167-168
Compost
    activator 46
    aerating 53
    bin 49
    brown matter 44
    building 44
    coffee grounds and 56
    for lawn 277-278
    free help 45
    green matter 44
    heating 51-52
    honey hole 52
    materials for 45-46
    readiness test 51
    straw as 49
    tea 48, 278
    turning 53
    watering 52-53
Concrete 356-357
Containers. *See also* Planters;
    Pots
    deodorant, for killing weeds
        303
    for air plants 235
    for terrariums 237
    for water gardens 338

for weeds 300
growing herbs in 199
growing vegetables in 178,
    195
    metal 242, 248
    picking plants for 221
Cooler 80, 220
Cooling costs, lowering 9-10
Corn 182, 315-316
Cosmos 128
Cover crop 36, 61, 304
Crape myrtle 102, 264
Crop calendar 21
Crop rotation 135, 172-174
Cucumbers 183
Curb appeal 3-4, 32, 258
Cutworms 309

D

Daffodils 102, 134, 138, 141
Dahlias 135
Daylilies 102, 140
De-icers, natural 18
Deadheading 137, 146
Decks 241, 335
Deer 321-322, 325, 327, 328
Deficiency
    iron 58, 275
    nitrogen 58, 275
    phosphorus 58-59, 275
Designs, landscape 4-5
Diaper, for watering plants
    218, 247
Dirt. *See* Soil
Dividing
    bulbs 102, 138-139
    perennials 103, 145
Dogs 27, 317, 323, 352
Dragonflies 344
Drainage 212

Dresser, for raised bed 29
Drought 15-16, 52, 106, 278, 288
Drywall, for improving soil 41
Dwarf plant 98

E

Earthworms. *See* Worms
Earwigs 312
Eggs, to repel deer 325
Eggshells 57, 190, 336
Elephant ears 137
Epsom salt 56
Erosion control 268, 280
Ethanol 57
Ethylene gas 138, 152, 234
Evergreens 3, 10, 58, 230, 251,
    256. *See also* Trees
Extension service 72

F

Fall
    gardening tasks in 24
    planting seeds in 122
    reseeding lawn in 282
    tilling 35-36
Fences
    beautifying 347-348
    for wind protection 354
    lattice 346
    security 351
    temporary 350
    to deter deer 321-322
    weeds and 303
Ferns 144
Fertilizer
    buttermilk as 57-58
    chemical-free 41
    coffee grounds as 128
    Epsom salt as 56

for bulbs 138
for houseplants 228
for lawns 274-277, 289
for roses 54, 58
for vines 271
free 55-57
manure as 55
measuring 60
types of 55
watering and 229
Fescue 283
Ficus 237
Fines, for paving 356, 358
Fish, for water gardens 339,
    341, 343
Fleas 309-310
Flower beds. *See* Raised beds
Flowers. *See also* Annuals;
    Perennials; specific flowers
    arranging 130, 131
    cutting 128-130
    drying 130, 131
    extending life of 152
    growing indoors 140
    low-maintenance 143
    mood and 141
    night-blooming 142
    second bloom 126, 150
    self-seeding 122-123
    slime and 141
    supporting 128, 135, 143
    to repel pests 305, 321
Fluorescent light 227-228
Fluoride 119
Foil
    as mulch 66
    to deter animals 257
Foliar feeding 58
Folklore, gardening 20
French marigolds 305

Frisbee 62, 332
Frost heave 360
Fruit. *See also* specific fruits
  exotic 165
  protecting from birds 156,
    158, 159, 160, 324
Fruit trees
  forcing buds 160-161
  pruning 161-163
  supporting 155
Fungus 150, 204, 264

G

Garden
  community 72
  cutting 130
  lighting 359
  moon 142
  natural 135
  paths. *See* Walkways
Gardening
  advice 166
  aids 43, 62
  baking soda and 150
  bargains 6
  beer and 57
  benefits of 170
  drought and 15-16
  flood and 16
  folklore 20
  hands-free 82
  in gutters 177
  in hard-to-grow areas 7
  in shade 7
  in water 338-345
  journal for 71
  memory and 9
  projects 126
  salt and 42
  seasonal tasks 23-24, 298

vinegar and 57, 60, 145, 151,
  297
vintage treasures 123
visual tricks 11, 12, 359
walking stick for 91
websites 5, 6-7, 14
worms for 39-40
Garlic
  for pest control 306
  harvesting 203
  storing 203
  to kill fungus 204
  to repel pests 136, 222
Geese 327-328
Geraniums 127-128
Girdling 326
Glove of death 304
Gloves 77
Glue, to seal wood cuts 149
Golf shoes, for aerating 278
Gophers 321
Grapevines 163-164
Grass. *See also* Lawn
  clippings 47, 63, 292
  feeding 276
  gas spilled on 294
  ideal height for 291-292
  low-maintenance 276-277
  ornamental 111
  seed 282-285
  shade and 280
  sprigs 286
  watering 287-290
  weeds and 282
Gravel 212, 360
Green manure 41
Greenhouse 89
Ground covers 267-268
Ground layering 101
Grounds, coffee 56

H

Hair, for compost 46
Hangers 17
Hanging baskets 218, 221-222, 242-243
Hard pruning 255-256, 262
Hardening off 93
Hardiness Zone maps 13-15
Hay 47. *See also* Straw
Heart rot 264
Heat Zone map 13-14
Heating costs, lowering 9-10
Hedges. *See also* Shrubs
  trimming 108, 109
Herbicides 47, 298, 304
  natural 297
Herbs. *See also* specific herbs
  as lawn cover 277
  culinary 124
  dangerous 204
  drying 206-207
  for healthy seasoning 202
  for rock wall 205
  freezing 203, 207
  making tea from 205
  planting 199-201
  spiral for 200
  storing 208
  to repel deer 327
Hexagons, sowing in 176
Honey, as rooting hormone 101
Hormone, in trees 163
Hose 118-119, 290
Houseplants. *See also* Plants
  fertilizing 228
  for cleaning the air 224
  for low light 226
  light and 226-228
  misting 225
  winter care for 229
Hubcaps, as planters 242

Hummingbirds 333-334, 335
Hyacinths 134, 137, 139
Hybrids 134
Hydrangeas 145

I

Ice chest. *See* Cooler
Ice, in water gardens 343
Impatiens 125
Incandescent light 227-228
Insects. *See* Bugs; Pests
Insulation, for plants 19, 147
Interplanting 169-170
Iris 102, 139
Iron, for plants 58, 145, 275
Irrigation 115
Ivy 240, 268, 272

J

Japanese beetles 149, 290, 316
Jars, strawberry 218
Journal, for gardening 71
Juneberries 160

K

Koi 339

L

Lacewings 307
Ladders, as an arbor 354
Ladybird Johnson Wildflower Center 125
Ladybugs 308
Landscape fabric 65
Landscaping
  choosing plants 6, 9-12
  designs 4-5

grouping plants 4
low-maintenance 2
materials 4
on slopes 7
professionals 23
to increase property values 258
to lower energy costs 9-10, 271
to solve problems 250
with edibles 5
Lawn. *See also* Grass
aerating 277-278, 286
compost for 277-278
edging 293
fertilizing 274-277, 289
herbs for 277
identifying pests in 279
mowing 291-294
repairing 280
seeding 282-286
thatch 277, 293
watering 287-290
Lead, in soil 196
Leaf mold, as peat moss substitute 214
Leaves
as fertilizer 275
for mulch 64, 278
in water gardens 342, 345
spraying 58
Lemons 165-166
Lettuce 177, 197
Light
for houseplants 226-228
for patios 358
for walkways 359
for window boxes 247
Lilies 133
Lime 59-60
Limestone 213

Liquid soap. *See* Soap

M

Magnolia 22
Mailbox 75, 272, 333
Manure
as fertilizer 55
contaminated 47
green 41
root vegetables and 182
to protect seedlings 92
Master gardener 166
Mealybugs 314
Melons 164-165
Memory, and gardening 9
Mice 326
Microwave, drying herbs in 206
Milk
as fungicide 188
for pest control 306
jug 116, 300
powdered 86
Minerals 40-41, 119-120
Mint 204
Mites 232-233
Moles 319-320
Mood, and flowers 141
Moon garden 142
Mosquitoes 344
Moss 104, 238, 280
Mothballs 318
Moths 310
Mousetrap 326
Mower, caring for 294
Mowing
around beds 32
lawn 291-294
to create mulch 64
Mr. Smarty Plants 125

Mulch
  fire-resistant 64-65
  free 62
  grass clippings as 63
  living 61
  measuring 62
  newspaper as 66
  pests and 63, 65
  plastic as 66-67
  seedlings and 92
  stone as 68
  straw as 65-66
  trees and 263
  weeds and 64, 302
  wood chips as 62
Mums 128
Music, to repel moles 320

N

N-P-K ratio 55
Nails, rusty 145
Native plants 3, 99
Newspaper
  collar 147
  for lining window boxes 247
  for mulch 66, 156
  for topsoil 35
  for weed control 148
Nicotine 309
Night-blooming flowers 142
Nitrogen 55, 275, 276

O

Oatmeal, to relieve itching 299
Oil, for cleaning tools 80
One Call Center 28
Optical illusions. *See* Visual
  tricks, for gardening
Orchids 233

Organic matter 50, 277. *See also*
  Compost
Ornamental grass 111

P

Paintbrush, to kill weeds 296,
  297
Pallet 49
Pantyhose 77, 109, 263, 317
Paperwhites 140-141
Paths. *See* Walkways
Patio 241, 358
Pavers 355-356, 360
Peanut butter, to attract mice
  326
Peanuts, packing 212
Peas 183
Peat moss 42, 214
Peat pot 103
Pepper, to repel pests 136, 313
Peppers 184
Perennials
  cold weather and 245
  dividing 103, 145
  fertilizing 59
  mixing with annuals 124-125
Permits 5
Pest control
  cedar for 312
  coffee for 308
  flowers for 305
  for ants 310, 334
  for aphids 305-307, 344
  for apple maggots 154-155
  for chiggers 281
  for coddling moths 154
  for fleas 309-310
  for mites 232-233
  for mosquitoes 311, 344
  for thrips 134

for ticks 281
garlic for 136, 306
milk for 306
orange peels for 306-307, 317
pantyhose for 317
pepper for 136
plants and 96, 309-310,
    325-326, 327
soap for 136
tea for 306
timing for 22
tobacco for 308-309
turpentine for 136
Pesticides 314
Pests
identifying 279
mulch and 63
Petunias 126-127
pH level
of soil 39, 56, 145
of water 56
Phenology 20
Phosphorus 55, 58-59, 275
Pickle juice 57
Pile, compost 44, 53
Pinching 146
Pine sap 74, 265
Pine straw 66. *See also* Straw
Pines 105
Planters. *See also* Containers;
    Pots
feet for 240-241
narrow 212
self-watering 217
toxic 184
unique 186, 219-220, 242-243
upside-down 192-193
Plant Hardiness Zone Map
    362-363
Plants. *See also* Houseplants;
    specific plants.
bare-root 96-97

blanket for 17
buying 94-98, 198, 223
cage to protect 321
calcium for 57, 190
cleaning 231
climbing 269-272
cold snaps and 16-17
companion 167-168
disease-resistant 97-98
dormant 95
for containers 221
for curbside beds 32
for landscaping 6, 9-12
for pest control 309-310,
    325-326, 327
for slopes 7, 335
for water gardens 341
free 98-99
grouping 4, 221
insulation for 19
invasive 8
iron for 58, 256-257
labeling 70, 86
low-maintenance 143, 230
native 3, 99
novelty 198
protecting 18, 87, 125-126,
    244-245, 355
removing pests 244
repotting 210-211
root-bound 96, 210
rotating 26, 135, 172-174
shielding from wind 354
supporting 128, 135, 143-144
thinning 138-139
ties for 180-181
to attract birds 331, 333-334
to attract butterflies 331
watering 127, 226, 247
Plastic
as mulch 66-67
for grass control 284

Plastic *(continued)*
  for warmth 16-17
  for weed control 25-26,
    296-297
Pods, seed 85
Poinsettias 233-234
Poison ivy 299
Polyculture 124
Ponds. *See* Water gardens
Popsicle sticks 70
Potassium 55
Potatoes 184-187
Potpourri 131
Pots. *See also* Containers;
  Planters
  cold weather and 245
  floating 339
  gravel for 212
  grouping 222
  growing moss on 238
  large 239-240, 244
  protecting from theft 240
  sterilizing 211
  terra-cotta 219, 240
Potting soil
  homemade 213-214
  refreshing 215
  soilless 195, 212-214
  sterilizing 215-216
Powdered milk, for storing
  seeds 86
Powdery mildew 188
Power tools 76, 112
Propagating
  grafting 103-104
  ground layering 101
  hardwood cuttings 101-102
  moss 104
  stem cuttings 100, 104
Pruning
  by pinching 146, 229-230,
    254
  cleanup 107, 111

during drought 106
fruit trees 161-163
ground covers 268
roses 149
shrubs 105, 106, 254-256
tools for 109-110
trees 107, 108, 262
Pumice soap 42
Pumpkins 164-165
Purslane 302
PVC pipe
  for composting 53
  for fertilizing 60
  for planting 204
  for watering 158, 218-219

R

Rabbits 322, 324
Raccoons 322
Rain barrel 113, 117-118
Rain shadow 349
Raised beds 8
  building 179, 180, 301
  dimensions for 26
  drainage for 29-30
  for comfort 27
  for vegetables 175-176
  materials for 28-29
Rake 79, 81, 279
Raspberries 158, 159
Red worms. *See* Worms
Reel mower 294
Rhododendrons 146, 152
Rock
  dust 40
  garden 334-335
  wall, herbs for 205
Rooting hormone 101
Rosemary 204-205
Roses 98, 147-151, 316

composting 48
cutting 111
fertilizing 54, 58
Rotation
  crop 172-174
  for plants 26, 151
Rototilling 36
Row cover 197
Rubber plant 110, 230
Rubbing alcohol
  to kill pests 314-315
  to kill weeds 297, 298
  to prevent poison ivy 299
Rust, on tools 80-81

S

Salt
  basil-flavored 202
  gardening and 42
  plants and 216-217, 297
Sand 42
  bulbs and 133
  sowing grass with 284
Sandbox, for dogs 323
Sandy soil 29-30, 280, 289
Sap 110, 265. *See also* Pine sap
Scales 314
Seasonal tasks 23-24
Seaweed 41
Seedlings
  grass 282
  natural pots for 88-89
  peat pots and 103
  protecting from cold 87, 92
  protecting from pests
    313-314, 318
  transplanting 93
  watering 88
Seeds
  for rock gardens 335

free 83, 124
grass 282-285, 293
homemade tape for 90
lemon 165-166
low-cost 83, 126
mail-order 285
nyjer 337
saving 84, 85
spacing 91
storing 84, 86
sunflower 46, 337
testing 84
tiny 83, 125, 284
tomato 188-189
weed 49, 301
when to plant 122
wildflower 123
Selenium 172
Shower cap 87
Shrubs. *See also* Hedges
  bare-root 96-97, 252
  flowering 254
  planting 251-253
  pruning 105-106, 254-256
  tea for 256-257
  watering 257
Silica gel 130
Skateboard, for gardening 43
Skin, protecting 60, 75, 125, 134
Slime, on flowers 141
Slope, watering on 115, 289-290
Slugs 63, 307, 308, 311
Snails 308, 318
Snake plant 230
Snow mold 291
Soaker hose 118, 302
Soap
  for pest control 279, 315
  for weed control 298-299
  homemade 42
  to deter animals 136

Sod 285, 286, 293
Soil
  acidic 39, 59
  alkaline 26, 39, 59
  amendments 40, 62
  clay 41, 280, 289
  cleaning off 125
  contamination 180, 196
  cooling 91
  for containers 212-214
  for raised bed 29
  lime for 59
  pH 39, 56
  readiness for planting 22, 35,
    171
  sandy 29-30, 280, 289
  testing 21, 37-39, 59, 216,
    274, 288
  toppers 222
  topsoil 35, 37
Soilless mixes 212-214
Spice rack, living 199
Spinach 197
Spools 82
Spring gardening 23
Sprinklers 18, 289
Squash bugs 313
Squirrels 136-137, 325, 331, 336
Stakes 112
Staking
  flowers 135, 144
  shrubs 109
  trees 262
  vegetables 180-181
Steps, building 361
Stone, as mulch 68
Storm damage, avoiding 10
Straw
  as compost 49
  as mulch 65-66
  chopping 37

  for planting potatoes
    184-185
  for raised beds 179
  to prevent pond algae 344
Strawberries
  mulching 156
  pyramid for 157
  watering 158, 218-219
Suckers 102, 254
Suet 333
Summer
  gardening tasks in 23
  mulching in 67
Sunflowers 129
  seeds 46, 337
Sweet peas 272
Sweet potatoes, ornamental
  187

T

Tea
  compost 48, 278
  for pest control 306
  for shrubs 256-257
  herbal 205
Termites 65
Terrariums 236
Thatch 277, 293
Thrips 134
Ticks, repelling 281
Tillandsia 235-236
Tilling 35-36, 297, 303
Timing tips
  for flowers 21
  for pest control 22
  for soil 35
  for vegetables 20
Tire, to protect plants 18
Toads 312
Tobacco mosaic virus 188
Tobacco, to control pests
  308-309
Tomatoes 188-194

Tools
    cleaning 74-75, 78, 110
    for comfort 79-80
    for measuring holes 90
    for pruning 109-110
    for weeding 301
    marking 73
    organizing 81-82
    power 76, 112
    rake 79, 81, 279
    rust on 80-81
    secondhand 73-74
    sharing 6-7, 74
    sharpening 82
    unusual 75-76
Toothbrush, for pollinating 188
Topiary 241, 272
Topsoil. *See* Soil
Transplanting
    annuals 127
    tomatoes 192
Trash can, for composting 48
Trees. *See also* Fruit trees
    bare-root 96-97
    black walnut warning 11, 64
    bud-suppressing hormone
        163
    buying 97
    deciduous 9, 106
    flowering 259
    free 258
    fruit, when to plant 260
    mulching 263, 266
    pine 105
    planting 260-261
    planting beneath 27-28
    protecting 265-266
    protecting from animals 326,
        328
    pruning 107, 108, 262
    removing stumps 264-265

    repairing wounds 263
    staking 262
    to attract birds 260
Trellis
    bamboo 351
    fan 347
    for beans 181
    for blackberries 159
    for grapes 163-164
    for melons 165
    for tomatoes 189
    from branches 174-175
    headboard as 348
    hinged 353
    placement of 197-198
    to hide eyesores 346
Tubers 133, 135, 243
Tulips 134, 137
Turpentine, to repel pests 136
Twine 77

U

Umbrella, to protect plants 18,
    125-126
Upside-down planters 192-193

V

Vacation, and plant care
    115-116, 120, 217
Vase, cleaning 130
Vegetables. *See also* specific
    vegetables
    dwarf varieties 177
    heirloom varieties 190
    money-saving 167
    organic 191
    plastic mulch for 67
    root 182
    rotating 172-174
    staking 180-181

Vegetables (*continued*)
  storing 194
Velcro 236, 270
Vermicompost 50
Vernalization 137
Vinegar 297
  for azaleas 57
  for rose fungus 151
  hydrangeas and 145
  to kill weeds 355
  to neutralize lime 60
  to repel ants 310
Vines
  decorating with 240, 272
  fertilizing 271
  flowering 269
  for decorating 272
  grape 163-164
  supporting 270, 272
Visual tricks, for gardening 11,
    12, 359
Volatile organic compounds
  (VOCs) 225

W

Wagon, for gardening 43
Walkways 355-361
Water bill, lowering 113, 289
Water gardens 338-345
Watering 3
  before laying mulch 64
  can 60, 117, 219
  cues 113-114, 120, 127, 225
  fertilizer and 229
  hanging plants 218
  lawn 115, 287-290
  on a slope 115, 289-290
  roses 151
  shrubs 257
  strawberries 157

  strawberry jars 218-219
  while on vacation 115-116,
    120, 217
WD-40 80, 294
Weeds 43
  container for 300
  controlling 296-304
  edible 302
  grass and 282
  mulch and 64, 302
  seeds from 49, 301
  vinegar for 355
Wheelbarrow
  as a planter 219
  cover for 43
Wheelchairs, paths for 357-358
Wildflowers 123
Windbreak, creating 10, 253,
  354
Window boxes 246-248
Winter
  caring for houseplants in
    229
  composting in 50-51
  gardening 24
  protecting grass in 281
  protecting plants in 244-245
Wireworms 315
Wisteria 271
Wood chips, as mulch 62
Wood, pressure-treated 180,
  350
Worms 39-40, 50

Z

Zones
  hardiness maps for 13-14,
    362-363
  selecting plants for 132